TEACHING MATHEMATICS IN MIDDLE SCHOOL

A Practical Guide

Stephen Krulik
Temple University
Philadelphia, Pennsylvania

Jesse Rudnick
Temple University
Philadelphia, Pennsylvania

Eric Milou
Rowan University
Glassboro, New Jersey

Boston ■ New York ■ San Francisco
Mexico City ■ Montreal ■ Toronto ■ London ■ Madrid ■ Munich ■ Paris
Hong Kong ■ Singapore ■ Tokyo ■ Cape Town ■ Sydney

The authors wish to thank the following reviewers:
Rena M. Shull, University of Houston
Karen Mae Lafferty, Morehead State University
Nicholas Holodick, King's College

Series Editor: Traci Mueller
Series Editorial Assistant: Erica Tromblay
Marketing Manager: Elizabeth Fogarty
Production Administrator: Annette Pagliaro
Editorial Production: Trinity Publishers Services
Composition Buyer: Linda Cox
Manufacturing Buyer: Megan Cochran
Cover Administrator: Kristina Mose-Libon
Electronic Composition: Omegatype Typography, Inc.

For related titles and support materials, visit our online catalog at
www.ablongman.com

Between the time Web site information is gathered and then published, it is not
unusual for some sites to have closed. Also, the transcription of URLs can result
in unintended typographical errors. The publisher would appreciate notification
where these errors occur so that they may be corrected in subsequent editions.

Library of Congress Cataloging-in-Publication Data

Krulik, Stephen.
    Teaching mathematics in middle school : a practical guide / Stephen
Krulik, Jesse Rudnick, Eric Milou.
        p. cm.
    Includes bibliographical references and index.
    ISBN 0-205-34327-9 (pbk.)
    1. Mathematics–Study and teaching (Middle school) I. Rudnick, Jesse A.
  II. Milou, Eric. III. Title.
QA11.2 .K78 2003
510'.71'2–dc21   2002074446

Printed in the United States of America
10   9   8   7   6   5   4   3   2   1   08   07   06   05   04   03   02

Contents

The Middle School: What's It All About?

CHAPTER 1

Why the Middle School? Origins and Issues

The original configuration for public schools in the United States was elementary school (grades K through 8) and secondary school (grades 9 through 12). In early times, many children completed their formal schooling at the end of grade 8. Those who were going on to college went to high school. The first major change in this configuration was the introduction of the junior high school (grades 7 through 9). This change was motivated by economic and social factors. As the United States mandated public education for all children, schools became overcrowded. It was more cost-effective to create another level of school—the junior high school—than to build both new elementary and new secondary schools. There was also a social concern that younger children in the primary grades would not benefit from interacting with early adolescents.

The creation of the junior high school brought with it programmatic concerns. The junior high school adopted the format of the secondary school. For the first time, early adolescents in grades 7 and 8 were introduced to subject matter departmentalization, as opposed to the self-contained classroom in which one teacher was responsible for teaching all subjects. Consequently, virtually all junior high school teachers held secondary certification in a specific subject field.

It has been apparent for some time that the junior high school is not meeting the needs of the early adolescent. Junior high school is often considered by many educators to be a replica of senior high school. As such, the emphasis has always been on organization rather than the curriculum. The junior high school has also failed to emphasize the social and developmental needs of the children who attend. In addition, it has long been recognized as being poorly equipped to enable the early adolescent to achieve. Educators felt that children in the early adolescent period (ages 10 through 14) constituted a distinct grouping that would be better served by separating them from students in the primary grades and in the senior high school. Concerns about these issues have contributed to the birth and growth of the middle school movement.

The middle school configuration also brought with it several major educational concerns about mathematics education. Research shows that in the middle grades many students become "turned off" to mathematics. The middle school mathematics curriculum has been poorly defined, especially in grades 7 and 8. Even with the junior high school model, the mathematics program for grades 7 and 8 was merely a continuation of the previously used elementary school program for grades 7 and 8. Grade 9 was devoted to Algebra I for the college-bound student, and general mathematics (whatever that was) for the other students. Textbook series continued to be developed for grades K through 8. Even in the beginning of the middle school program, the mathematics textbooks used for grades 5 through 8 were taken from a K–8 basal series. Looking at the mathematics textbooks, it was difficult, if not impossible, to distinguish the math program for grade 7 from that for grade 8. This began to change with the publication of the National

Council of Teachers of Mathematics' *Curriculum and Evaluation Standards for School Mathematics* (1989). However, another problem remained. Most teachers teaching mathematics were elementary certified and not mathematics certified, and few, if any, had mathematics skills. Those who were certified as secondary mathematics teachers lacked the training and skills to deal with the needs of early adolescents.

The middle school has only recently begun to receive the attention of professional educators, largely as a result of concerted efforts by the National Council of Teachers of Mathematics (NCTM) and other professional organizations, foundations, and national agencies. As more is learned about the psychology of the early adolescent and how the early adolescent learns, the middle school has taken on a new and important role in education. The need to provide developmentally appropriate educational experiences for young adolescents is becoming more and more apparent.

Many states now offer, or are contemplating offering, a certificate specifically for the middle school, as is the case with elementary school and senior high school. Colleges of education and other teacher preparation institutions are taking a leadership role by designing and offering full programs to prepare mathematics teachers for the middle school. These programs mandate courses in educational psychology (with an emphasis on the early adolescent) and a methods course designed specifically for the middle school mathematics teacher, as well as a sufficient number and variety of mathematics courses to ensure subject matter competency. Some institutions are creating programs with a double-focused major (i.e., mathematics/science) requiring competency in both areas. Normally, this double major constitutes eighteen semester hours in each subject area. Being certified in two subjects provides school administrators with personnel flexibility.

MATHEMATICS AND THEORIES OF LEARNING

Before discussing specifics of teaching mathematics to children, it is important to briefly review what learning theorists have had to say about the learning of mathematics and especially how the early adolescent learns. The purpose here is to survey the ideas of some of the better-known learning theorists who had an impact on the teaching of mathematics.

Piaget: Stages of Intellectual Development

Many teachers feel that learning concepts in mathematics is an instant occurrence, like a lightbulb suddenly being turned on. Jean Piaget (1973) showed that something quite different takes place. Piaget was one of the most important learning theorists in the twentieth century. His work showing that children's intellectual development occurs in stages had a major impact on the teaching of mathematics at all levels of instruction. According to Piaget, a child moves along a continuum through a series of stages and well-defined levels of learning.

1. *Sensory motor period.* This stage, usually present in the first eighteen months to two years of a child's life, takes place when language skills are first beginning to form. The child moves from reflexes and seemingly spontaneous behavior to habits and then to intelligent behavior. Objects are conceived to continue to exist even when they are out of the child's sight.

2. *Preoperative period.* This stage ranges from about age 2 through age 7 and is the period when the child begins to communicate with other people. The child is just beginning to think in symbolic terms. The object itself need no longer be present; rather, a picture of the object is sufficient.

3. *Concrete operational period.* This stage usually begins at ages 6 or 7 and continues until about age 11. The child first begins to use logical classification, numbers, and cause-and-effect relationships. The child begins to count objects and to recognize degrees of quantity such as "more than," "less than," "the same as," and so on.

4. *Formal operational period.* This period extends from about age 11 through age 15. Now the child begins to draw conclusions from statements. This is when the child's hypothesis and deduction skills begin to shape formal patterns of thought. The child begins to think logically about abstract problems.

The ages for each stage vary greatly, even though the order in which these stages occur is fixed. Many of your students may still be in the concrete operational period. If so, you likely will need to work in a mathematics laboratory or with hands-on materials, or manipulatives. Your children must be active participants in their own learning rather than merely sitting back passively while someone (the teacher) presents new material. Basically, Piaget's work reinforces the idea that learning proceeds from the concrete to the abstract and that rather than giving children a concept, they should be allowed to "discover" the concept through several carefully selected investigations. Piaget's work led to the laboratory movement in mathematics education.

Bruner: Discovery Learning

When Jerome Bruner (1977) examined how children learn mathematics, he found three phases that occurred almost at the same time: (1) *acquisition* of new information, (2) *transformation* of knowledge to make use of the new information, and (3) *evaluation,* or checking to see if the task has been accomplished.

Bruner's work (along with that of Piaget) led to the extensive use of manipulatives, or hands-on materials. Bruner suggested that learning begins with an action, a *concrete stage.* The child manipulates objects and in the process develops the concepts underlying the materials. For example, students beginning to add integers can use chips of two different colors to represent positive and negative numbers. Thus, they are using a hands-on approach to the topic and acting on real objects in a concrete way. Bruner's second stage, usually referred to as the *pictorial stage,* permits the student to represent physical objects with drawings. The final stage is the *symbolic* or *abstract stage* in which objects are completely replaced by symbols or by words that may or may not be directly related to the objects. Thus, the student can solve the addition problem of $(+3) + (-7) = (-4)$ by applying a system of abstract thought, without resorting to any aids or hands-on materials. Bruner's work contributed to the discovery learning movement in which the process is more important than the end product.

Dienes: Analytical and Constructive Thinking

Zoltan Dienes was a student of Piaget's and a colleague of Bruner's. He was an English mathematician who turned to psychology to learn how children learn mathematics.

According to Dienes, there are two kinds of thinking that occur when children attempt to learn mathematics. He refers to these as (1) *analytical thinking,* in which children work from one step to the next in a systematic, logical manner, and (2) *constructive thinking,* in which children leave the realm of logical thought and begin to "create" their own mathematics. Dienes encourages mathematics teachers to create learning situations that emphasize the use of constructive thinking rather than logical thinking. He suggests that children be given unrestricted *free play* with selected manipulatives. These should provide different embodiments of the same concept so that students can begin to extrapolate the common concepts. Based on these commonalities or patterns, students begin to *generalize* the concept. Next, students begin to move through a *representation* stage, using pictures and words to describe the concept under consideration. Students then move to a *symbolization* stage in which they describe the concept in mathematical symbols and language. Finally, students move to a *formalization* stage in which the rules and structure of the concept are formalized either verbally or with paper and pencil.

Vygotsky: Learning as a Social Activity

Lev Vygotsky (1962) was a Russian psychologist who discovered that children learn best in a social setting. He believed that children are constantly building and rebuilding their knowledge. Children begin by realizing that objects have names and that these names are usually unique. Eventually, children come to realize that a name may represent an action or a complex skill. Vygotsky's research showed that children are best capable of internalizing complex knowledge when they are involved in discussion and activities—that is, being guided by a series of good questions by a teacher. In other words, the child builds new knowledge based on prior knowledge and experiences. Children should be free to experiment in a nonthreatening environment that has been enriched with mathematical concepts. The child should feel free to try new things and to learn new things from others. Vygotsky suggested that children need time to think and to think out loud. The teacher must not tell answers but rather guide the students' responses to promote transfer from what was known previously to what is to be learned.

Vygotsky felt that tools contribute to the ease of our everyday living. Similarly, children can increase their intellectual capacities by utilizing tools. For example, the calculator would probably be welcomed by followers of Vygotsky as a tool for enriching intellectual capacity rather than as a device that creates dependency.

Constructivism

The constructivist movement is a relatively new one in mathematics education. The movement grew out of the work of Piaget, Bruner, and Dienes, although they themselves never used this term. According to the constructivists, knowledge cannot be learned passively—that is, it cannot be transmitted from one person to another by "telling." Instead, all knowledge is created or constructed through activities that are experienced and then reflected on. Students should be given the opportunity to develop their own mathematical ideas by interacting with their environment. According to G. M. Bodner (1986), to achieve effective instruction, the teacher must "disturb" the student's environment—that is, provide a stimulus. How students make sense of this stimulus is the path to knowledge rather than simply learning facts. Knowledge is constructed by the learner.

Many of us have learned mathematical rules by memory. For example, you probably remember the FOIL method for multiplying two binomials, in which you take the sum of four products. That is, to multiply $(a + b)(c + d)$, we take the product of the **F**irst terms in each binomial, (ac), the **L**ast terms (bd), the **O**uter terms (ad), and the **I**nner terms (bc). We then take their sum. Thus, the final product is $ac + ad + bc + bd$. Or, to divide one fraction by another, you invert the second fraction and multiply. But why do we do this? For most of us, these are simply meaningless rules that work, rules we have memorized. To the constructivist, conceptual understanding must come first.

Constructivists suggest that the students should, in most cases, work together. This social process provides an opportunity for students to enhance their abilities to communicate in mathematics, as suggested by the NCTM in their process standards (as discussed more fully in Chapter 2). That is not to say that the teacher should *never* use direct instruction. There will always be lessons that can and should be taught through teacher presentations. The computational algorithms cannot really be "discovered." However, the student-centered classroom, rather than the teacher-centered classroom, is basic to the constructivist approach. The role of the teacher is that of a choreographer or orchestrator of experiences, rather than that of an authority who "tells all." The teacher is a guide rather than someone who lectures. Indeed, it is the questions the teacher asks that lead students to discover or construct new knowledge.

A classroom taught in a constructivist manner and a classroom in which teaching is based on NCTM *Standards* are closely related. In fact, it is a question as to which movement leads which—the constructivists or those who advocate a standards-based approach to teaching and learning.

The Van Hieles: Levels of Learning in Geometry

Geometry has in recent years become very important in the middle school. Due to the emphasis placed by the NCTM on geometry and its inclusion on state tests, classes in geometry are increasing in middle school. Two researchers have had a significant impact on the way geometry is taught. Pierre Marie van Hiele and Dina van Heile-Geldof developed a set of stages of geometric development through which students pass. The importance of their work lies in the fact that the geometric level at which the student is operating need not necessarily be related to the chronological age of the student. The stages are not necessarily age related but rather reflect the student's experiences. This means that you can significantly enhance a child's geometric development by using appropriate activities as you teach geometry. It is important that you keep in mind that these levels are sequential in nature—that is, to arrive at any level (after Level 0), the student must pass through all intervening levels.

Level 0:
Visualization/Recognition

At this level, students are able to recognize and name geometric shapes based solely on the visual characteristics of the figure. The primary thinking tool is direct visual observation. At this level, the student thinks of a rectangle as being a rectangle because "it looks like a rectangle" or "it looks like a door." The child might recognize a square in its usual position (i.e., sides parallel to the horizontal and vertical) but not recognize it if it were rotated through 45 degrees. Students at this level usually put objects together because they look alike. The teacher must develop activities that involve sorting, identifying, and classifying.

Level 1: Analysis/ Description

At this level, students begin to organize shapes by common properties and move beyond simple recognition. For example, they can now consider what makes a figure a square and can comprehend that it is properties that put a collection of objects together. At this stage, students recognize that a class of shapes have certain properties and any member of the class must have these properties—that is, shapes "belong" to a category because of their properties. However, students at this level do not recognize properties spontaneously but must be guided. Many middle school students function at this level. As a teacher, you should develop activities that concentrate on properties of figures and discuss classifying figures based on their properties. You might prepare a worksheet on which you show a series of figures that have a variety of properties in common. Ask students to categorize them any way they wish, and then ask them to explain their classification system.

Level 2: Informal Deduction/Abstract Relational

Students now begin to understand informal deduction, which allows conclusions to be drawn based on other known facts. This understanding occurs without the rigor of mathematical proof. Certain truths are accepted, and these, in turn, lead to other truths. Students at this level can offer a formal definition of a class of shapes. Students make observations beyond the properties themselves and begin to focus on logical arguments about shapes and properties. As a teacher, you can make lists of properties and discuss necessary and sufficient conditions for these properties. Also, you can begin to examine converses of statements—for example, "All squares are rectangles" and "All rectangles are squares." Ask such questions as "If a figure is a rectangle, must it be a square?" and "If a figure is a square, must it be a rectangle?" Students can begin to create informal proofs; however, they are not yet ready to see the need for axiomatic proofs.

Level 3: Deduction

At this level, students begin to construct a formal system based on postulates, definitions, and theorems. Students also begin to recognize the need for a formal system that rests on a minimal basis of statements. The formal deduction incorporates geometric proof, logic, and the creation of alternate proofs of theorems. This is the level of formal geometry courses that usually take place in high school or ninth grade. Conclusions are now based on logic rather than intuition.

Level 4: Rigor/Formal Axiomatic

Students functioning at this level are usually able to understand geometry in the abstract sense. This is usually the level of most college students who major in mathematics and begin to investigate other geometries. Students now focus on the system itself and not just the deductions of that system.

The work of the Van Hieles reinforces the need to involve middle school students in activities in geometry that employ hands-on manipulatives—blocks, puzzles, beads, tiles, paper, and so on. The levels in the van Hiele model are not indicators of *what* students know, but rather of *how* they are thinking.

MIDDLE SCHOOL ISSUES

The middle school mathematics teacher is faced with a number of issues and challenges: (1) the special stresses and features of the developmental stage of early adolescence, (2) the requirement to include the special child in the curriculum, and (3) the issue of gender equity in the classroom.

Early Adolescence

The term *early adolescent* is a relatively new one and only appeared in the literature in the 1970s. Prior to that time, children from ages 10 through 14 were usually referred to as preadolescents. Today, however, early adolescence is now widely recognized as a developmental period between early childhood and adolescence. As more was learned about early adolescents, a body of knowledge about the middle school child began to develop. The early adolescent period has been defined as occurring from about age 10 through age 14. Middle school educators now recognize that we must provide developmentally appropriate activities for these students. These activities must not only provide opportunities for new experiences and social changes, but also must offer early adolescents the structure, routines, and limits that their developmental age requires.

The early adolescent years are extremely volatile, being marked by rapid, dramatic, and extreme changes, both physically as well as mentally. These students begin to search for independence and freedom yet still depend on adult authority for direction. There is increased social awareness, and peer pressure becomes an increasing factor. Students often will defy the adult authority they look to for guidance. Many people consider early adolescents as rowdy, noisy, inattentive, and inherently misbehaving. Indeed, this group is often referred to as too old to be children and too young to be adolescents. As a result, teachers often consider these students extremely difficult to teach, a stereotype that is inaccurate at best. These changes from the typically docile child in the elementary school to the more questioning middle school child, as well as the child's social or peer interactions, must be carefully considered when developing strategies for teaching mathematics. For example, the teacher must consider how to provide opportunities for cooperative groups to work together. Students must constantly be encouraged to feel better about themselves and to take an active role in their own learning, without fear of embarrassment or ridicule.

As the students reach the middle grades (5 through 8), they become more able to carry out long-term projects, deal with controversial topics, and pursue a discussion of interesting problems and problem situations. Once again, it is crucial that the classroom atmosphere must be nonthreatening and relaxed. Students should feel free to voice their opinions without fear of ridicule. In this period, cognitive changes allow for higher levels of abstract thinking. Students begin to think hypothetically, critically, and abstractly. They are able to use cognitive skills to solve real-world problems. What is most important is that they learn to think about thinking—to develop metacognition. Middle school students must become more confident in their own ability to learn and move gradually from the concrete to the higher levels of abstract reasoning. Every child wants to succeed. You, as the authority figure in the classroom, must provide opportunities for students to be recognized for their accomplishments and to develop feelings of adequacy. You must provide situations in which they can begin to reason critically and engage in higher levels of cognitive thought. Your students must be helped to develop their problem-solving skills and their reasoning power.

Inclusion: The Special Child

If we are to meet the needs of all children as the standards suggest, and as set forth in the Individuals with Disabilities Education Act (IDEA), then we must examine our teaching practices with children with both learning and physical disabilities. While teachers are not expected to be expert in all types of disabilities, many students will come to the classroom with special learning issues relating to memory, speech, auditory, and visual problems and, in many cases, a lack of the ability to integrate abstract ideas. For these students, there are some important considerations to keep in mind:

- Students with disabilities are not necessarily slow or retarded; many are mentally capable of learning mathematics. According to Feigenbaum, "Students with learning disabilities can learn algebra when the environment focuses on their needs and learning styles."

- Learning disabilities often cannot be remediated.

- Instructional modifications are necessary to accommodate the specific needs of LD children (children with learning disabilities).

For many years, it was the practice to place learning disabled children or children with special needs in a self-contained classroom with a small number of students and one teacher who would work with these children on a one-to-one basis. When the Individuals with Disabilities Education Act (IDEA; PL 101-476) was passed, it became the practice to include these children in what is referred to as the "least restrictive environment." This term has gradually come to mean including these students in the regular classroom and providing them with the help they need to learn the material. This approach is known as inclusion. As a classroom teacher, you may have one or more of these children in your mathematics class. It is important that you learn something about how to work with these students within your regular class setting.

First of all, you should learn what support is available to you by meeting with the school's instructional support team or child study team. Each student with disabilities should have an individualized educational plan (IEP) that sets specific goals for the student. These plans are updated every year and inform you as to what kinds of weaknesses the child has experienced in the past as well as what attempts have been made to compensate for them. You must be familiar with the goals and objectives included in these plans; they are legal documents and the guidelines must be followed.

The usual procedure is to have the teacher work with the class and an aide or an assistant teacher work directly with the child with disabilities. However, "recent research indicates that poor or traditional instruction contributes to the mathematics difficulties of many learning disabled students" (Rafferty, Heinenbach, and Helms, 1999, p. 55).

In many cases, a special education instructor is available for supplementary work with the children. Find out all you can about the LD children who are in your class, what their disabilities and strengths are, what special needs they have, and what you should do to help them learn mathematics. Keep in mind that you are not expected to change the mathematics content you teach; it is clear that these children can learn. What you must do is pay specific attention to how these children learn best and design your instructional model to maximize their strengths and minimize their weaknesses. Be certain to include them in all small group activities. By assigning a student mentor to work closely with these children, both students will profit. (These peer mentors can be used during any part of the mathematics classroom instruction.) Learning disabilities can include perceptual and memory deficits as well as attention disorders and physical disabilities.

Perceptual Deficits   These deficits comprise the most common learning disabilities and include both visual and auditory problems. These children have trouble recognizing the component parts of what they see or hear. Some have reversal problems, and see things as a mirror image of what is being presented. Many have problems with organizing their work; as a result their papers are often messy and their writings are disorganized.

Some suggestions for working with children with these kinds of disabilities include:

- Keep the child seated near your desk and near to the chalkboard.

- Repeat major ideas and concepts.

- Carefully structure worksheet pages for the child.

- Provide the child with graph paper. The grid helps in aligning numbers so the child can organize the work.

- Use physical models rather than simply referring to pictures in the text.

- Remind these students to pay attention if their minds begin to wander. (Be certain to do this without causing them any embarrassment.)

Memory Deficits   Students with memory deficits have trouble recalling things. Children who have a short-term memory disorder often cannot recall things even as they are copying them from the chalkboard. Lengthy, verbal directions pose a problem, since they often forget what they have just seen or heard. Children who have a long-term memory disorder often cannot recall having learned something as little as a day or two later. These children especially have trouble memorizing and retaining the basic arithmetic facts. Have a calculator readily available for them to use at will. Insisting on their learning the basic algorithms and facts of arithmetic will only place them under undue pressure and possibly prohibit them from learning any mathematics as they struggle to memorize these facts. Their inability to retain items in memory makes it extremely difficult for them to recognize patterns in many cases.

Some suggestions for working with these children include:

- Offer one instruction at a time rather than an entire series of instructions at once. You might consider writing out these instructions as a series of short, individual steps.

- Show examples of how to apply a given algorithm rather than teach the entire algorithm in the abstract.

- Make sure a calculator is available at all times.

For children with both perceptual and memory deficits, the extensive use of colored chalk is suggested. Keep a supply of colored pencils available so that students can copy the colors used on the board during a presentation.

Students with ADD and ADHD   Some of your students will be identified as having attention deficit disorder (ADD) or attention deficit hyperactivity disorder (ADHD). These children are not always easy to recognize. They usually have difficulty maintaining their attention span, and some forms of hyperactivity are often present. For these students, clear routines should be established, and they must understand exactly what is expected of them. You can channel the hyperactivity of these children by involving them in classroom activities that include hands-on and active participation rather than having them sit quietly in their seats to work on a long set of drill-and-practice problems. Remember, these children require a modified instructional approach (which may be listed in their IEP). Your assignments should be kept short. Rather than a long, single problem, you should divide the problem up into several short, easy-to-follow tasks. If these students seem to be "wandering," simply walk over and quietly talk to them.

Students with Physical Disabilities

Physical disabilities are another category of disabilities that bear careful consideration and planning. These disabilities usually fall into three major categories: difficulties in hearing, visual disabilities, and disabled students in wheelchairs.

Hard-of-Hearing Students.   If you have a hard-of-hearing student in your mathematics class, first determine how the child communicates. There are basically three methods: American Sign Language, vocalization, or total communication (a combination of the first two).

If the student uses American Sign Language to communicate, the school will usually assign a special signer or interpreter to work with the student in your class. This may upset the dynamics of your class for a while, since other students may be distracted by the signer. However, be assured that this distraction will quickly vanish as students grow accustomed to the new situation.

In working with the hard-of-hearing students, be certain that you face them when talking. Many have learned to read lips. Assign a buddy student in class who can check to see that the student has understood the classwork. Above all, put everything you can into written form. Many teachers remember to put the notes that are on the board into writing but forget to put into writing any additional instructions given to the class orally.

If the child's hearing is extremely impaired, you might ask about an auditory trainer. This is a device that the teacher and the student both wear. As you teach, the student "hears" you through this device.

Students with Visual Disabilities.   Always seat these students near the front of the room, giving them a clear, unobstructed view of the chalkboard. Even though these children wear glasses, this does not mean that they can see clearly from anywhere in the room. You should check these students' notes periodically to make certain they are getting all the material. Furthermore, you should consider reproducing the class notes in extra-large type (on your computer) for students with vision problems. You also can assign a reader who will come into your class and read material to the student. You might contact the American Society for the Blind to see if there are any copies of your textbook available on tape or in braille (if the student reads braille).

There is a great deal of advanced technology available for visually impaired students. Many have laptop computers with magnification. Ask the special education teacher in your school to find out what else is available to these students.

Wheelchair-Confined Students.   These students must have an accessible classroom. In some cases, this might involve moving the class to the first floor of your school if no elevator is readily available. There have also been great advances in recent years in the technology for these children. Most have laptop computers. Some use laptops with a pointer and enter the material by pressing the keys with a stick or pointer. Some use a "talking machine"; using a pointer, the student presses an appropriate key and the computer speaks. Find out what is available for these students.

Other ways to help include putting the student's desk on blocks to raise the desk so that the wheelchair can slide under it. Also when you talk to students in wheelchairs, try putting yourself at their eye level. Having the teacher tower above them is very imposing and distracting to these students.

Special considerations must be given to LD children when grading and returning homework and test papers. Too many red marks will reduce their self-esteem, which is necessary for them to achieve. Classroom organization and classroom routines are the key. If everything follows in order and the papers and materials are always in the same place each day, you will have gone a long way to helping students with disabilities.

Gender Equity

For many years, it was not considered feminine for girls to be good in mathematics. Indeed, parents often would tell their daughters not to excel in mathematics; it was considered a male subject. As a result, it was not at all unusual for girls to drop out of mathematics classes as soon as their minimum requirements had been fulfilled. Thus, as with any self-fulfilling prophecy, girls who expected to not succeed in mathematics did not succeed. This led to feelings of incompetence, low self-esteem, and the conviction that they could never succeed in mathematics no matter how hard they might try. In many cases, female students did not feel that mathematics could play an important role in their everyday lives. Women college students do not take as many advanced mathematics courses as do their male counterparts. However, long before college, the idea that females cannot excel in mathematics begins. It is in the middle grades, when adolescents experience so many physical and hormonal changes, that the teacher's role in dispelling these myths is crucial.

As a teacher of mathematics in middle school, there are several things you can do to help eliminate gender inequity and ensure mathematics power for all students: First, encourage wide participation in class discussions by both genders. Do not allow male students to dominate the discussion. Second, ask equally demanding questions of all your students and encourage all to think, reason, and enter the class discussion. Female students often will respond to open-ended questions, those that allow for more creative solutions. Third, become aware of your students' attitudes toward mathematics. Talk about mathematics in a nonthreatening manner, to put both sexes at ease. The anxieties that females (and males) often feel about mathematics are not unique to any one group; all students have them at one time or another. Talking about them puts math anxieties into the proper perspective. On the other hand, you must also be careful to not lower your expectations of students by trying to relieve their anxieties. Students can usually sense when you lower your expectations, and this can have the exact opposite effect, causing them to doubt their own abilities. Finally, let your female students know that you do not give them grades; anything they receive, they have earned. Your female students must learn to trust that they do have the ability to succeed in mathematics.

Activities

1. Have you ever considered the reasons why you decided to become a middle school mathematics teacher? Write a brief paragraph giving your reasons for becoming a mathematics teacher. Then write another paragraph explaining why you chose to teach in the middle school.

2. "Practice makes perfect" is a well-known adage. Discuss the role of rote practice of skills in the middle school mathematics classroom.

3. You have one student in your seventh-grade class who is special. She is extremely gifted. You cannot accelerate her into the next grade. What kind of program would you develop for this child?

4. Whenever you ask the class to divide itself into working groups of five students, the girls all seem to group themselves with the girls, and the boys with the boys. How would you handle this situation?

5. Interview three or four of your classmates who attended a middle school. Ask them what they remember. Did they feel that their middle school years were productive in learning mathematics?

Bibliography

Becker, Joanne R. "Differential Treatment of Females and Males in Mathematics Classes." *Journal for Research in Mathematics Education* 12 (January 1981): 40–53.

Bodner, G. M. *Constructivism: A Theory of Knowledge.* Washington, DC: Wiley, 1986.

Bruner, Jerome. *The Process of Education.* Cambridge, MA: Harvard University Press, 1977.

Choate, Joyce S. *Successful Inclusive Teaching.* Needham Heights, MA: Allyn and Bacon, 1997.

Feigenbaum, Ruth. "Algebra for Students with Learning Disabilities." *The Mathematics Teacher* (2000), 39 (4).

Fennema, Elizabeth, and Carpenter, Thomas P. " Sex-Related Differences in Mathematics: Results from the National Assessment." *Mathematics Teacher* 74 (October 1981): 554–559.

Henrion, Claudia. *Women in Mathematics: The Addition of Difference.* Bloomington: Indiana University Press, 1998.

Kline, M. *Why Johnny Can't Add.* New York: St. Martin's Press, 1973.

Leitzel, James R. C. (Ed.). *A Call for Change: Recommendations for the Mathematical Preparation of Teachers of Mathematics.* Washington, DC: Mathematical Association of America, 1991.

National Council of Teachers of Mathematics. *Curriculum and Evaluation Standards.* Reston, VA: Author, 1989.

Piaget, Jean. *To Understand Is to Invent.* New York: Viking, 1973.

Rafferty, C. D., Heinenbach, M., and Helms, H. "Leveling the Playing Field Through Active Engagement." *Middle School Journal* (March 1999): 55.

Stevenson, Chris. *Teaching Ten- to Fourteen-Year-Olds.* Boston, MA: Allyn and Bacon, 2002.

Thornton, C., and Bley, N. S. *Windows of Opportunity: Mathematics for Students with Special Needs.* Reston VA: National Council of Teachers of Mathematics, 1994.

Trentacosta, Janet, and Kenney, Margaret J. (Eds.). *Multicultural and Gender Equity in the Mathematics Classroom.* Reston, VA: National Council of Teachers of Mathematics, 1997.

Vygotsky, L. *Thought and Language.* Cambridge, MA: MIT Press, 1962.

Zaslovsky, Claudia. *Women in Mathematics: The Addition of Difference.* Bloomington: Indiana University Press, 1998.

Related Research

Ball, D. L. (1990). The mathematical understandings that preservice teachers bring to teacher education. *Elementary School Journal* 90: 449–466.

Beaton, A. E., Mullis, L. V. S., Martin, M. O., Gonzalez, E. J., Kelly, D. L., & Smith, T. A. (1997). *TIMSS: Mathematics achievement in the middle school years.* Chestnut Hill: Boston College.

Brooks, J. G., & Brooks, M. G. (1997). *Constructivism: An ASCD professional inquiry kit.* Alexandria, VA: Association for Supervision and Curriculum Development.

Brooks, J. G., & Brooks, M. G. (1993). *In search of understanding: The case for constructivist classrooms.* Alexandria, VA: Association for Supervision and Curriculum Development.

Brown, I., Jr., & Inouye, D. K. (1978). Learned helplessness through modeling: The role of perceived similarity in competence. *Journal of Personality and Social Psychology* 36: 900–908.

Bruner, J. S. (1973). *The relevance of education.* New York: Norton.

Bruner, J. S. (1966). *Toward a theory of instruction.* New York: Norton.

Cobb, P. (1988). The tension between theories of learning and instruction in mathematics education. *Educational Psychologist* 23 (2): 87–103.

Fennema, E., & Franke, M. L. (1992). Teachers' knowledge and its impact. In D. Grouws (Ed.), *Handbook of research on mathematics teaching and learning* (pp. 147–164). Reston, VA: National Council of Teachers of Mathematics.

Ford, M. E. (1992). *Motivating humans: Goals, emotions, and personal agency beliefs.* Newbury Park, CA: Sage.

Fuys, D., Geddes, D., & Tischler, R. (1988). *The van Hiele model of thinking in geometry among adolescents.* JRME monograph number 3. Reston, VA: National Council of Teachers of Mathematics.

Grouws, D. A. (Ed.). (1992). *Handbook of research on mathematics teaching and learning.* Reston, VA: National Council of Teachers of Mathematics.

Hembree, R. (1990). The nature, effects, and relief of mathematics anxiety. *Journal for Research in Mathematics Education* 21: 33–46.

Linchevski, L., & Kutscher, B. (1998). Tell me with whom you're learning, and I'll tell you how much you've learned: Mixed-ability versus same-ability grouping in mathematics. *Journal for Research in Mathematics Education* 29: 533–554.

Malone, T. W., & Lepper, M. R. (1987). Making learning fun: A taxonomy of intrinsic motivations for learning. In R. Snow & M. Farr (Eds.), *Aptitude, learning and instruction,* vol. 3: *Cognitive and affective process analyses* (pp. 223–253). Hillsdale, NJ: Lawrence Erlbaum.

Nicholls, J. G. (1984). Achievement motivation: Conceptions of ability, subjective experience, task choice, and performance. *Psychological Review* 91 (3): 328–346.

Rogers, K. B. (1998). Using current research to make "good" decisions about grouping. *NASSP Bulletin, 82,* 38–46.

Skemp, R. R. (1979). *Intelligence, learning, and action: A foundation for theory and practice in education.* New York: Wiley.

Skemp, R. R. (1971). *The psychology of learning mathematics.* Middlesex, England: Pelican.

Tymoczko, Thomas. (Ed.). (1998). *New directions in the philosophy of mathematics: An anthology.* Princeton: Princeton University Press.

CHAPTER 2

The Middle School Mathematics Curriculum

HISTORICAL BACKGROUND

Before examining the mathematics curriculum for today's middle schools, it is useful to review mathematics programs as they have evolved over time. In the United States there is no national curriculum. Each state, city, or school district can include virtually anything they wish in the school curriculum. In spite of this freedom, there is a great deal of uniformity in what is presented. In general, the textbook determines what is taught. Most states and local school districts have developed frameworks or curriculum guides that spell out what is to be taught at each grade level. However, these are either modeled from textbooks or the textbooks are written to meet the frameworks. But from which sources were these texts and frameworks drawn? Several movements in the field have shaped the current curriculum: New Math, Back to Basics, and NCTM's *Agenda for Action*.

New Math

For the first fifty years of the twentieth century, there were few changes in the mathematics curriculum. Textbook writers decided independently what they would include in their texts, and their choices comprised the school mathematics programs. This situation changed shortly after World War II and the launching of the Russian *Sputnik*. The scientific revolution had begun, and the U.S. government as well as several private foundations felt that the school mathematics curriculum had to be updated, expanded, and improved. Several major projects were formulated and funded to develop a new mathematics curriculum and model textbooks for use in grades K through 12. Some of the more influential groups involved were the School Mathematics Study Group (SMSG), the University of Illinois Committee on School Mathematics (UICSM), and the Greater Cleveland Mathematics Program (GCMP). For the first time, there was an organized effort to create a common mathematics program for the schools throughout the United States. The result was New Math. The goal of the New Math movement was to increase the mathematics content being taught in the schools, to make it more rigorous, and to introduce abstractions much earlier in the curriculum. New textbooks were created and written, and found their way into many schools. Students were exposed to set notation, numeration systems with bases other than 10, and an increased emphasis on notation and mathematical language. The movement did not survive. First, it was too abstract. Second, many teachers were not able to cope with the content. Finally, it did not enhance the children's computational skills, which many people regard as critical. Another important reason for the demise of New Math was the failure to involve the public and parents in the changes being made. The program was completely developed and controlled by college-level mathematicians and mathematics educators. When children brought their homework home, parents were faced with material that was completely unfamiliar to them.

Thus, the New Math movement died, but not without having a lasting influence on school mathematics. Even today, the NCTM Standards reflect many of the concepts of the New Math movement. Ideas that were an integral part of the New Math era remain in mathematics textbooks and are now a vital part of the curriculum.

Back to Basics

The Back-to-Basics movement developed as a reaction to the New Math movement. The curriculum returned to its basis in rote learning, memorization, and drill and practice. This movement, too, came to an end, partly because test scores revealed that students had not improved in basic skills and were doing very poorly in their understanding of concepts and problem solving. However, the major reason for the demise of the Back-to-Basics movement was the protest and opposition of mathematics educators across the nation, in particular, the National Council of Supervisors of Mathematics (NCSM) and the National Council of Teachers of Mathematics (NCTM). In 1978, NCSM published a position paper on basic skills entitled *The Ten Basic Skills of Mathematics* in which it urged that the mathematics curriculum move forward, not back to basics. It stated that "the skills of yesterday are not the ones that today's students will need when they are adults. They will face a world of change in which they must be able to solve many different kinds of problems."

The ten skill areas are:

1. **Problem Solving.** Students should be able to solve problems in situations which are new to them.

2. **Applying Mathematics to Everyday Situations.** Students should be able to use mathematics to deal with situations they face daily in an ever-changing world.

3. **Alertness to Reasonableness of Results.** Students should learn to check if their answers are "in the ballpark."

4. **Estimation and Approximation.** Students should learn to estimate quantity, length, distance, weight, and so on.

5. **Appropriate Computational Skills.** Students should be able to use the four basic operations with whole numbers and decimals, and they should be able to do computations with simple fractions and percents.

6. **Geometry.** Students should know basic properties of simple geometric figures.

7. **Measurement.** Students should be able to measure in both the metric and customary systems.

8. **Tables, Charts, and Graphs.** Students should be able to read and make simple tables, graphs, and charts.

9. **Using Mathematics to Predict.** Students should know how mathematics is used to find the likelihood of future events.

10. **Computer Literacy.** Students should know about the many uses of computers in society and should be aware of what computers can do and cannot do.

When NCSM issued this position statement, it also discussed the role of computation in the curriculum. It claimed that computation skills were important but that most long computations should be done with a calculator. Though teaching computational skills alone was of little use, when taught along with other skills, facility with computation added to students' overall mathematical ability.

NCTM's Agenda for Action

The second stimulus for the termination of the Back-to-Basics movement occurred in 1980, when the NCTM, the major professional organization of mathematics educators in the United States and Canada, released a publication entitled *An Agenda for Action: Curriculum for the 1980s.* This publication consisted of a set of recommendations for the teaching of mathematics, as follows:

1. Problem solving must be the focus of school mathematics.

2. The concept of basic skills in mathematics must encompass more than computational facility.

3. Mathematics programs must take full advantage of the power of calculators and computers at all grade levels.

4. Stringent standards of both effectiveness and efficiency must be applied to the teaching of mathematics.

5. A wider range of measures than conventional testing must evaluate the success of mathematics programs and student learning.

6. More mathematics study must be required for all students, and a flexible curriculum with a greater range of options should be designed to accommodate the diverse needs of the student population.

7. Mathematics teachers must demand of themselves and their colleagues a high level of professionalism.

8. Public support for mathematics instruction must be raised to a level commensurate with the importance of mathematical understanding to individuals and society.

These two publications, the position paper of the NCSM and the *Agenda* of the NCTM, initiated the current changes in the school mathematics curriculum. A landmark date, 1980, marked the initiation of a school mathematics curriculum that would focus on problem solving, reasoning, and other process skills along with important mathematical concepts and skills from many branches of mathematics. This marked the beginning of the time period in which the content of school mathematics would be greatly influenced—indeed, virtually determined—by professional organizations of mathematics educators. Since that time, the NCTM has put out four additional major publications: *Curriculum and Evaluation Standards for School Mathematics* (1989), *Professional Standards for Teaching Mathematics* (1991), *Assessment Standards for Teaching Mathematics* (1995), and *Principles and Standards for School Mathematics* (2000).

WHAT WAS THE MIDDLE SCHOOL MATHEMATICS CURRICULUM?

Before the creation of the middle school, the mathematics curriculum for grades 5 through 8 was part of the K–8 elementary curriculum. In many school districts, a junior high school existed to include grades 7 through 9. Grades 7 and 8 pursued the elementary school curriculum, and in most cases, the study of algebra was begun in grade 9. For those students not planning to attend college, algebra was replaced by a course entitled General Mathematics. This general math curriculum merely extended what had been previously taught in grades K through 8, with additional exercises that tried to relate the mathematics to the real world.

This elementary school curriculum, originally designed to meet the needs of nineteenth-century students, was devoted almost entirely to the study of arithmetic, consisting mainly of rules and procedures for computing with whole numbers, decimals, and fractions. Shape identification and elements of metric geometry were included, but algebra, statistics, probability, and number theory were left out. In grades 7 and 8, ratio, proportion, and percent were introduced. These were the only new topics included in the curriculum for those grade levels. In fact, a study of popular textbooks of the time, conducted by J. R. Flanders in 1987, revealed that in grades 7 and 8 only 30 percent of the pages introduced any new material.

In the classroom, the basic technique for learning was memory, practice, and more practice. No emphasis was placed on thinking or reasoning. Word problems, often irrelevant, were included to show an application of the mathematics topic being studied and to provide practice in the skill. For example, if the topic just taught was the simultaneous solution of two linear equations in two variables, the word problem might be a mixture of two kinds of coffee or a problem involving the rate, time, and distance of two trains. The teacher presented the problem, explained it, and then showed the student how to "do it." This was followed in class by several more illustrations of the same type of problem, which were then followed by a homework assignment of many more problems of the same type. Thus, the students were taught to "type" problems, and were given an algorithm, or method specific for doing that type of problem. As long as there were no changes in the problem at exam time, the students did well on the test. The students were not required to think through the problem. Instead the teacher showed them how to do it. The main goal was to get the correct answer, not to think about what the problem involved.

These were the conditions that existed at the end of the Back-to-Basics movement. The two position statements of the NCSM and the NCTM, along with the subsequent efforts of the NCTM, have produced significant changes in the school mathematics curriculum.

WHAT IS THE MIDDLE SCHOOL MATHEMATICS CURRICULUM?

The middle school mathematics curriculum can now be discussed because the middle school has been fairly well established as a separate entity. Many states have already established separate certification for middle school teachers, and other states are moving in this direction. However, the middle school mathematics curriculum is still integrated within the K–12 curriculum and, as such, must be viewed as part of the whole.

By far the greatest influence on today's mathematics curriculum is the efforts of the NCTM. The NCTM Standards (established in their four publications) have provided and are continuing to provide the guidelines for most current textbook series, state frameworks, and curriculum guides.

But before looking at exactly what the NCTM recommends and at the evolving curriculum, some questions need to be addressed. Is there really a need to change the mathematics program? Why change a program that has served so many people so well for so long? Isn't this change just for change's sake? The answer to this last question is an emphatic NO! The traditional curriculum served the needs of an America that was engaged primarily in agriculture and industry. Our current America is subsumed in a scientific explosion and a fast-paced information age. The complex demands placed on each individual today by these factors have created a radical change in how we view mathematics, what mathematics should be taught, and how we should teach mathematics. Employers today want employees who can apply several strategies to solve an unfamiliar problem situation. People today are constantly confronted by situations that require sound reasoning, logical deduction, and the ability to analyze and interpret data. Everyone today must be able to use calculators, computers, and other technological devices. They must have the ability to estimate and a keen number sense. Addressing these needs is not possible through the traditional mathematics curriculum. These social and technological changes require a change in the mathematics curriculum.

THE NCTM STANDARDS

In this book, *Curriculum and Evaluation Standards for School Mathematics* (1989) is integrated with the *Principles and Standards for School Mathematics* (2000). The *Standards 2000* is a refined and updated revision of the original standards. The NCTM states that *Standards 2000* extends the vision of the original standards and offers a rich resource for those trying to improve mathematics education. The 2000 edition contains electronic enhancements as well as additional engaging examples in the content areas. There is also an electronic version of the *Standards 2000*. The basic recommendations of the 2000 document differ little from the original 1989 publication, but there are several organizational changes, as seen in the table.

	1989 Standards	*2000 Standards*
Content grade bands	K–4, 5–8, 9–12	pre-K–2, 3–5, 6–8, 9–12
Process standards	Mathematics as problem solving Mathematics as communication Mathematics as reasoning Mathematical connections	Problem solving Reasoning and proof Communication Connections Representation
Content standards	Number and number relationships Number systems and theory Computation and estimation Patterns and functions Algebra Statistics Probability Geometry Measurement	Number and operations Algebra Geometry Measurement Data analysis

The middle school is a critical period in the mathematics development of the early adolescent. In the overview of *Standards 2000,* the authors state: "The middle grades represent a significant turning point in students' lives. During the middle grades, students solidify conceptions about themselves as learners of mathematics. They arrive at conclusions about their competence in mathematics, their attitude, their interests, and their motivation. These conceptions will influence how they approach the study of mathematics in later years, which in turn will affect their later careers and personal opportunities" (p. 17).

Probably the most radical and significant component of the 1989 *Standards* was the first four standards put forth and extended across all grade levels. These standards were referred to as process standards and dealt with problem solving, connections, reasoning, and communications. In *Standards 2000,* a fifth process standard, representation, was added. For the first time in the history of school mathematics, it was suggested that classroom time be specifically devoted to helping children develop reasoning skills, learn problem-solving strategies, see the connections between the various branches of mathematics and between mathematics and other disciplines, and learn to use mathematics and mathematical terms in their everyday lives. The standards bear more close examination to see how they address curriculum issues.

Process Standards

In presenting the standards, a 5–8 grade band is used because it corresponds to the middle school period. The four process standards—problem solving, communication, reasoning, and connections—of the 1989 standards are set forth as well as the 2000 addition, representation.

Problem Solving   Problem solving is the cornerstone of mathematics. Computational and algorithmic skills are of little value if the problem is not understood and if a path to the answer is not known. Middle school students should be presented with ample opportunity to resolve problem situations and to develop their own problem-solving strategies. Not only is problem solving a topic of study, but it is also a process that should pervade the entire study of mathematics, and is also a teaching strategy. It is the context in which concepts and skills should be taught and learned.

In grades 5 through 8 the Standards expect students to:

1. Use problem-solving approaches to investigate and understand mathematical content

2. Formulate problems from within and outside mathematics

3. Develop and apply a variety of strategies to solve problems, with emphasis on multistep and nonroutine problems

4. Verify and interpret results with respect to the original problem situation

5. Generalize solutions and strategies to new problem situations

6. Acquire confidence in using mathematics meaningfully

Communication   Communication skills have long been neglected in mathematics classrooms. Students should be able to communicate intelligently to their classmates and others about the solutions they have attempted and the mathematics they are learning. The ability to communicate will add to their understanding of mathematics. Children who can read, write, listen, and communicate about mathematics will be better able to deal successfully with the scientific era in which they live.

In grades 5 through 8, the Standards expect students to:

1. Model situations using oral, written, concrete, pictorial, graphical, and algebraic methods

2. Reflect on and clarify their own thinking about mathematical ideas and situations

3. Develop common understandings of mathematical ideas, including the role of definitions

4. Use the skills of reading, listening, and viewing to interpret and evaluate mathematical ideas

5. Discuss mathematical ideas and make conjectures and convincing arguments

6. Appreciate the value of mathematical notation and its role in the development of mathematical ideas

Reasoning   Reasoning is fundamental to mathematics. The development of reasoning is a primary instructional goal of all education, and nowhere is it more important than in mathematics. Children must be able to draw logical conclusions from sets of data, determine inconsistencies, and make and demonstrate the validity of conjectures. This is probably the most important skill a person must possess to successfully meet the demands of current society. Reasoning is an integral part of the problem-solving process. The middle school is a crucial period of development for children. It is the time in which many students move from the concrete to the abstract. Concrete examples may still be necessary for new relationships, but this is the time that many students can move to more formal logic.

In grades 5 through 8, the Standards expect students to:

1. Recognize and apply deductive and inductive reasoning

2. Understand and apply reasoning processes, with special attention to spatial reasoning and reasoning with proportions and graphs

3. Make and evaluate mathematical conjectures and arguments

4. Validate their own thinking

5. Appreciate the pervasive use and power of reasoning as part of mathematics

Connections   For many years, the middle school mathematics program consisted mainly of a continuation and extension of the material studied in the primary grades. This material was mainly the further development of computational and algorithmic skills. To most students, mathematics consisted of a set of isolated topics.

It is important that students experience mathematics as an integrated whole, not a set of independent topics. Mathematics also should be seen as relevant and connected to other disciplines and to situations students face outside of school. Through mathematics they can model real-world situations and situations that confront them in other school activities.

In grades 5 through 8, the Standards expect students to:

1. See mathematics as an integrated whole

2. Explore problems and describe results using graphical, numerical, physical, algebraic, and verbal models or representations

3. Use a mathematical idea to further their understanding of other mathematical ideas

4. Apply mathematical thinking and modeling to solve problems that arise in other disciplines, such as art, music, psychology, science, and business

5. Value the role of mathematics in our culture and society

Representation The ability to represent or simulate a problem situation in real life is a vital skill. The simulation can be concrete or a symbolic representation using paper and pencil. It can utilize manipulative materials, be a line drawing, or take the form of a chart, graph, table, or equation. Simulating a problem situation helps students understand what is going on and also communicates their thought process to other classmates as well as to the teacher. The process of representation should begin in the primary grades and be continued throughout the school years. The middle school grades are a particularly important time, because during this period the student moves from concrete modeling to symbolic representation, which is the process of mathematics.

In grades 5 through 8, the Standards expect students to

1. Create and use representations to organize, record, and communicate mathematical ideas

2. Select, apply, and translate among mathematical representations to solve problems

3. Use representations to model and interpret physical, social, and mathematical phenomena

These five process standards attempt to expand school mathematics programs beyond traditional content. For the first time, mathematics textbook pages are devoted to problem solving, reasoning, connections, communication, and representations. The content standards deal with traditional mathematics but recommend a significant change in the grade placement and mathematics content. NCTM has taken a bold stand on the grade placement of certain topics and on the sophistication level required by students to master the content. In particular, the recommendations regarding algebra and geometry are quite ambitious. In many respects, the recommendations are reminiscent of the New Math era. They are not quite as rigorous but are nevertheless much more sophisticated than what was previously set forth.

The Content Standards

The ten content areas in the 1989 *Standards* are presented, because they provide a better differentiation of the subject matter, particularly for the beginning teacher.

Number and Number Relationships The study of numbers, the fundamental operations with numbers and the relationship between numbers, has always been the bread and butter of the elementary school mathematics program. Most mathematics educators do not find fault with this aspect of the current program. There are many, however, that feel that too much time is spent on the computational algorithms and not enough time given to conceptual development and an understanding of the relationships between the numbers.

In grades 5 through 8, the Standards expect students to:

1. Understand, represent, and use numbers in a variety of equivalent forms (integer, fraction, decimal, percent, exponential, and scientific notational) in real-world and mathematical problem situations

2. Develop number sense for whole numbers, fractions, decimals, integers, and rational numbers and find their location on the number line

3. Understand and apply ratios, proportions, and percents in a wide variety of situations

4. Investigate relationships among fractions, decimals, and percents

5. Represent numerical relationships in one- and two-dimensional graphs

Number Systems and Number Theory

Instruction in grades 5 through 8 typically devotes an inordinate amount of time to computation and very little time to fostering understanding of the basic structure of number systems and underlying structure of arithmetic. Students should see mathematics as as a coherent body of knowledge, not merely as a collection of isolated facts and processes.

In grades 5 through 8, the Standards expect students to:

1. Understand and appreciate the need for numbers beyond the whole numbers

2. Develop and use order relations for whole numbers, fractions, decimals, integers, and rational numbers

3. Extend their understanding of whole numbers operations to fractions, decimals, integers, and rational numbers

4. Understand the basic operations and how they are related to one another

5. Develop and apply number theory concepts (e.g., primes, factors, and multiples) in real-world and mathematical problem situations

Computation and Estimation

Computation is still a very important part of mathematics education but the means of computation has changed. Inexpensive calculators are now used for computations that were formerly done with paper and pencil. Paper-and-pencil calculation is still an important skill to teach, but computational skills should not dominate the curriculum. In the past, children who had not mastered basic arithmetic skills often were held back from studying more complex and meaningful mathematics. This is wrong! The ability to compute with paper and pencil is not a prerequisite for achievement in mathematics. The ability to compute with paper and pencil is important, but not necessary. Rather, the student should learn to choose an appropriate method of computation when computation is called for. That is, which method is most appropriate for a given situation? Is it using a calculator for complex calculations such as $483 \times 5.26 + \sqrt{19}$, or, is it mental calculation such as 9×7? Or, is paper and pencil more appropriate for something like $432 + 567 + 23$? Or, perhaps estimation is sufficient. Large portions of classroom time should not be devoted to the development of human calculators. The NCTM standards suggest that much of the time previously devoted to mastering computational skills should be given over to having students problem solve, develop procedures, evaluate their own work, and interpret the computations done by machines. The use of technology for computation does demand that students be able to use estimation skills. They must be able to determine if the answer obtained by the computational device is "in the ballpark." Thus, time must be devoted to helping students develop their estimation skills. Such skills will offer significant advantages to children in endeavors beyond the classroom.

In grades 5 through 8, the Standards expect students to:

1. Compute with whole numbers, fractions, decimals, integers, and rational numbers

2. Develop, analyze, and explain procedures for computation and techniques for estimation

3. Use the properties of commutativity, associativity, and distributivity to simplify computation

4. Develop, analyze, and explain methods for solving proportions

5. Select and use an appropriate method for computing from among mental arithmetic, paper-and-pencil, calculator, and computer methods

6. Use computation, estimation, and proportion to solve problems

7. Use estimation to check the reasonableness of results

Patterns and Functions   Patterns and functions are major themes of mathematics. W. W. Sawyer, a well-known mathematician, once said that mathematics was a search for all patterns. Patterns appear all around us in nature, in science, and in human behavior. Students should be able to recognize and describe patterns and predict the behavior of the pattern or of the event described by the pattern. In the primary grades, students observe patterns that exist in concrete objects such as strings of beads, rows of shapes, and patterns of color. They also are exposed to patterns of numbers, such as even or odd natural numbers. In grades 5 through 8, the skill of pattern recognition must be extended to functional relationships in which a change in one variable causes a change in a dependent variable. Students can gain experience in patterns and functions by making and examining graphs, charts, expressions, and equations. Pattern recognition also plays an important role in problem solving. Finding the pattern is a problem-solving strategy that can be used to resolve perplexing arithmetic and geometric problems.

In grades 5 through 8, the Standards expect students to:

1. Describe, extend, analyze, and generate a wide variety of patterns

2. Describe and represent relationships with tables, graphs, and rules

3. Analyze functional relationships to explain how a change in one quantity results in a change in another

4. Use patterns and functions to represent and solve problems

Algebra   Perhaps the greatest change being suggested in the middle school mathematics curriculum is the extent to which algebra is included; it is a major component that permeates the entire middle school program. Algebra is the bridge between the concrete mathematics of elementary school and the abstract mathematics of the senior high school, university, and research institution. Algebra is the language of mathematics—the common denominator of virtually all branches of mathematics. Algebraic symbolization is the way in which mathematicians represent and describe the phenomena they are investigating. Teachers need to equip students with the power to represent, in algebraic terms, the quantitative problems they face daily in and out of class. All students need to develop the ability to use variables in expressions and equations to represent the problem situations they are investigating. The algebra included in today's school programs goes well beyond the factorization of polynomials and the solution of linear and quadratic equations. Algebra is a way of thinking; it aids students in analyzing, representing, and solving problems and gives them the ability to focus on relationships in general terms, as opposed to focusing on answers when dealing with specifics, as in arithmetic.

In grades 5 through 8, the Standards expect students to:

1. Understand the concepts of variable, expression, and equation

2. Represent situations and number patterns with tables, graphs, verbal rules, and equations and explore the interrelationships of these representations

3. Analyze tables and graphs to identify properties and relationships

4. Develop confidence in solving linear equations using concrete, informal, and formal methods

5. Investigate inequalities and nonlinear equations informally

6. Apply algebraic methods to solve a variety of real-world and mathematical problems

Statistics   Not too long ago, statistics and statisticians seemed to be living in a world apart from that of the ordinary citizen. Nowadays, in the age of information and technology, the ordinary citizen is inundated with statistical information through the newspapers, in advertising, on television, and from schools in the form of test results, school rankings, and student achievement. It is necessary that our students understand how data are obtained and processed. They must also be able to interpret the findings and conclusions of statistical presentations in whatever form they are presented. A knowledge of statistics is necessary if students are to become intelligent citizens and consumers. Students also need to learn to identify how data are obtained and processed. Middle school students are actively involved in the statistical process when they formulate questions; gather, process, and analyze data; and present and explain their findings by means of tables, charts, and graphs.

In grades 5 through 8, the Standards expect students to:

1. Systematically collect, organize, and describe data

2. Construct, read, and interpret tables, charts, and graphs, including line and bar graphs, histograms, box plots, and scatter plots

3. Make inferences and convincing arguments based on data analysis

4. Evaluate arguments based on data analysis

5. Develop an appreciation for statistical methods as powerful means for decision making

Probability   As with statistics, today's citizens must have an understanding of probability. We are constantly confronted in the news media and in ordinary conversation with statements such as, "The chance of winning the state lottery is 1 in 6 million," "The odds of Big Red winning the Derby are 4 to 3," "The probability of precipitation (POP) tomorrow is 40%." Children in the middle school grades are interested in games, as are most people. Involving students in experiments—such as tossing coins, rolling dice, pulling colored balls from a bag, or matching cards—can lead to an understanding of the relationship between numerical expressions denoting probability and the conditions that lead to those expressions. These experiments and their outcomes also provide students with real-world applications of fractions, decimals, ratios, and percents.

In grades 5 through 8, the Standards expect students to:

1. Model situations by devising and carrying out experiments or simulations to determine probabilities

2. Model situations by constructing a sample space to determine probabilities

3. Appreciate the power of using a probability model by comparing experimental results with mathematical expectations

4. Make predictions and test conjectures based on experimental or theoretical probabilities

5. Develop an appreciation for the pervasive use of probability in the real world

Geometry   The mathematics program of the middle school grades has always included some geometry. Students were taught to recognize and identify several plane figures, such as rectangles, squares, isosceles and equilateral triangles, trapezoids, and circles. The metric properties of perimeter, circumference, and area were also introduced.

The current Standards greatly expand these areas. Three-dimensional figures are now included in geometry in middle school, along with the associated topics of surface area and volume. The concepts of congruence and similarity are introduced and provide applications of ratio and proportion. Right triangles, the Pythagorean theorem, and angle measurement are also investigated. Coordinate geometry is included as another way to represent and examine shapes. However, the most significant addition is the inclusion of the basic notions of logic and logical inference. Validating conclusions and inferences with the use of if-then statements fosters the goals of the process standard of reasoning. These recommendations are intended to form a bridge between the concrete elementary school material and the more abstract and sophisticated secondary school mathematics.

In grades 5 through 8, the Standards expect students to:

1. Identify, describe, compare, and classify geometric figures, including congruence and similarity

2. Visualize and represent geometric figures, with special attention to developing spatial sense

3. Know the relationship between angles, side lengths, perimeter, area, and volume of similar figures

4. Explore transformations of geometric figures

5. Specify locations and describe spatial relationships using coordinate geometry and other representational systems

6. Represent and solve problems using geometric models

7. Understand and apply geometric properties and relationships

8. Develop an appreciation of geometry as a means of describing the physical world

Measurement   Measurement is not new to students. They use measurement when they solve metric problems in geometry as well as in many of their out-of-school activities. The new notion, introduced by the current standards, is that all measurements are approximations: absolutes do not appear in measurement. The concepts of approximations, orders of precision, accuracy, and tolerances are new and of great importance. Students should be actively involved in using various measuring instruments such as rulers, tapes, protractors, scales, balances, pedometers, speedometers, and so on. They should experience firsthand that the results obtained from using these instruments are all approximations and not absolutes.

In grades 5 through 8, the Standards expect students to:

1. Extend their understanding of the process of measurement

2. Estimate, make, and use measurement to describe and compare phenomena

3. Select appropriate units and tools to measure to the degree of accuracy required in a particular situation

4. Understand the structure and use of systems of measurement

5. Extend their understanding of the concepts of perimeter, area, volume, angle measure, capacity, and weight and mass

6. Develop the concept of rates and other derived and indirect measurements

7. Develop formulas and procedures for determining measures to solve problems

DISCRETE MATHEMATICS

During the 1990s, there was increased interest in an area of mathematics referred to as discrete mathematics. Discrete mathematics deals with counting arrangements of distinct objects and includes a wide variety of topics and techniques that arise in everyday life. Discrete mathematics is used by many decision makers, from government employees to those in health care, transportation, and telecommunications.

Topics from discrete mathematics are beginning to appear in some textbooks in the middle school. Much of this material has been a part of school mathematics programs but was not identified as discrete mathematics. Some examples of discrete mathematics problems are:

• How to count the number of different toppings for a pizza.

• How to find the best route from one city to another.

• How to best schedule a list of tasks to be done.

Five major themes of discrete mathematics should be addressed in the middle school grades:

1. Systematic counting and listing

2. Modeling with graphs and networks

3. Iterative and repetitive patterns

4. Following and devising a list of instructions or algorithms

5. Using algorithms to find solutions to real-world problems

SOME STANDARDS-BASED MIDDLE GRADE CURRICULA

Five middle school curriculum projects were funded by the National Science Foundation (NSF). These were intended to develop comprehensive standards-based curricula for grades 5 through 8. Each curriculum represents a comprehensive program and can stand alone.

Connected Mathematics

The Connected Mathematics Project (CMP) has as its main focus developing student knowledge of mathematics that is rich in connections. These connections are made between mathematics and its applications to other disciplines, and between mathematics developed in the elementary school and the goals of secondary school mathematics. CMP was designated as an Exemplary Program by the U.S. Department of Education.

Example: In one unit entitled "Prime Time," students learn the basics of number theory, often in a game setting. They study multiples, prime and composite numbers, even and odd numbers, square numbers, greatest common factors, and least common multiples. They discover the Fundamental Theorem of Arithmetic and understand why 1 is neither a prime nor a composite number. They connect the area and dimensions of a rectangle with products and factors, developing strategies for finding factors and multiples of a whole number. They learn to solve problems involving factors and multiples, using a variety of strategies.

Mathematics in Context

Mathematics in Context is a comprehensive mathematics curriculum for the middle grades. The development of the curriculum units represents a collaboration between research and development teams at the Freudenthal Institute at the University of Utrecht in the Netherlands, research teams at the University of Wisconsin, and a group of middle school teachers. A total of forty units have been developed for grades 5 through 8. These units are unique in that they make extensive use of realistic content and settings. Each of the units uses a theme based on a problem situation that should be of interest to students.

Example: For example, one unit is based on tiling a floor. This unit provides a wealth of mathematical applications and experiences, including similarity, ratio and proportion, scaling, measurement, and scale drawings.

MathScape

The MathScape curriculum builds on a central theme of mathematics as a human experience. Throughout the curriculum, students experience mathematics as it is used for planning, predicting, exploring, explaining, deciding, and other activities fundamental to human endeavors throughout the world and history. The pedagogy of this curriculum reflects a view of learning as a process of constructing one's own knowledge and emphasizes the importance of social context for learning mathematics in the middle school.

Example: One unit, entitled "Designing Spaces," explores different methods for representing three-dimensional structures with two-dimensional drawings. Students build a house with cubes, create a set of building plans, explore the properties of sides and angles, use a protractor to measure angles, actually build a model home, and create building designs with certain specifications. They identify structures that are made up of prisms and pyramids.

MATHThematics

The Middle Grades MATHThematics (STEM) curriculum is designed to provide teachers with curricular materials that are mathematically accurate, utilize technology, and provide students with bridges joining the fields of science and mathematics. The materials are designed to integrate communication skills into mathematics by providing opportunities for students to use reading, writing, and speaking as tools for learning mathematics. MATHThematics materials are problem centered, application based, and use technology where appropriate. Many of the lessons are designed to be project oriented and have students work cooperatively. Nontraditional assessment techniques are used throughout the materials.

Example: One example is the unit "Wonders of the World." In this unit, students use integers to represent real-world situations such as:

- Using benchmarks to estimate Fahrenheit and Celsius temperatures

- Developing and applying formulas for the area of a parallelogram, a circle, and a triangle

- Plotting points and writing the coordinates of points from a given coordinate grid

- Recognizing and identifying the parts of pyramids, cylinders, prisms

- Developing three-dimensional visualization skills by predicting the shape a net will form when assembled

MMAP/Pathways

Pathways to Algebra and Geometry is a two-year comprehensive middle school curriculum based on the Middle School Mathematics through Applications Program (MMAP). MMAP was developed at the Institute for Research on Learning and was designated as a Promising Program by the U.S. Department of Education. MMAP has developed a comprehensive middle school mathematics curriculum centered around applications projects that involve students in real-world problem solving and require students to learn and use mathematics as necessary.

Example: In a unit involving guppies, students assume the role of population biologists. Each student plays a role in the group, and a community of population biologists is formed. Through group work, shared goals, and discourse, mathematical problems emerge. Because understanding mathematics can be helpful in solving a real problem, mathematics is seen to be functional. Discussion about the problem takes place, and new mathematical understandings emerge. Skills are taught when needed.

THE ROLE OF THE MATHEMATICS TEACHER

The mathematics teacher in the middle grades has responsibility to provide the experiences necessary for students to work with significant mathematical ideas; to build their confidence, knowledge, and appropriate skills; and to communicate their ideas to others. The role of the teacher has changed. Teachers are no longer "tellers"—

explainers and presenters—but rather facilitators and choreographers of experiences and, above all, listeners. Where once teachers told students how to do the problem, they now encourage students to examine and make sense of the information presented and resolve the situation in any way they can. When students ask you "Why does this work?" or "How do we know . . . ?" or "What if we change this to . . . ?" they are beginning to make use of their creative reasoning skills. They should be encouraged to seek proof and verification of their own work rather than asking the teacher "Is this right?" or "Is this how it should be done?"

Your career as a middle school mathematics teacher must be developed with these recommendations as background. If middle school students can be challenged in their mathematics classes, taught to solve problems as they arise, helped to form hypotheses and verify them, and learn to think logically and to reason, then they will find mathematics to be alive, engaging, and satisfying as they progress through school and life.

Activities

1. Examine a copy of the NCTM *Agenda for Action*. Do you feel that the document was a failure? Did it leave a legacy for students in the twenty-first century?

2. You are approached by the parents of one of your students. The parents claim that their child is very talented in mathematics. You agree.

   a. How would you respond to the parents?

   b. What are some of the things you might decide to do to keep this child from becoming bored in class?

3. You are approached by the parents of one of your students. The parents claim that their child is rather slow in grasping new concepts in mathematics and has trouble keeping up with the "new mathematics" of the *Standards*. You agree.

   a. How would you respond to the parents?

   b. What are some of the things you might decide to do to keep this child from falling behind in mathematics?

4. What is meant by the term "process standards"? How do these differ from the "content standards" as stated in NCTM's *Principles and Standards for School Mathematics?*

5. In many middle school classrooms, the textbook determines the curriculum. Explain how you might blend your textbook with NCTM's *Principles and Standards for School Mathematics* to create a curriculum on which to base your teaching.

6. As the twentieth century drew to a close, there was once again an outcry to go "back to basics." What is your position on the discussion of reform versus basics?

7. Examine an eighth-grade mathematics textbook written since 1995. How is it different from your mathematics textbook when you were in the eighth grade?

8. What is meant by the word *process* as it is used by the NCTM in stating the "process standards"?

9. What mathematics do you think is important for middle school students? Do you agree or disagree with the *2000 Standards*?

10. Discuss the difference between understanding a concept and understanding a skill. For example, what is the difference between understanding how to add two fractions with unlike denominators and understanding why we add them in this manner?

11. Compare the goals, objectives, and subject matter content of the New Math movement as put forth by the School Mathematics Study Group (SMSG) and those of the current standards movement as expounded by the NCTM *Principles and Standards.*

12. Most textbook companies claim that their current basal series for grades K through 8 comply with NCTM *Standards.* Select several middle school textbooks and carefully examine them. Choose one or two standards and judge the extent to which the texts meet the standards.

Bibliography

Bishop, Wayne. "The California Mathematics Standards: They're Not Only Right; They're the Law." *Phi Delta Kappan* 80, no. 6 (February 1999): 439–440.

Chappell, M. F. "Geometry in the Middle Grades: From Its Past to the Present." *Mathematics Teaching in the Middle School* 6, no. 9 (May 2001): 517–519.

Edwards, Thomas G. "Some 'Big Ideas' of Algebra in the Middle Grades." *Mathematics Teaching in the Middle School* 6, no.1 (September 2000): 26–31.

Johnson, I. D. "Standards-Based Teaching: Alive and Well in Portugal." *Mathematics Teaching in the Middle School* 6, no. 9 (May 2001): 538–542.

Lambdin, D. V., Lynch, R. K., and McDaniel, H. "Algebra in the Middle Grades." *Mathematics Teaching in the Middle School* 6, no. 3 (November 2000): 195–197.

Merrow, John. "Undermining Standards." *Phi Delta Kappan* (May 2001): 653–659.

Meyer, M. R., Dekker, T., and Querelle, N. "Context in Mathematics Curricula." *Mathematics Teaching in the Middle School* 6, no. 9 (May 2001): 522–527.

National Council of Supervisors of Mathematics. *The Ten Basic Skills of Mathematics.* Minneapolis, MN: Author, 1978.

National Council of Teachers of Mathematics. *An Agenda for Action: Curriculum for the 1980s.* Reston VA: Author, 1980.

National Council of Teachers of Mathematics. *Curriculum and Evaluation Standards for School Mathematics.* Reston, VA: Author, 1989.

National Council of Teachers of Mathematics. *Professional Standards for Teaching Mathematics.* Reston, VA: Author, 1991.

National Council of Teachers of Mathematics. *Assessment Standards for Teaching Mathematics.* Reston, VA: Author, 1995.

National Council of Teachers of Mathematics. *Principles and Standards for School Mathematics: An Overview.* Reston, VA: Author, 2000.

O'Brien, Thomas C. "Parrot Math." *Phi Delta Kappan* 80, no. 6 (February 1999): 434–438.

Related Research

Anderson, R. D. (1995). Curriculum reform: Dilemmas and promise. *Phi Delta Kappan 77* (1): 33–36.

Battista, M. T. (1994). Teacher beliefs and the reform movement in mathematics education. *Phi Delta Kappan, 75* (6): 462–463, 466–470.

Conference Board of the Mathematical Sciences. (1983). *The mathematical sciences curriculum K–12: What is still fundamental and what is not.* Report to the NSB Commission on Precollege Education in Mathematics, Science, and Technology, Washington, DC.

Dossey, J. A. (1991). Discrete mathematics: The math for our time. In M. J. Kenney (Ed.), *Yearbook of the NCTM: Discrete mathematics across the curriculum, K–12* (pp. 1–9). Reston, VA: National Council of Teachers of Mathematics.

Garet, M. S., & Mills, V. L. (1995). Changes in teaching practices: The effects of the curriculum and evaluation standards. *Mathematics Teacher, 88* (5): 380–88.

Hiebert, J. (1999). Relationships between research and the NCTM standards. *Journal for Research in Mathematics Education, 30* (1), 3–19.

Hirsch, C. R. (Ed.). (1985). *1985 yearbook of the NCTM: The secondary school mathematics curriculum.* Reston, VA: National Council of Teachers of Mathematics.

Hirschhorn, D. B., et al. (1995). Rethinking the first two years of high school mathematics with the UCSMP. *Mathematics Teacher, 88* (8), 640–647.

Meiring, S. P., Rubenstein, R. N., Schultz, J. E., Lange, J., & Chambers, D. L. (1992). *A core curriculum: Making mathematics count for everyone.* Reston, VA: Author.

National Council of Teachers of Mathematics. (2000). *Principles and standards for school mathematics.* Reston, VA: Author.

National Council of Teachers of Mathematics. (1991). *Professional standards for teaching mathematics.* Reston, VA: Author.

National Council of Teachers of Mathematics. (1989). *Curriculum and evaluation standards for school mathematics.* Reston, VA: Author.

National Research Council. (1989). *Everybody counts: A report to the nation on the future of mathematics education.* Washington, DC: National Academy.

Paul, E., & Richbart, L. (1985). New York state's new three-year sequence for high school mathematics. In C. R. Hirsch (Ed.), *1985 yearbook of the NCTM: The secondary school mathematics curriculum* (pp. 200–210). Reston, VA: National Council of Teachers of Mathematics.

Smith, S. Z., et al. (1993). What the NCTM standards look like in one classroom. *Educational Leadership, 50* (8), 4–7.

Steen, L. A. (Ed.). *(1990). On the shoulders of giants: New approaches to numeracy.* Washington, DC: National Academy.

The Middle School Classroom: Your Home Away from Home

CHAPTER 3

Organizing Your Classroom

Each class of students you teach will usually spend a minimum of three hours per week in your mathematics classroom. This means that they will have ample time to notice the physical aspects of your room—how it looks. Are the walls depressingly empty, or are they filled with interesting and unusual mathematically based displays, articles, and posters? Is the room messy, with piles of papers and books everywhere, or is everything in its appropriate place? Does the room reflect that mathematics is taking place here? Are bulletin boards used to display student work, or are they left empty? Are the chairs in neat rows, or are they grouped? Are there calculators readily available whenever students want to use them? Are there computers and a software library? Are manipulatives readily accessible? Since you will be spending your day in this classroom, it is your job to make it feel friendly, accessible, and interesting— a place students will want to come into daily, rather than a room from which they can hardly wait to escape. Although it may sound unimportant, the physical appearance of a mathematics classroom must be conducive to teaching and learning mathematics. As the 1989 *Standards* state, the classroom environment informs students that mathematics is important, that the teacher has placed value on what is taking place in the classroom.

Organizing your classroom consists of two aspects: the physical environment and the pedagogical setting.

PHYSICAL ENVIRONMENT

Remember, classrooms are for students: your room should provide the best physical environment for learning mathematics and it should reflect the interests of your students. Keep in mind that the physical environment stimulates learning: if the learning environment improves, so will the learning that takes place therein. Furthermore, the physical environment affects your students' behavior and consequently it will also affect their learning. Whatever classroom you are assigned to, you can make the environment rich and conducive to learning mathematics.

Desks and Tables

Unless your classroom has desks that are bolted to the floor in neat rows, you will have to make a decision as to how you want your classroom arranged. Desks arranged in neat rows suggests that this will be a class that is lecture oriented, one in which students will have to pay careful attention, take notes, and not talk. If you wish to send a message that your room will involve student teamwork and discussion, you might push two desks together to form a pair of class "buddies," or arrange a number of desks together to form a cluster, with students facing one another. These arrangements help foster interaction among students. On the other hand, you might wish to change the desk arrangement from time to time, as the task dictates. This can be done by the students at the time or you can do it in advance. (Weigh the disadvantage of the noise and confusion of dragging tables across the room versus the advantage of having students feel they are participating in the activity.)

One teacher decided she would change the physical arrangement of desks within her classroom to provide a new experience for her students who were just entering middle school. She placed her own desk in one corner of the room and then arranged the students' desks in a triangular format as shown below. The students were able to view the chalkboards with minimal shifting of desks, and she had access to her own minilaboratory of materials in the back of the room, along with the class library.

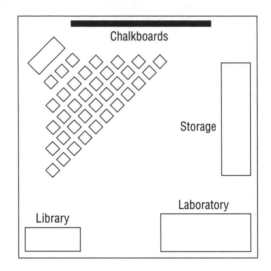

Bulletin Boards

Bulletin boards play a prominent role in every classroom. Before the 1980s, every mathematics classroom had a great deal of chalkboard space, and few, if any, bulletin boards in the room. Now, in many classrooms, this is quite different. In fact, some classrooms have the exact opposite: a great deal of bulletin board space and few chalkboards to write on. Some bulletin board space can be devoted to basic, routine matters, such as posting weekly assignments, schedules, calendars, notices, and so on. However, your bulletin boards should be used primarily to encourage an interest in mathematics on the part of your students. The boards should be interesting, colorful, attractive, and should be changed every few weeks. One teacher we know has posted the value of π to 200 decimal places across the front of his classroom. This certainly attracts the attention of his students when they enter the classroom.

Many teachers are aided in the task of producing colorful, interesting bulletin board displays by their students, who readily volunteer. This activity is a true learning experience for the students and provides an excellent opportunity for some students (who seldom receive recognition for academic achievement) to gain some recognition and perhaps become motivated to greater learning. Finding ways to praise and motivate the low achiever is a problem that constantly faces all teachers. Helping to set up a bulletin board display is also a good challenge for more gifted students.

If you are not artistic in nature, here is a technique you might use to put letters on your bulletin boards. Print the title of the exhibit on ordinary paper. Or obtain stick-on letters and put the title on paper in this way. Next, make a transparency for the overhead projector of the printed sheet. If you now project this onto a large sheet of paper, you can trace over the title or words onto the paper. Color them in and use this at the top of the bulletin board. The same technique can be used to make simple line drawings for an exhibit.

You might wish to show a display of some of the various historical number systems. For example, you could display Egyptian hieroglyphic numerals, Roman numerals, and Babylonian cuneiform numerals. Then ask the students to write the number 1,557 in all three systems.

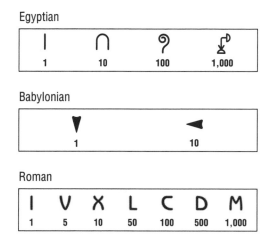

This kind of bulletin board exhibit is instructive and intrigues the students. At the same time, it challenges them to do some investigative work to write the number in three different systems. It can also be the motivation to begin a discussion on a place value system (ours) versus an additive system.

Another display that students find interesting is to use the bulletin board to introduce them to some of the topics of basic topology. For example, you might show the following drawings on the bulletin board and ask students if they can make the drawing in one continuous line without lifting their pencil from the paper. You could follow this exercise up with a discussion on Euler and his use of vertices and arcs to determine whether or not the drawing could be done with one continuous line.

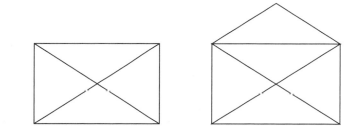

Another use of your bulletin board could be to display pictures of some famous mathematicians and have the class write reports on their lives. Some of the more interesting ones might include Newton, Gauss, Archimedes, Euclid, Euler, Kovaleski, Bannister, and so on. A history of mathematics textbook would provide a list of some of the more prominent men and women of mathematics for your students to write about.

Some teachers make use of the bulletin board to provide a Problem of the Week. Students are presented with a problem for them to try at home or during free time. Students must turn in their complete solution by the end of the week. The teacher can offer an incentive for the first three or four correct solutions.

The physical environment of your classroom is very important to your students' learning of mathematics. The physical environment contains a hidden motivation to the students about the importance of learning mathematics and about what is important and what is not. Think back to your mathematics classroom when you attended middle school or junior high school. Was it a room with dusty chalkboards and cluttered piles of old papers and textbooks? Was the room attractive? Was there anything on the bulletin boards to indicate that it was a mathematics classroom? How were the desks (or tables) arranged? Did you want to come to class? Was your room conducive to learning mathematics?

PEDAGOGICAL SETTING

The art of teaching mathematics (and it is an art) is a difficult one. Teachers are professionals and as such are called on to make important decisions on an ongoing basis. Your mathematics classroom must be nonthreatening. Every student must feel comfortable and willing to make suggestions, put forth ideas, and take part in discussions. You must be prepared to deal with every spontaneous question students ask and to accept these as a part of the curriculum, not as interruptions. You must make no value judgments but listen carefully to students' ideas and use their questions and comments as springboards to further the learning process. Sometimes the questions the students ask will change the entire direction of your lesson. You will have to make a split-second decision as to the worth of this new, unexpected direction and whether to pursue it in depth immediately or to put it aside (tactfully) for later discussion.

Instructional Organization

Teaching mathematics to middle school adolescents requires that you make use of a wide variety of techniques in organizing your daily lessons. Students feel secure when some routines are followed on a daily basis, when they know what to expect. While some classroom routines are important and should be conducted every day, students should also expect you to provide the organizational setting most appropriate for them to learn the particular mathematics at hand.

Middle school students tend to talk a great deal. As their world expands to encompass new discoveries and understandings, they are constantly trying to communicate these newest ideas to their friends and classmates. One of your major tasks is to channel these new attempts at communication so that the students apply them to sharing their mathematical thinking with others. A successful teacher in the middle school grades is one who can inspire students to explain their own work so well that everyone in the room understands it (including you, the teacher).

First, you must be flexible in how you organize your classroom. The days are gone when desks stood in neat rows, with students sitting quietly at them, watching you present the topic of the day, day after day after day. This mode of instruction does not usually fit well with the in-depth discussions necessary when resolving the problem-solving situations prevalent in today's classroom. Today, teachers have a much wider variety of organizational strategies at their disposal. As orchestrator of your students' classroom experiences, your job entails finding and using the particular strategy that most appropriately matches the mathematical content being taught with the learning style of your students.

Chalk-Talk Instruction

We are not saying that chalk-talk, or whole class, instruction—with the teacher at the center of the lesson—should never be used. In fact, this model of instruction is still one of the most valuable and widely used by mathematics teachers. For example, you would not expect to show a videotape ten different times to ten small groups of students. This would hardly be an efficient use of time, neither yours nor the students'.

There will be times when the chalk-talk model of instruction will be called for. This is particularly true when an algorithm or skill is being taught, such as multiplication of fractions, for example. In a situation such as this, the teacher might decide to present the algorithmic skill to the class as a whole and then divide the class up into groups for practice. This kind of lesson is expository, with the teacher engaged in extensive, directed teaching. Even here, however, when using the teacher-centered, whole class instruction as a teaching strategy, you must carefully prepare the lesson in advance.

Specific questions to ask should be considered, prepared, and written down. These should be questions that require more than a simple yes or no or one-word answer. The questions should challenge students, engage them in thinking, and encourage them to use the knowledge they possess to expand what they already know, to build on it, and acquire the new idea or skill being presented. For example, rather than ask "Is triangle ABC a right triangle?" it would be better to ask "What kind of triangle is ABC and how do you know?" The former gives students a 50-50 chance of guessing correctly. The latter requires students to decide what kind of a triangle ABC is and then explain how they arrived at this conclusion.

Once you have asked a question, be certain to pause before calling on anyone. Be patient. Give the class some time to think about what you have asked. Arriving at a good answer usually takes time. Listen to their responses carefully, asking them to clarify or justify their ideas. How you react to a student response, the very words you use and even the look on your face, can set a definite tone for the rest of the lesson. For example, when a student provides an answer (either correct or incorrect), rather than saying "How did you get that?" (which has a confrontational tone to it), it can be better to say "Could you share your thinking with the rest of us?" which is a much more friendly and encouraging response. If a student's response is incorrect and shows a lack of understanding of the material, a negative response might discourage the student from volunteering to take part in the future.

Don't call on students as a punitive act. Calling on someone who obviously does not know the answer, does not understand the material, or is not paying attention will only serve to embarrass that student and may even provoke a verbal confrontation. (More about questioning approaches is presented in Chapter 5, "The Art of Questioning.")

Difficult or out-of-the-ordinary computation problems should not be presented in the initial presentation. Rather, your explanation should be straightforward, to the point, and presented in a manner that the students will understand and be able to call on when needed.

In general, the whole class model of instruction should be used for topics that can be presented to all your students at the same time (this assumes that all of the students have the necessary prerequisites for the new topic) or when all students need some continuous guidance on the part of the teacher. Concept information, vocabulary, and examples to illustrate the concept should be provided by the teacher.

Partners

One specific grouping of students that is easy to accomplish is that of partners, or having students work together in pairs. This organizational technique leads to the least moving about, lends itself to having students communicate with each other, and makes it easy for you, the teacher, to listen to the students explain their work to each other as you move about the room. When asking students to work in pairs or as partners, you may want to group them simply by who is sitting next to whom. This pairing is quickly done, usually requires minimal moving of furniture, and enables you to call a halt to the discussion when the activity has been completed. One disadvantage of this approach is that students often want to sit next to friends. As a result, what may be intended as a mathematical discussion can easily turn into a social chat. Part of your task is to move about the room, listening to the discussions and possibly even asking a pointed question to one student pair (or more than one pair) to help get them back on track.

A possible task that lends itself well to pairs of students working together is to give them a geometric figure and ask them to write down all they can about the figure. This might involve perimeter, area, parallel lines, equal angle measures, and so on. Then, as a whole class activity, you should take the time to allow each pair of students to report on their findings.

Another excellent use of student pairs is for checking a homework assignment. Rather than spend valuable class time by having students put all the problems on the board (many of which were correctly done by everyone), the student pairs can examine each other's work and make corrections and suggestions as you move from group to group, determining which problems were difficult enough to warrant spending class time on them. (See Chapter 10.)

Cooperative Learning Groups

Most of the typical classroom experience on any given day is more than 50 percent teacher talk. This usually means that a student, on average, talks less than one minute during any given class period. This is hardly a situation conducive to helping students learn to communicate mathematical ideas or exercise their thinking skills. It is a widely accepted fact that students learn better when they take part in an active discussion rather than listening to someone else. You can divide your class into small cooperative learning groups of three to five students. If your class has thirty-five students, for example, you might have seven groups with five students in each. This will enable seven students to talk at one time, increasing the amount of student-student interaction.

Much of the research indicates that students who learn in a cooperative group setting exhibit

- much longer-term retention

- an increase in their higher-order process skills

- an increased ability to work well with other students

- an increase in their own self-esteem

- an increased ability to communicate

- a greater appreciation for the subject matter

If you decide to organize your class into cooperative learning groups, you should keep some things in mind. First of all, do not allow students to form their own groups. You should assign the members to each team. You know your own students best—which of them are good readers and which are not, which are outgoing and which are introspective, which will get along and which will not. In some situations, you might decide to group the students with the same relative ability in each group. Other times, it might be better to mix a higher-ability student, a lower-ability student, and two average-ability students in each group. Be certain to include male and female students in each group and make the membership of each group as ethnically diverse as possible. Once you have established these groups, keep them intact for a period of a month or so. A team usually needs a few days to learn how to work together, accept personality differences, and develop some cohesiveness. You might permit the groups to decide on a group name to add to the fun of working together.

Notice that working in cooperative learning groups is *not* the same as simple group work. Teachers have always used group learning. In group learning, a problem is assigned to a group of students, who work to resolve the problem. This can often be done by one student in the group who may have a quicker grasp of the material. Group participation is not usual in this setting. Cooperative learning groups, on the other hand, have a group goal, and students collaborate with one another to attain the goal. Members of the group are dependent on one another. Members are expected to bring their assigned work to the group so that the task can be completed. Each student must be prepared for the give-and-take of group participation. Students must assume the responsibility for keeping each other focused on the task at hand, and each member of the group is equally responsible for mastering the task.

In a cooperative learning group, each student should have a specific assigned task. For example, one student might be designated as the *group leader,* the one who chairs the discussion. A second student might be the *recorder,* someone who keeps a record of the groups' discussion. A third might be designated as the *presenter,* the one who will be called on to present the group's findings to the rest of the class. The fourth (and fifth) student might be designated as the *materials person(s),* the student who has the responsibility for gathering and returning any materials the group might need in its work. These tasks should be rotated on a regular basis so that every student has the opportunity to act in all capacities.

Expect some noise, disorder, and possibly some "organized chaos" when you begin to work with cooperative learning groups. If students have not worked in this setting before, they may resist group work and wish to continue working alone. Students need time to adjust to working in a cooperative or collaborative environment. You may have to keep the groups separated so that each group can work comfortably without any interference from the other groups. You will have to develop some technique to get the attention of all your students. Sometimes they become so engrossed in what they are doing that they tend to ignore the teacher's attempts to call the class together. One technique that works well is to have a small bell on your desk and ring it once or twice in the classroom to get students' attention. Another technique is to simply hold your hand up and have the students do the same when they see you. As students raise their own hands, the rest of the class will see this happening and do the same until all have raised their hands and have become quiet waiting for further instructions.

Once the groups are ready to proceed, you must present the task clearly, making certain that everyone understands the directions and what they are to do. In addition, the groups should know how much time they will be allowed to complete the task. Is this a one-period assignment, or will the groups have a week to complete their work?

For example, suppose the group task is to determine the probability of rolling a 4 on a die and, at the same time, pulling a red chip from a bag that contains one red chip, one white chip, and one blue chip. The group leader might suggest how the task could be accomplished—that is, how to actually do it. At the same time this student could assign the task of obtaining a die and three chips to the materials person. Once the materials have been assembled, the leader could roll the die, the materials person could pull a chip from a bag, the recorder could keep track of what takes place, and so on. Finally, the reporter would prepare the results to be explained to the class. The groups may not obtain the correct results in all cases. It is your role to see that the correct answer is finally obtained and that erroneous findings do not remain in students' minds. In this problem, for example, some of the groups (or you) might suggest writing out the sample space. The sample space would include eighteen items:

1R	1W	1B	2R	2W	2B	3R	3W	3B
4R	4W	4B	5R	5W	5B	6R	6W	6B

Since only one of these eighteen is correct (namely, 4R) the probability is 1/18.

Some teachers do not always include the role of reporter in their groups. Rather, the teacher reserves the right to call on any member of the group to report the group's findings to the class. This helps ensure that all members of the group comprehend what is taking place and understand the group's solution.

Despite the extra planning that cooperative learning groups require, plus the additional class time it takes, this strategy of organization is justified, considering the following positive outcomes that result:

- Increased mathematical communication skills

- A possible variety of approaches to a problem situation

- Increased student participation

- Increased opportunity for all students to succeed

- A social aspect to learning mathematics

Discovery Learning

This teaching strategy is most often used in a laboratory or exploration type of setting. The classroom is usually extremely noisy, with students moving around from place to place. You must provide each student, or group of students, with a set of directions and/or questions designed to lead them in their discovery process. The procedure is not really as open as it sounds. Rather, it is a process of *guided discovery,* in which the teacher has orchestrated the lesson to help students discover what it is they should be discovering. It is important while students are "discovering" that you walk around the room to make certain that they are not arriving at some incorrect solution. Unless students are going off on a completely erroneous tangent in their work, do not interrupt them. Rather, let them proceed until they realize that what they are doing will not lead them to the correct results. If, after a few more minutes, you see that they are not moving in the right direction, you might ask a leading question of the group to help out. Above all, never tell the group that what they are doing is wrong. Instead, lead them toward the correct resolution.

Jigsaw

Jigsaw is a procedure in which students are given the task of learning something new and then teaching it to other students. For example, suppose you have a classroom with eighteen students. Begin by placing the students in six groups of three, called the "primary groups" (groups A through F in the figure below). The task of the students in each group is to master one single aspect of a given situation or one particular problem. Once the three students in each group have accomplished this, the class is now regrouped into the *secondary groups* (groups 1 through 3 in the figure). This time there are three groups of six such that each group of six includes *one student from each of the six primary groups*. Now the six students in the group teach what they learned in their primary groups to the other students. Thus, each student is now teaching what was learned before. (Of course, you can reverse the groups—that is, begin with three groups of six students each and have them move into six groups of three students each in the second step.)

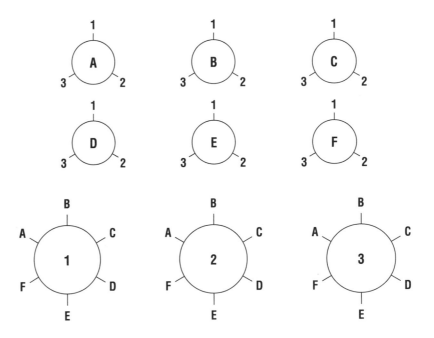

For an example, the six primary groups are each given a different problem to solve, each of which illustrates a different problem-solving strategy (groups 1 through 6). The teacher moves around the room listening to each group and offering suggestions when needed. When the teacher sees that the groups have solved their problems and that they understand the solutions well enough to explain them, the class is divided into groups of six, each group containing one student from each of the original groups (groups A, B, C). The students now explain their problems to the others and make certain that all students can explain the solutions and strategies used. After all groups have finished, the teacher can call on any student in the class to explain the solution to any problem.

TEACHING TOOLS AND RESOURCES

Chalkboards

The one single aid most often neglected by many beginning teachers is the chalkboard. You likely will have one or more chalkboards in your classroom. It is the one device that you will probably make use of every day. The board may be in one of several colors; black, green, and tan are the most common. If you are to take full advantage of the chalkboard, there are several things to consider.

Most chalkboards are made with steel backing, which enables you to put pictures, models, and so on directly on the board by using small magnets.

Your board may have one or more sections ruled into a graph grid. Sometimes, instead of a permanent grid, you may have a "window shade." This is a stencil with holes cut for the grid. Simply pull down the shade and go over it with a chalk-filled eraser. The chalk will settle into the holes and create a grid board that can easily be erased when you are finished with it. This is exceptionally valuable when your board space is limited.

Be careful not to write all over your chalkboard in random places. Rather, begin writing at the leftmost part of the board and work from left to right. Also, erase from left to write when you do erase the work. This allows students who are taking some notes to keep the newest material on the board. Be careful, too, not to write uphill or downhill and to write in large, legible letters. Many beginning teachers write with very small letters that are not readable by students who are sitting in the back of the room. Many also have a tendency to let their writing move upward as they write. Try it for yourself! Go into an empty classroom; write a word problem of several lines of text and formulas on the board. Now go to the rear of the room and examine what you have just written. It takes a bit of practice to keep your writing neat and in straight lines. Be certain that what you have written is large enough and clear enough to be read from the back of the room.

Make extensive use of colored chalk. Use it to identify key ideas in your lesson, to add attractiveness to drawings, and to emphasize common or overlapping elements in two figures or sets. You can also use colored chalk when solving a problem. Given facts can be written in one color; deduced facts can be written in another.

Overhead Projectors

With the exception of the hand-held calculator, no one single technological development has so influenced the way we teach mathematics as the overhead projector. The projector was originally designed during World War II for use in hospitals, for bedridden patients. The projector would throw images on the ceilings for patients to read, hence the name "overhead." Nowadays, however, the overhead projector is aimed at a large vertical screen, although it can be used directly on the chalkboard in your classroom.

The main advantage of the overhead projector is its simplicity of use. You place a transparency on the horizontal glass stage of the overhead, turn on the machine, and adjust the focus. That's it! The image is projected onto the screen or chalkboard over your shoulder. You use the overhead facing the class, and this allows you to watch your students and see their facial expressions as you teach and as they speak. By turning the overhead on and off several times, you can easily attract the students' attention to what is taking place.

There are many other advantages in using the overhead projector. You do not have to turn off the lights in your room when you use the overhead. This allows students to take notes while the lesson is taking place. Furthermore, the overhead permits you to write on a horizontal plane, rather than on the vertical chalkboard. This is a much more natural way to write. In addition, you can prepare complex drawings, diagrams, and even write out long problems in advance, which saves a great deal of class time. The transparencies can easily be labeled and stored for use again; there is no need to draw the same diagram every time.

Transparencies are usually $8\frac{1}{2}$" × 11" sheets of clear plastic. You or the student who is at the overhead simply writes on the plastic with a felt-tipped pen or marker. Color can be added to emphasize certain parts of the drawing. For example, if you are working in geometry with a pair of overlapping triangles, you can draw each of the triangles with a different colored pen to make the overlapping parts more apparent.

Physical Models

Students in the middle grades are especially in need of hands-on materials. You can have your students make models of geometric solids for a discussion of three-space figures. The templates for some of these models are available in the book *Teaching Middle School Mathematics: Activities, Materials and Problems* (2000) by Stephen Krulik and Jesse Rudnick. You can purchase other models to illustrate factoring, solving equations, and so on. Store these in a place in your classroom where they will be readily accessible to the students and yourself whenever they are needed.

Classroom Libraries

In your room, you might wish to establish a class library. In this library or reading corner, you might put textbooks other than the one you are currently using with your students. These resources enable students to look up an approach to a concept or a skill other than the one in the textbook. This is exceptionally valuable, especially if they are having trouble understanding the approach presented. You can get these textbooks by writing directly to the publishers on your school stationery and requesting them.

You can keep some of the many books on the history of mathematics in this reading corner. Many are written at a level appropriate for the middle school student. An excellent book is *Agnesi to Zeno* by S. Smith (Key Curriculum Press). There are many others as well.

There are many other books which could easily be part of your reading corner for students. *Flatlands* by Edwin Abbott (Dover Publications) is the fictional story of life in a two-dimensional world in which all the characters are polygons. Although the book was written in Victorian England, it is a story your students may find interesting. *The Greedy Titans* by Marilyn Burns (Scholastic Publications) is the story of a triangle who, when he becomes bored, asks for an additional side and angle. In turn, he becomes a quadrilateral, a pentagon, and finally a circle. It's a very interesting book for younger middle school children in grades 4 and 5.

The Magic School Bus: Lost in the Solar System by Joanna Cole (Scholastic Publications) is an excellent book for grades 5 and 6. It establishes the need for ratios and proportions as the characters travel from one planet to another. For example, a student who weighs 85 pounds on earth only weighs 77 pounds on Venus and weighs 247 pounds on Jupiter. You can ask your students to calculate the weight of their parents and themselves on each of these planets.

Of course, *Gulliver's Travels* by Jonathan Swift is a classic that can be read by students in grades 7 and 8. The story of Gulliver and the Lilliputians is well known; there have been several movie versions of this classic. Again, the ideas of ratio and proportion are suggested.

For some interesting materials on informal geometry, consider the book *Sam Loyd's Book of Tangrams* by Peter Van Note (Dover Publications). In this book, tangrams are used to model fraction comparisons and to construct geometric figures such as triangles of different sizes, polygons, and so on using the tangram pieces.

You should read the book *How to Use Children's Literature to Teach Mathematics* by Rosamund Welchman Tischler (National Council of Teachers of Mathematics). This book is an excellent source of suggested literature appropriate for different grade levels and explores how each book can be used in the mathematics classroom. As one example, the author considers the song "The Twelve Days of Christmas" as a source of some interesting problems for students in grade 6. For instance, how many presents were brought on the seventh day? On the fifth day? How many were brought on all twelve days?

Keep a personal collection of books as well. Develop your own personal library. You already have the first volume in your collection—this book. Send for catalogs from the many companies that publish supplementary materials and books for teachers. Companies such as Dale Seymour Press, Creative Publications, McGraw-Hill/ Wright division, and J. Weston Walsh are just a few who will gladly send you beautifully illustrated catalogs on request.

You should also own a copy of the 1989 Standards and *Standards 2000*. Many of the *Addenda Series* books, also published by the National Council of Teachers of Mathematics, offer a myriad of ideas for teaching middle school mathematics. Some of the titles in this series appropriate for your use include *Geometry in the Middle Grades, Dealing with Data and Change, Developing Number Sense,* and *Understanding Rational Numbers and Proportions*. Write to the NCTM, 1906 Association Drive, Reston, VA 22091, for a catalog of these and other publications in the series. Some of the yearbooks published annually by the NCTM will be described in the catalog. Several apply directly to middle school mathematics teaching.

Remember, your classroom is your home away from home. In the normal school year, the average teacher spends 675 hours in the classroom. Each of your students will spend approximately 135 hours a year in the classroom. It is your responsibility to make this room an environment in which your students will learn, one to which they will be anxious to come. It should be pleasant to the eye as well as a center for learning.

Activities

1. Select a topic in sixth-grade mathematics. Examine two textbooks to see how the topic is presented in each. Then explain how you might develop this same topic using a cooperative learning group strategy.

2. Examine a seventh-grade textbook and its accompanying teacher's guide to see what suggestions are given for adapting the instruction to different styles of presentation. Tell how you would organize your class to teach this topic.

3. The school guidance counselor informs you that a student in your class wishes to be changed to another teacher. The student claims that your room is too noisy to work. How would you respond?

4. You notice that whenever you divide the class into cooperative learning groups, the same students seem to be doing all the work in the group. How would you handle this situation?

5. The guidance counselor has been called by a parent who tells him that you are holding his child back by making her work in a group with slower students. How would you respond?

6. You ask the class to write a letter to a friend, explaining how they should go about adding $\frac{1}{3} + \frac{1}{4}$. One student objects, saying that this is a mathematics class, not an English class. How would you respond?

7. Prepare a list of some of the items you might include in the mathematics laboratory corner of your classroom. You might examine some catalogs from companies that supply materials for mathematics instruction to help you.

Bibliography

Artzt, Alice F., and Newman, Claire M. *How to Use Cooperative Learning in the Mathematics Class.* Reston, VA: National Council of Teachers of Mathematics, 1992.

Baines, Lawrence A., and Stanley, Gregory. "We *Still* Want to See the Teacher." *Phi Delta Kappan* 82 (May 2001): 695–696.

Farivar, Sydney, and Webb, Noreen M. "Helping and Getting Help—Essential Skills for Effective Group Problem Solving." *Arithmetic Teacher* 41 (May 1994): 521–524.

Larson, Carol Novilla. "Organizing for Mathematics Instruction." *Arithmetic Teacher* 31 (September 1983): 16–20.

Sherin, Miriam G., Louis, David, and Mendez, Edith P. "Students' Building on One Another's Mathematical Ideas." *Mathematics Teaching in the Middle School* 6 (November 2000): 186–189.

Related Research

Burns, Marilyn. (1981). Groups of four: Solving the management problem. *Learning 10* (2): 46–51.

Copeland, Richard W. *How children learn mathematics.* Englewood Cliffs, NJ: Merrill/Prentice Hall, 1984.

National Council of Teachers of Mathematics. (1963). *Enrichment mathematics for the grades.* Reston, VA: Author.

Evertson, Carolyn M., et al. (1989). *Classroom management for elementary teachers.* Englewood Cliffs, NJ: Prentice Hall.

Johnson, David W., & Johnson, Roger T. (1987). *Learning together and alone: Cooperative, competitive, and individualistic learning.* Englewood Cliffs, NJ: Prentice Hall.

Johnson, David W., Johnson, Roger T., & Johnson Holubec, Edythe. (1986). *Circles of learning: Cooperation in the Classroom.* Edina, MN: Interaction.

Rosenshine, Barak, & Stevens, Robert. (1986). Teaching functions in Merlin C. Wittrock (Ed.), *Handbook of research on teaching.* Englewood Cliffs, NJ: Merrill/Prentice Hall.

Sheffield, Linda J. (Ed.). (1999). *Developing mathematically promising students.* Reston, VA. National Council of Teachers of Mathematics.

Sheffield, Linda J., Bennett, Jennie, Abal, Manuel Berrioz, DeArmond, Margaret, & Weilheimer, Richard. (1995). *Report of the NCTM task force on the mathematically promising.* Reston, VA: National Council of Teachers of Mathematics.

National Council of Teachers of Mathematics. (1972). *The slow learner in mathematics.* Reston, VA: Author.

CHAPTER 4

Planning for Instruction: What Do I Do Now?

Your teaching will only be as good as your planning. It is virtually impossible for anyone to be spontaneous every day and still present a successful, interesting lesson. Planning involves careful thinking about what it is you will be teaching, researching the topic to find out what problems you can expect, deciding how best to present the topic, and finally, after the lesson has been taught, reviewing what went well and what went wrong and why. As the *Standards 2000* say, "Effective mathematics teaching requires understanding what students know and need to learn and then challenging and supporting them to learn it well" (p. 4). For the new teacher, this can be a very stressful process unless it is undertaken in a careful, systematic manner.

BEFORE SCHOOL STARTS

Planning for instruction in mathematics should begin even before school starts. You should visit the school and obtain a copy of the syllabus or course outline for each class you will be teaching. In fact, it would be a good idea to obtain the school mathematics curriculum guides for each of the grades. This will enable you to see what has preceded and what will follow your particular mathematics class. By scanning through these curriculum guides or texts for the grade immediately preceding the one you will be teaching, you will see what students are supposed to have learned before, but don't assume that everyone has learned it. What is most important is to gather as much information as possible about the students and the courses you are going to teach. After all, mathematics knowledge is built as a series of "blocks"; without the proper foundation, no blocks can be added successfully.

In many middle schools, the textbook *is* the curriculum. Thus, you should obtain copies of all the texts being used in your school. In fact, if at all possible, you should try to obtain as many different textbooks for each course as you can. From these, you can discover new and different approaches to teaching a given topic. If you attend a professional meeting that features book publishers and exhibits, you will see many different textbooks for each grade level. Most publishers will be glad to send you a sample copy of their text for possible adoption. A word of caution, however. Since the sequence of topics may differ from book to book, be certain that anything you decide to try fits into the order of topics you are teaching.

ONCE SCHOOL STARTS

It is an excellent idea to ask the department chairperson (if the position exists) or experienced teachers if they will allow you to sit in their classroom and observe them teach. If they agree, sit in regularly and take careful notes. Notice the way topics are introduced, the motivational techniques that are used, and the "unusual" ways to teach a topic. If possible, sit down with the teacher and discuss why a certain approach was used. Did any problems arise? If so, how were they anticipated and dealt with?

A lesson is a planned learning experience or series of experiences designed by the teacher to convey the skill and the concepts the students are to master. In planning your lessons, many things must be considered. Chapter 1 discussed how children in middle school learn mathematics. Learning theory must be taken into consideration when planning your lessons. The following eight considerations derive from learning theory and must be taken into account when developing a lesson plan.

1. *Build your lesson on the previous knowledge your students bring to class.* Learning mathematics is a continuum; each new concept or idea depends on the concepts and ideas that have preceded it.

2. *Make use of hands-on materials and manipulatives.* Your students should explore mathematics as they learn it. You should include in your lesson, when appropriate, the manipulatives that best enable students to discover the concept. You should become familiar with these materials in advance to avoid any difficulties that might arise when students use them.

3. *Involve your students as active participants.* Early adolescents learn mathematics best by actively taking part in the lesson, not by merely listening. Your lessons should be of the hands-on type, both physically and/or mentally. Active participation does not only mean physically doing something; it can also mean mental involvement, thinking about the topic and actively considering the mathematics involved.

4. *Your lessons must be developmental.* The lesson should proceed from the concrete to patterns and commonalities, then to the concept under consideration, and, finally, to verbalization. Middle school students pass through most of these stages each time they learn something new.

5. *Practice the art of asking good questions.* Every one of the questions you ask in class should have a definite purpose. Questions should be thought provoking, requiring more than one-word answers. Prepare a list of questions vital to the learning and understanding of the topic under consideration. If the students don't ask these questions, make certain that you do.

6. *Provide the opportunity for your students to practice their communication skills.* Most middle school students are weakest in the ability to communicate their ideas. What good does it do for students to know how to do something if they cannot communicate this idea to you and to other students? A good lesson provides students with a chance to talk to other students, to talk to the teacher, and to present their ideas in a verbal manner.

7. *Teach your students the art of metacognition.* When children begin to think about their own thought processes, they begin to understand what they are doing. The concepts they have discovered become clarified.

8. *Evaluate your lesson afterward and identify ways to improve it.* Every lesson must be carefully designed, carefully implemented, and carefully assessed afterward.

THE UNIT PLAN

Unfortunately, many teachers fail to consider unit planning. Rather, they plan on a day-by-day basis and let the textbook decide what constitutes a unit. No single lesson should take place in a vacuum. Every daily lesson should fit into some overall unit plan. Each day's work is an integral part of an overall longer unit of work. There are subtle bits of information in each lesson that must be considered as a whole and tied together if the students are to master the concepts. How you connect these bits of information provides the cohesiveness for your mathematics instruction and makes your class more than a series of disjointed lessons with no connections.

There are probably as many different formats of the unit plan as there are textbooks on teaching mathematics, but they all have one thing in common. They all have a broader overall goal than the daily lesson plan, and all require that content and pedagogy be synthesized to achieve this goal. You will need a different approach when planning the unit plan than when planning your daily lessons. There are several things which you must consider when developing a unit plan:

1. **Objectives:** What is it I want my students to know when they finish this unit? What are the specific objectives, and how do they fit into the course objectives? What concepts should they have mastered? What skills should they have mastered?

2. **Content:** What are the major ideas of the unit? How are these ideas related to what units have come before and what units come afterward? What background do my students need? Do I have to review anything first?

3. **Methodology:** Do the ideas lend themselves to group discussion? Do they lend themselves to experimentation and discovery? What kinds of student activities and assignments are appropriate for this unit?

4. **Evaluation:** Are my objectives observable? Can I evaluate with a paper-and-pencil test? Are student reports appropriate? What other kinds of assessment can I use?

After using this four-point planning structure to block out the unit plan, the individual daily lessons will gain a direction and will even be partially planned.

THE DAILY LESSON PLAN

The teacher who enters the classroom without an orderly, carefully defined and developed lesson plan risks wasting a great deal of time and effort. Working out the daily plan crystallizes the lesson in your own mind and allows you to see any pitfalls that might occur in class.

As noted earlier, the first five minutes of class will establish the tone for the entire class period. Your lesson is not self-starting. Rather, it will require some extensive planning on your part. Don't always begin a lesson by going over the previous evening's homework. Instead, you might use some of the five-minute openers found in Chapter 8.

The daily lesson plan should include what you are going to do, how you are going to do it, and what you expect your students to do and achieve during that class period. Many beginning teachers plan carefully for what *they* are going to do but forget to plan for what *the students* are going to do. Keep in mind that the daily lesson plan is only a guide, a blueprint. It must be flexible. Expect to modify it as the lesson proceeds. Circumstances will arise that call for modification. Questions will be asked, unusual approaches to a problem will have to be explained, time will be taken to review something that was forgotten—all these events will cause you to change your plan on the spot.

Keep your lesson plans in a plan book and keep a separate plan book for every course you teach. This will enable you to have a guide to what has come before and what will come after. These plans will also be invaluable when you write new lesson plans next year. And you should write a new set of lesson plans every year. The previous year's plans will not do. The level of the class will be different, and you will have learned some things to do and not do from your past year's experience. You will have learned what worked well, what worked not so well, and what flopped and should be dropped from consideration next year.

As you write your lesson plans, you likely will find your lessons falling into three categories: the exploratory (or discovery) lesson, the guided discovery lesson, and the chalk-talk or direct instruction lesson. In each of these, your role will change with the purpose of the lesson.

Exploratory (or Discovery) Lesson

This type of lesson is most used when you wish to develop a new concept or make use of problem-solving skills. This lesson permits students to investigate the concept on their own. As the teacher, you must carefully identify the task students are being assigned so that all students understand what they are expected to do. Students then will generate their own ideas and perform their own experiments or activities as they try to discover the concept under consideration. Your role is to serve as a director or choreographer to help ensure that your students are moving in the right direction. This kind of lesson must be gotten underway quickly, otherwise the students will begin to talk and to mill around waiting for direction. In your lesson plan, be certain to list some key questions you will ask to ascertain how successful the students were in discovering the concepts. A basic danger when using this kind of lesson is that students might come up with some erroneous, rather than correct, concepts. However, as students' discoveries are discussed in class, you can correct any errors.

Guided Discovery Lesson

This kind of lesson is similar to the exploratory lesson. The main difference lies in the role of the teacher. In the exploratory lesson, your role was primarily one of observer. You introduced the topic, raised some questions, and then walked around the room, supervising what the students were doing. Hopefully, they found what you wanted them to discover. The guided discovery lesson is a more teacher-centered lesson. You are in control; you introduce the topic to the students and lead the class in a discussion of how to approach the topic and how to solve the problem. The experiments may be set up in advance. As students perform them, they discover what you have predetermined they will discover. If this goal or concept is not discovered, you must lead them to it. There is less chance of the students failing to meet your goals in this kind of lesson.

Chalk-Talk Lesson

This is the most familiar kind of lesson, the one you probably remember best from your own middle school or junior high school days. It is a lesson that is best used when you are explaining a new skill or algorithm. This lesson is teacher centered. You begin by going over the previous day's assignment, introducing the new topic, explaining it to the class, and then demonstrating the new skill with several examples. The students then practice the skill or concept using several additional examples. The lesson is easily planned, since you are in charge and know exactly where the lesson is going.

One major concern of most beginning teachers is that they will run out of things to say and do before the class period ends. Don't worry! You will quickly find out that the opposite is far more likely to occur—that is, there will usually not be sufficient time to carry out everything you planned to do. Any well-planned lesson that involves student participation will take much more time than you expected. Most teachers tend to overestimate what they will be able to do in one class period.

THE UNIVERSAL LESSON PLAN

Your lesson plan should follow some definite format. The consistency thus provided will permit you to examine the various parts of the lesson from time to time. There really is no one particular format to follow. Your school may suggest a format; if so, use that one. If not, any one will do. The universal lesson plan provides one format option. This format will probably be the "bread-and-butter" lesson plan you will follow, regardless of the type of lesson you are planning to teach. This plan has proved to be successful, but you may want to vary this basic plan from time to time.

A suggested outline for the universal daily lesson plan follows. (Not all the suggested parts need be in every lesson.)

1. **Objectives.** The objectives of your lesson should be based on your background knowledge of the students. For example, before you can teach percent, your students must be well versed in working with fractions, decimals, and ratios. If you don't consider their backgrounds, you might find yourself introducing concepts and skills that will only confuse them or cause difficulties in their attempts to master the new material. Ask yourself three questions: (1) What is it that you wish to achieve in this lesson? (2) What are the concepts and skills you want them to learn? and (3) Do they have the appropriate background? Be certain that you are *very* familiar with the mathematics content of the lesson. In this way, you can easily respond to any questions that students might raise. If you are not sure of your students' backgrounds, ask some questions and find out.

2. **Materials.** If any special materials are needed, list them here. This will alert you to arrange for them to be delivered to your class or for you to pick

them up before class starts. Such items would include hardware, such as a computer, a projector and screen to show a film, or software such as scissors, rulers, compasses, manipulatives, games, and so on.

3. **Motivational Activity (Introduction).** The initial activity for the day's lesson should be carefully thought through and written down. In some classes, this may be part of the five-minute warm-up (as discussed in Chapter 8). In others, it may simply be a "Preclass" or a "Do Now" problem. This could be a problem based on the previous day's work or a review exercise. It might be some task that you wish students to perform as soon as they are seated. These activities help students get seated and settled down. But motivation for the lesson is more than merely getting the lesson started. A "Do Now" problem will get the students' attention and permit you to start the lesson. However, it is rare that it will get the students interested in what comes next.

   Don't always tell students what you are going to teach them. Instead of saying "Today we will begin a lesson on linear graphing," you might ask students to perform an experiment and collect data. After putting the data into tabular form, you could help students plot the data and obtain a line graph.

4. **Exploration and Development.** In this section the bulk of your lesson will be described. Here you create the appropriate learning environment to make your students want to learn the topic. This is where your role as an "orchestrator" takes place. What experiences will you use to develop the lesson? Will you use a group discussion? Will it be a teacher-talk lesson? Will you use a discovery approach? What key questions will you ask? (Obviously, you cannot list every question that will be asked; only the most important ones should appear here.)

5. **Practice.** After the concept or skill has been developed, students will need to practice using the concept or skill. Model problems selected to bring out the points taught should be given, completed, and discussed. The first problem or few problems should be direct and to the point—no unusual approaches at this time. However, if the class shows mastery, the next problem or two can bring in other topics connected to the first ones. (Work the problems out first. Nothing is as disconcerting as having unforeseen difficulties with a problem—sometimes merely computational quirks that will obscure the intent of the problem.)

6. **Summary.** The conclusion of every lesson should be a summary or review of the major concepts or skills developed in the lesson. This is usually a brief review of what was accomplished in class during the period and brings closure to the lesson. Hopefully, this summary will include the goals you had set for the lesson in your lesson plan. At this point, the parts of the lesson come together. This review can take several different forms. For instance, you can have students state the major points and list or show them on the chalkboard or overhead screen. Or you can call on several students, asking carefully constructed questions designed to bring out the material. Some teachers ask students to write what they have learned that day in their journals.

   Don't ask "Does everyone understand the lesson?" or "Are there any questions?" You probably won't get anyone to respond.

7. **Homework.** Your lesson will require some follow-up on the part of the students in order to sharpen their mastery of the new topic, concept, or skill. The homework assignment should be carefully constructed and included as part of your lesson plan. (See Chapter 10 for more on homework.)

THE EIGHT-STEP LESSON PLAN FORMAT

Another widely known format is that suggested by Madeline Hunter. It consists of the following eight steps:

1. **Anticipatory Set.** The teacher focuses the start of the lesson on what will be learned. It's helpful to base the current lesson on what happened previously. This phase of the lesson gets the students' attention.

2. **Objective and Purpose.** Here the teacher tells students what they will be able to do when they complete the lesson. Some teachers feel that students learn more effectively when they know what they are supposed to be learning. Obviously, this will affect any kind of discovery lesson you intend to use and should be ignored when this kind of lesson is being implemented.

3. **Input.** The new knowledge, process, or skill is presented to the students in an effective manner. This could be through discovery, discussion, reading, listening, observing, and so on.

4. **Modeling.** In this phase of the lesson, you will demonstrate what you are presenting in a manner similar to what the students will do afterward. It is important for the students to see what it is that they are to learn.

5. **Checking for Understanding.** It is important to make sure that students understand what was presented. This can be done in a variety of ways. One of the most typical is to ask questions and examine students' faces as they attempt to answer.

6. **Guided Practice.** Here students begin practicing the new skill or concept under direct teacher supervision. As the students work, you move around the room examining their work, making suggestions and comments.

7. **Independent Practice.** When you are sure that your students understand the new material, you can assign independent practice. This can be done in class (if time permits) or may be assigned for homework.

8. **Closure.** Here you review, summarize, or wrap up the lesson. It is often helpful to briefly comment on tomorrow's lesson; this makes today's lesson an integral part of the unit.

ACCOMMODATING STUDENTS WITH VARYING ABILITIES

Every textbook usually has exercises designed to address a range of student abilities. When designing your lesson plans, the abilities of the students in your class must be taken into consideration. Most teachers feel that they should "teach to the middle."

That is, the lesson should be aimed at the students with average ability. While it is true that this method will often reach the majority of your students, you cannot ignore the upper- and lower-ability students in your class. The *Standards* suggest that all students be exposed to the same mathematics.

The equity principle in *Standards 2000* suggests that "excellence in mathematics education requires equity—high expectations and strong support for all students" (p. 3). This does not mean that the levels of instruction will be the same. Rather, when trying to challenge the gifted student, you will need to enrich the topic. For example, when teaching the finding of area, the gifted student might be given a floor plan and asked to compute the area. If the shape is irregular, so much the better. The student must then develop a plan to find this area, since routine formulas will not work. Challenge gifted students; force them to use their minds and be creative.

Slower students can also be given "special tasks" to help them achieve. Often, the use of a manipulative device to illustrate a concept will help the slower middle school student comprehend the concept or skill. You will have to anticipate these needs as you plan your lesson and provide materials and time accordingly.

The use of small groups will facilitate the opportunity for students of varying abilities to work together with their peers and move either faster or slower as necessary.

Regardless of the format you decide to use, you must plan. This cannot be emphasized enough. Every teacher, even the most experienced, must plan. As you gain experience, you will begin to anticipate what will happen in class and how you should react. You will also gain a better feel for the timing of your lesson. As you continue teaching, be certain to stay current in the field. Become active in your local and state mathematics education organizations. You can find new ideas and new materials by attending the meetings of the National Council of Teachers of Mathematics as well as those of your own local, regional, and state organizations. These meetings will provide you with the latest ideas and materials to help you plan your lessons and address student concerns.

Activities

1. "The textbook is the curriculum." Do you agree or disagree with this statement? Support your answer.

2. Prepare a unit plan for a series of lessons on addition, subtraction, multiplication, and division of fractions.

3. Select a topic from a textbook in elementary algebra. List the specific outcomes you will want your students to achieve.

4. Select a topic in elementary algebra. Examine how this topic is taught in three different textbooks. Which approach did you like best? Why? What did you like or dislike about each approach?

5. Examine a textbook in sixth-grade mathematics. Discuss what provisions have been made to accommodate students with different abilities.

6. Pick three different topics you know you will have to teach during the school year. For each of the three, decide which type of approach you will use: exploratory, guided discovery, or chalk talk. Write a lesson plan for each. Be sure to use all three approaches.

7. Select a topic for enriching instruction in a seventh-grade honors class. Explain how you would treat the topic and develop a lesson plan for presenting this topic in your class.

8. Examine a sixth-grade textbook from the 1950s and determine how the text discusses the topic of percent. Now examine a post-*Standards* sixth-grade textbook (from the mid 1990s). Compare how these textbooks treat this topic.

Bibliography

Easterday, K. E., Henry, L. L., and Simpson, F. M. *Activities for Junior High School and Middle School Mathematics.* Reston, VA: National Council of Teachers of Mathematics, 1981.

Larson, Carol N. "Organizing for Mathematics Instruction." *Arithmetic Teacher* 31 (December 1983): 16–20.

National Council of Teachers of Mathematics. *Principles and Standards for School Mathematics: An Overview.* Reston VA: Author, 2000.

Rathmell, Edward C. "Planning for Instruction Involves Focusing on Children's Thinking." *Arithmetic Teacher* 41 (February, 1994): 290–291.

Stecher, Brian, Bohrnstedt, G., Kirst, Michael, McRobbie, Joan, and Williams, T. "Class-Size Reduction in California. A Story of Hope, Promise, and Unintended Consequences." *Phi Delta Kappan* 82 (May 2001): 670–674.

Stern, Frances. "Choosing Problems with Entry Points for All Students." *Mathematics Teaching in the Middle School* 6, no. 1 (September 2001): 8–11.

Related Research

Bitter, G. (1997). *Understanding teaching: Implementing the NCTM professional standards for teaching mathematics CD-ROM series.* Tempe: Arizona State University. (Available through the Association for Supervision and Curriculum Development.)

Borich, G. D. (1996). *Effective teaching methods.* New York: Merrill.

Classroom Connect. (1997). *Teaching grades K–12 with the Internet: Internet lesson plans and classroom activities.* Lancaster, PA: Author.

Duquette, G. (Ed.). (1997). *Classroom methods and strategies for teaching at the secondary level.* Lewiston, NY: Edwin Mellen.

Gronlund, N. E. (1995). *How to write and use instructional objectives.* Englewood Cliffs, NJ: Merrill.

Gronlund, N. E. (1985). *Stating objectives for classroom instruction.* New York: Macmillan.

Harris, D. E., Carr, J. E, Flynn, T., Petit, M., & Rigney, S. (1996). *How to use standards in the classroom.* Alexandria, VA: Association for Supervision and Curriculum Development.

Henak, R. M. (1984). *Lesson planning for meaningful variety in teaching.* Washington, DC: National Education Association.

Lesson design and reflection. *Mathematics Teaching in the Middle School* 1 (8): 648–652.

Ornstein, A. C. (1990). *The systematic design of instruction.* New York: HarperCollins.

Ridley, L. L. (1995). When a lesson bombs: Hints and suggestions for teachers. *Teaching Exceptional Children* 27 (4): 66–67.

Schoaff, E. K. (1993). How to develop a mathematics lesson using technology. *Journal of Computers in Mathematics and Science Teaching 12* (1): 19–27.

Schoenfeld, A. H. (1998). On theory and models: The case of teaching-in-context. In S. Berenson, K. Dawkins, M. Blanton, W. Coulombe, J. Kolb, K. Norwood, & L. Stiff (Eds.), *Proceedings of the twentieth annual meeting of the North American chapter of the International Group for the Psychology of Mathematics Education.*

CHAPTER 5

The Art of Questioning: Don't Always Trust Your Instincts

In the *Professional Standards for Teaching Mathematics* (1991), the National Council of Teachers of Mathematics discusses the idea of discourse in the mathematics classroom. According to the authors, discourse is "central to what students learn about mathematics as a domain of human inquiry with characteristic ways of knowing." Discourse refers to the way ideas are exchanged in verbal counterpoint. Within this section, they state further that the "teacher's role is to initiate and orchestrate this kind of discourse and to use it skillfully to foster student learning" (p. 34). Standard 2, The Teacher's Role in Discourse, begins by stating that "the teacher of mathematics should orchestrate discourse by posing questions and tasks that elicit, engage, and challenge each student's thinking" (p. 35).

When you were still a young child, you learned by asking questions such as "Why is the sky blue?" "Why does this work?" Today, most of the learning that takes place in the mathematics classroom is the result of the questions that are asked by the teacher. Effective, clear, and critical questioning is an art. Even the manner and tone of voice in which the question is asked will directly influence student response. For example, when a student presents an answer to a particular problem, the teacher might say "Show us how you got that." To many students, this comment, depending on the tone of voice in which it is said, can be almost confrontational in nature. Notice how much more relaxed the student would be if the teacher said instead, in a pleasant manner, "Would you share your thinking with us?"

WHY WE ASK QUESTIONS

Since formal education began, teachers have used questioning as a basic form of helping their students learn new material. In the Aristotelian school in ancient Greece, learning proceeded by having students respond to a series of questions posed by the teacher. But why do we ask questions today? First, we want to find out if our students are paying attention. Second, we want to know if our students are learning what is being discussed in class. Finally, if we really want our students to be interested in what we are teaching, we ask questions. Today, questioning is used extensively in a particular learning situation, and it often becomes the primary method of instruction. Basically, teachers ask two kinds of questions: (1) questions that elicit a factual response, such as asking students to perform an algorithmic skill (these are relatively low-level questions), and (2) questions that encourage thinking, such as asking students to explain how they carried out the solution process to a problem (these are higher-level questions).

In the *Professional Standards for Teaching Mathematics* (1991), five reasons are listed for why teachers should ask questions in a mathematics classroom:

1. Helping students work together to make sense of mathematics

2. Helping students to rely more on themselves to determine whether something is mathematically correct

3. Helping students to learn to reason mathematically

4. Helping students learn to conjecture, invent, and solve problems

5. Helping students to connect mathematics, its ideas and its applications (pp. 3–4)

ASKING GOOD QUESTIONS

When you attempt to orchestrate discourse within your classroom, it is important to carefully ask "good" questions. Several things must be kept in mind. First, you should ask many questions. By paying careful attention to the students' responses, you can incorporate their answers as you formulate your next questions, making students feel a part of the lesson. You must always be positive about students' responses. Your classroom must be a nonthreatening environment. Students must feel free to join in the discussion. Avoid any outright rejection of a student's response; find something worthwhile in every response. Use student responses to move the discourse to the next step in the topic development. Try to ask as many open-ended questions as possible so that your students are encouraged to think.

Questions fall into two major categories: convergent and divergent. Convergent questions tend to converge on a single answer. Divergent questions usually have a wide variety of responses or a single correct response with a variety of ways of getting to that response. Regardless of the type, each question you ask should have a specific purpose. Some of the purposes for asking questions are:

- To elicit a relationship or comparison—for example, "How does an isosceles triangle compare with an equilateral triangle?"

- To have the student state a fact—for example, "How many sides has an octagon?"

- To elicit an example or illustration—for example, "Find a pair of parallel lines in the given figure."

- To develop an analysis or discussion—for example, "Tell us all what is taking place in the problem" or "Do you agree or disagree with Johnny's answer? Why or why not?"

- To apply an idea or a formula—for example, "What is the area of the circle with radius 7?"

- To summarize what has been learned—for example, "What are the kinds of factoring we have learned today?"

- To lead the students to a higher level of thinking—for example, "What do you think would happen to the area of the circle if we add 5 to the radius? If we doubled the radius?" or "What do you think would happen to the time it takes to go from Boston to Springfield if you increase your speed from 45 to 55 miles per hour?"

Good questions require planning. Obviously, you cannot plan all of your questions in advance. No one knows what responses earlier questions will generate in a given lesson. However, the key questions in your lesson must be thought out ahead of time. Questions should be clear, concise, and unambiguous and should lead to learning and promote thinking. Effective questions are aimed at a specific purpose and are clearly stated, brief, and thought provoking. Questions must also be asked at the level of the students in the class and in everyday language they can understand.

Follow-Up Responses

After asking a question, there are certain follow-up phrases and questions you can use to continue the discussion and help students give more than one-word answers. Many students will not volunteer even a one-word answer because they know that you will probably follow up their answer with a question that strikes terror in their hearts, namely "Why?" Instead, you might consider using some of these alternatives:

- How did you decide on that?
- Would you please elaborate for others in the class who might not see that?
- Please give us your insights on that.
- Please share your thinking with the rest of us.
- How did you reason to find that?
- Can you talk about that in everyday language?
- What made you think of that?
- Jane, can you explain Paul's answer in your own words?

QUESTIONS TO AVOID

There are certain kinds of questions you as a teacher should avoid. These questions rarely help move the lesson along and almost never supply you with any information about what the students are or are not learning. In many cases, these questions are the ones that first occur to us. They are almost instinctive. In this case, you need to ignore your instincts. Avoid these types of questions:

1. **Yes-no questions.** Even if the student answers correctly, no one else in the class will know how the answer was achieved. Very little is gained by asking a student "Is this a quadrilateral?" Even if students have no idea of what a quadrilateral is, they have a 50 percent chance of being correct with either answer. Better to ask "What kind of polygon is ABCD?" If you ask students "Is triangle RST an isosceles triangle?" they will assume you want the

answer yes; why else would you have asked this question? A much better question is "What type of triangle is triangle RST?" To this question, you might get a variety of answers, such as scalene, obtuse, and acute as well as isosceles.

2. **Elliptical questions.** These are questions such as "What do you know about percent?" These questions are usually too vague to elicit any meaningful response. They usually lack sufficient specificity to elicit a meaningful answer. Asking a question such as "What about adding these fractions?" will not generate an answer of value to the student or the class. It is better to be more specific and ask something such as "Why did we find a common denominator in this problem?" A question such as "What about these lines?" can lend itself to a wisecrack. It's better to ask "How do we know these lines are perpendicular?"

3. **Leading questions.** These usually give away part of the answer, "leading" the student toward the response you wish. If you ask a student "How do similar triangles help us form equal ratios?" you have given away much of the knowledge you wish to elicit from the student. A better way to ask the question would be "In triangles ABC and RST, how do we know that the ratios AB:BC and RS:ST are equal?" Similarly, it makes little sense to ask "Is 5 a factor of 45?" It would be better to ask "By what number should 5 be multiplied to give 45?" Why waste time asking "This is a right triangle, isn't it?" Who would challenge your question by saying no?

4. **Guessing questions.** Avoid questions that encourage speculation rather than careful thought. "How many faces do you think an icosahedron has?" can invite students to guess at any number without any idea about what an icosahedron is or its properties. (This is quite different from making an " 'intelligent' guess and test" which is a valid strategy for solving problems.)

5. **Multiple questions.** Don't change your question in midstream before the student has a chance to think and answer. Sometimes you may begin to ask a question and then realize that you have not been specific enough to obtain the correct answer. For example, "Can you find the perimeter of that square? What is the length of each side?" A student may be ready to answer your first question but may not have assimilated the second. As a result, the student may become confused. Similarly, two questions tied together often can be confusing. For example, "What is the lowest common denominator for these two fractions?" and "What do we multiply each fraction by to give them equivalent denominators?" are really two distinct questions. Each should be asked separately; the second should be asked only after the first has been answered correctly.

6. **Vague questions.** Questions such as "Does everyone understand?" or "Are there any questions?" are virtually useless, since they rarely elicit any response of value. Rather than ask "Does everyone understand this?" a much better question would be one that assesses the extent of understanding and is directed to a specific student. Asking "Are there any questions on last night's homework?" will usually elicit a great deal of noise and confusion, as some students call out yes, some call out no, and others just look around to see what the rest of the class is doing. Instead, you can ask for a volun-

teer to come to the board to explain a particular problem you think might have been confusing to the class. This might produce responses that could help other students clarify their own thinking about the assignment.

7. **Teacher-oriented questions.** These questions tend to separate the teacher from the rest of the class, rather than making the teacher a part of the learning community. Asking "Who can tell *me* what the first equation should be?" tells the class that this is a me-you classroom. It is better to use the words *we* and *us* when discussing a problem. For example, rather than saying "What should I do next to solve this?" the teacher should say "What should be our next step?" or "What should we do next to solve this?"

DO'S AND DON'TS FOR QUESTIONING

Don't repeat student answers. If you do, the class will gradually learn that this is a teacher-talk lesson and will ignore each other's responses, since they are going to be repeated by you anyway. If you wish to have a specific point emphasized, ask another student to repeat the answer. For example, "Mary, would you repeat what Jim has just said?" or "Sally, would you explain what Jim just told us in your own words?" Very often, having a student explain someone else's response will clarify it for the other students far better than you could.

Don't ask questions designed to embarrass a student. Why ask a question when you know the student is not paying attention or does not know the answer? You'll probably get a response such as "What?" or "Huh?" neither of which is of much help. Embarrassing students will simply cause them to feel angry toward you and possibly encourage further classroom disruption. After all, middle school students are very much afraid of being embarrassed in front of their peers.

Don't always ask students to prove a statement true. When students are asked to prove something, they make the assumption that the statement is true. Since we will be asking students to make conjectures and then test their validity, it is better to ask them to explain why their statement is either true or false. Many of the hypotheses students advance will not be true. Disproving a statement is an acceptable form of proof.

Don't let your facial expressions give away the answer. When a student answers incorrectly, it was never done on purpose. Preadolescents do not want to be incorrect in front of their peers. A wrong answer can mean that what has been presented so far is not making sense to the students and should be gone over in more detail.

Don't accept chorus answers to your questions. It is simple for any one student to "hide" by being part of a chorus. You will rarely obtain any information of value, since you will not be able to determine who knows what or who answered the question. Instead, ask the question, pause, and then call on one student to answer. You can involve other students in the discussion by asking whether they agree or disagree with the first student's answer and why. For instance, asking "What is the sum of 3Y and 4Y, class?" will yield a response of "7Y." But how many students really would recognize the method of addition in another setting? And how many are waiting to see what the brightest students will answer before they join in?

Do ask a lot of questions in your lessons. Begin by asking a question that will engage the attention of the students. Then continue by using a variety of questions, some calling for thought, some asking for facts, some requesting a summary of what has been done.

Do accept and build on student answers as much as possible. Even when a student's answer is outside the realm of the response you are looking for, try to find some part of the answer that can be used.

Do ask open-ended questions. As was stated earlier, open-ended questions permit your students to respond in a variety of ways. For example, if students are given a rectangle with the measure of the sides 5" and 12", rather than asking for the perimeter or the area, you might ask them to prepare a list of all the things they can tell about the rectangle. You can be certain that the area and the perimeter will be two of the things on their lists, along with some others as well. You might ask "Which is the larger quantity, x or –x?" This will lead the class into a rather lengthy discussion of positive and negative numbers.

Do ask questions that encourage students to make conjectures and experiment with the ideas of the lesson. For example, "In what other ways can we look at this problem?" or "Are there any other situations in which we might be able to use this algorithm?" Ask students to create problems of their own using some of the information just learned. Have them explain their reasoning and state some of the hypotheses they have made.

Do use your questions to involve all students in the learning process. If all they had to do to learn was to listen to you, why not tape record your lessons and sit at your desk, reading a magazine?

Although the focus here has been on oral discourse and what to do with responses to your questions, written responses are also important. Not only are written responses a necessary part of mathematics, but they are also required on tests. Consequently, it is good to provide your students with many opportunities to respond in writing to convergent and divergent questions.

USING ANSWERS

If you are going to use questions as a basic method of teaching, then using the answers you receive is just as important. Here again is where your instincts may lead you astray. When students do not understand what the lesson is about, some teachers try to talk louder, even to the point of shouting at the students. Others pound on the chalkboard while emphasizing their answer. Even using the single word "Think!" isn't helpful. Sarcasm, of course, should never be used. Saying something like "I don't understand it. Last year's class had no trouble" or "Who taught you last year?" is not going to help students learn. Instead, it will surely turn them off for at least the rest of that day if not longer.

Instead, ask yourself "Why didn't anyone respond to my questions? Is it because they really didn't learn what I was teaching? Maybe no one understands it." Or perhaps the question was too difficult at this point in the lesson. Students might be afraid of being wrong and so be afraid to take part.

When you want to get some meaningful responses, you might say "What questions can I answer for you?" or "Now you can ask me some questions."

Praising student responses will sometimes give the students that necessary boost to help them continue learning. However, praise must be meaningful. Too many teachers say "That's good!" or "OK!" or "Fine!" routinely. As a result, praise is overdone and becomes meaningless to the students. It may even give students a wrong impression of their ability. And it can put a halt to any meaningful discussion and stop students from listening to one another. The word "Good!" ends the discussion on that topic! The class now knows that the response given was the one the teacher was looking for. Rather than foreclose the question, try using approaches such as "Why do you believe that to be correct?" or " What would happen if we replaced 6 with x?" or "How was your solution similar to the one Leslie put on the board?" or "How might we generalize the solution?" Reducing the number of verbal responses you give can help students delve more deeply into the problem at hand. Of course, you will want to praise students for a particularly interesting, unusual, or mathematically different (but correct) response. But don't smother your students with meaningless praise.

On the other hand, even a wrong answer can provide the jumping-off point for a fruitful discussion. Asking another student to modify an answer or to embellish or add to it will help the student who gave the erroneous response get back on track in the discussion. Using the response gives it worth and makes the student feel a part of the discussion.

CONVERGENT QUESTIONS AND DIVERGENT QUESTIONS

In the hands of a competent, thoughtful teacher, a simple convergent question can lead to a series of responses that create a valuable learning experience. The first scenario demonstrates how this might be done using a convergent question.

TEACHER: "We have triangle ABC, with AB = AC = 6 inches, and vertex angle BAC containing 40 degrees. *How many degrees are there in angle B?"* (convergent question)

(The students work on the problem in small groups for a few minutes. Maria, a spokesperson for one of the groups, raises her hand and is called on by the teacher.)

MARIA: "We got 70 degrees."

TEACHER: "That sounds reasonable. Tell us how your group got that."

MARIA: "We know it is isosceles."

TEACHER: "How did you know that?"

MARIA: "It said that AB = AC = 6 inches."

TEACHER: "And how did that help?"

MARIA: "Then the two angles are equal."

TEACHER: "Johnny, you were in Maria's group. Which two angles is Maria talking about?"

JOHNNY: "Angle B and angle C, the base angles."

TEACHER: "What makes them equal?"

JOHNNY: "They're opposite the equal sides."

TEACHER: "Very good, Johnny. OK, Leslie, why don't you go on?"

LESLIE: "We took 40 degrees from 180 degrees. That left 140 degrees."

TEACHER: "But where did the 180 degrees come from?"

LESLIE: "We knew that the angles of any triangle equal 180 degrees."

TEACHER: "You mean the sum of the angles of any triangle contains 180 degrees?"

LESLIE: "Yes."

TEACHER:	"Go on, Leslie."
LESLIE:	"Well, 180 degrees – 40 degrees = 140 degrees. And half of 140 degrees is 70 degrees."
TEACHER:	"Very nicely done."

Notice what this brief discourse reveals about geometry. First, the properties of an isosceles triangle were reviewed. Second, the students used their knowledge about the sum of the measures of the angles in any triangle. Finally, there was computation practice in subtraction and division.

In the second senario the same problem is approached using a divergent question.

TEACHER:	"We have triangle ABC, with AB = AC = 6 inches, and vertex angle BAC that contains 40 degrees. *What can you tell us about the triangle?*" (divergent question)

(Students work alone for a few minutes, creating a list of their findings.)

TEACHER:	"Who will begin?"
ANTHONY:	"The triangle is isosceles."
TEACHER:	"How do you know that?"
ANTHONY:	"Because it has two equal sides, and any triangle with two equal sides is isosceles."
TEACHER:	"Very nice, Anthony. Jonathan, what else can you tell us?"
JONATHAN:	"The base angles are equal."
TEACHER:	"What do you mean by the base angles?"
JONATHAN:	"Angle B and angle C—at the bottom of the triangle."
TEACHER:	"Can anyone say that differently?"

(Liu raises his hand, and the teacher calls on him.)

LIU:	"The two angles opposite the two equal sides contain the same number of degrees or are equal."
TEACHER:	"Nice, Liu. What else did you find?"
LIU:	"All three angles add up to 180 degrees."
TEACHER:	"Good. Does anyone have something else?"
SARAH:	"Yes. I know that angle B and angle C each contain 70 degrees."
TEACHER:	"That's interesting, Sarah. Share your reasoning with us."
SARAH:	"Well, 180 degrees – 40 degrees = 140 degrees. Since they're equal, I divided by 2, and angle B is 70 degrees and angle C is 70 degrees."
TEACHER:	"Mark, do you agree with Sarah?"
MARK:	"That's what I got, too."

(The teacher sees Jonathan's hand up and calls on him.)

JONATHAN:	"Base BC = 4 inches."
TEACHER:	"How did you get that?"
JONATHAN:	"Well, the angle at A is the smallest angle of the triangle, so the side opposite it is the shortest side."

TEACHER:	"But why is it 4 inches?"
MARTHA:	"He's right. It is the smallest side. But we can't tell exactly how much it is. We know it is less than 6 inches."

This discourse reveals an exciting discussion of geometry by the class. The same properties explored in the first scenario are also discussed here. However, this type of discussion permitted Jonathan to bring in additional information as he used his critical and creative thinking skills. The teacher never said he was wrong but permitted other students to find the error.

Activities

1. Why is it better to call on a student by name after asking the question, rather than before?

2. A student you have called on says "I didn't hear the question." How would you respond?

3. A student makes an error in answering your question by multiplying two numbers instead of adding them. How would you respond?

4. A student you have called on says "I don't know." How do you respond?

5. Pick a topic from a seventh-grade textbook. Make a list of five or six questions you would ask to stimulate discussion during the lesson.

6. One student in your Elementary Algebra class keeps calling out the answers whenever you ask a question. The answers are usually correct. How would you handle this situation?

7. State whether or not you consider each of the following to be a good question. If you feel it is not a good question, explain why not. Then change the question to make it a good one.

   a. What is $\sqrt{4} + \sqrt{9}$, class?

   b. In triangle ABC, when we bisect angle A, angle DAB contains the same number of degrees as angle what?

   c. Who can tell me the sum of the two fractions?

   d. Is the sum of these two fractions $\frac{13}{5}$?

   e. What is the greatest common factor for the two numbers, and what do we get when we divide by it?

Bibliography

Burns, Marilyn. "The Art of Questioning." *Arithmetic Teacher* 22 (February 1985): 14–16.

Chuska, Kenneth R. *Improving Classroom Questions.* Bloomington, IN: Phi Delta Kappa, 2001.

National Council of Teachers of Mathematics. *Professional Standards for Teaching Mathematics.* Reston, VA: Author, 1991.

Schmalz, Rosemary. "Categorizing of Questions That Mathematics Teachers Ask." *Mathematics Teacher* 66 (1973): 619.

Wilen, W. W. *Questioning Skills for Teachers.* Washington, DC: National Education Association, 1987.

CHAPTER 6

Technology in the Middle School Mathematics Class

There is no question that in the twenty-first century technology will have an increasing impact on society in general and education in particular, especially in the middle school. Technology is an essential part of teaching and learning of mathematics. Technology influences the mathematics that is taught and enhances students learning. Calculators and computers are changing the mathematical landscape, and your classroom needs to reflect such change. Mathematics educators must explore ways to direct technology toward more effective instruction. The National Council of Teachers of Mathematics states in its *1995–1996 Handbook* that "the use of the tools of technology is integral to the learning and teaching of mathematics" (p. 24). With the appropriate use of technology, students can learn mathematics by making and testing conjectures, by engaging in tasks that would otherwise be impossible (often due to the complexity of the numbers involved), and by looking more closely at the underlying structures of mathematics. Moreover, the explosion of the Internet (the World Wide Web) has brought information retrieval to a new level. Students can quickly find answers to questions that are not in their textbooks; can search out problems, puzzles, and so on; and can seek help with their homework. For example, most middle school students know the tests for divisibility by 2, by 3, and by 5. But what is the rule for divisibility by 7? This can be found quite easily on the Internet.

We are not suggesting that this technology should replace mental mathematics or paper-and-pencil computational skills, but rather it can enhance understanding of mathematics. Students need to explore both old and new (to them) mathematics with calculators and computers. They must become proficient in using technology in much the same way as it is used by adults—that is, as an aid to solving real-world problems. The NCTM has long advocated the use of calculators at all levels of mathematics. As suggested in its *Curriculum and Evaluation Standards for School Mathematics* (1989), these tools have changed the very nature of the problems important to mathematics and the methods used to investigate those problems. Furthermore, the availability of such technologies raises questions about what is, what can, and what should be taught in the mathematics classroom.

The NCTM (1989) recommends that:

1. Appropriate calculators should be available to all students at all times.

2. A computer should be available in every classroom for demonstration purposes.

3. Every student should have access to a computer for individual and group work.

4. Students should learn to use the computer as a tool for processing information and performing calculations to investigate and solve problems. (p. 9)

However, the availability of such technologies does not suggest that students will no longer need to know mathematical facts and algorithms. On the contrary, they will need to know their facts even more, in order to determine how best to use these new tools.

CALCULATORS

Using a calculator or computer to assist with mathematics is similar to using a word processor to assist in English. No one would claim that the word processor has replaced the need for the knowledge of spelling or grammar rules. Similarly, no one should argue that the calculator replaces the need for the knowledge of mathematical facts. In fact, the availability of technology offers students and teachers the chance to de-emphasize rote memorization and to focus on problem solving and reasoning. The calculator can remove the drudgery of complex calculations. However, no calculator can think for itself, and a student who blindly pushes buttons will not benefit from this tool. It is knowledge of basic facts and algorithms that will enable a student to estimate whether or not the answer arrived at is "in the ballpark." As the saying goes, garbage in results in garbage out. Calculators are merely a tool to help students solve problems. They eliminate tedious computations that often discourage many students. Extensive research is available that shows that calculators, used appropriately, enhance learning and thinking but do not replace it.

Because of the tremendous pace of calculator development, many parents and teachers did not have the benefit of calculators and had to work out all computation with paper and pencil, often a long and tedious exercise. Thus, many parents argue against the use of technology in mathematics, since they had to memorize algorithms, practice drills, and do paper-and-pencil manipulations. It is important to note that calculators do not replace all algorithms and all paper-and-pencil computations. When those methods are the most appropriate for solving problems, they are used. Such skills as knowing the multiplication table will always be necessary despite technology. But the fact is that calculators are more efficient and accurate for performing many "messy" computations (such as 3.5×2.75) than paper and pencil. Calculators will never replace the human mind when it comes to understanding a problem-solving situation. Proper calculator usage in conjunction with mental mathematics, estimation, and paper-and-pencil manipulations is needed for solving real problems.

Picking the Right Calculator

Calculators now come in many different styles and are equipped with an extensive range of capabilities and prices. Two basic questions that teachers and curriculum developers must ask when incorporating calculators in the middle school mathematics classroom are "How sophisticated do these calculators have to be?" and "What calculator is appropriate for middle school students?" For middle school use, a calculator must have these minimum requirements:

- Algebraic logic (follows PEMDAS)

- Exponent key (to do powers and square roots)

- At least one memory

- Straightforward way to clear all memory and programs

- Fraction and decimal capabilities

Graphing calculators, many designed with the middle school classroom in mind, have all of these capabilities and the additional capability of making tables and statistical charts and graphing functions. In addition, many functions that were once strictly the province of the computer are now readily available in relatively inexpensive hand-held calculators. Such calculators should be available to students as part of their everyday mathematics tool kit, much like a pencil, paper, ruler, and compass. Indeed, many people now regard the calculator as a sort of "electronic pencil"—always available for use when needed.

The World Wide Web can be used to explore the latest calculator models available. Below are three of the major calculator manufacturers and their respective Web sites:

- Texas Instruments—http://education.ti.com

- Casio—http://www.casio.com/calculators/

- Hewlett Packard—http://www.hp.com/calculators/

Teaching and Calculators

Calculators should be used both as computational tools and as problem-solving aids. One of your major tasks as a middle school mathematics teacher is to help your students decide when it is appropriate to use their calculator, when it is appropriate to use mental mathematics, or when the paper-and-pencil algorithm is the best option. (One would hardly use a calculator to multiply 9×8.) Above all, you must treat the calculator as an integral part of your teaching, not merely as an add-on extra to be used when you decide to use it.

In some cases, the calculator will be essential to the activity being considered. Without a calculator, some problems would probably be too complex to solve and you would probably have to omit them. In other cases, even though the activity could be completed without the use of a calculator, using a calculator could free students from the drudgery of making complicated calculations and allow them to focus on the concepts being taught.

The calculator likely will cause some changes in the middle school curriculum. For example, it is now more important to learn decimals at an early age than fractions. By the time students are in middle school, they should have an understanding of the two forms for fractions. By sixth grade, they should be interchangeable.

In order to develop an understanding of the calculator, your students need to be taught what their calculators are capable of doing and how the individual keys work. It stands to reason that intelligent use of calculators begins with being taught how to use them. Begin by having the students work on their own or in small groups to explore what the individual keys do. You can then direct some of the actual keystroke patterns for particular operations. Encourage students to learn and use the appropriate vocabulary of the calculator as they work with it. It is extremely important to focus on the order that the buttons must be pushed to obtain the desired results. A beginning exploration activity could include several arithmetic expressions to be evaluated with a calculator, such as:

(1) $10 - 4 \times 2 =$

(2) $8 + 3 \cdot 2^3 =$

(3) $8 + 6 - 4 =$

(4) $\dfrac{8 + 2 \cdot 3}{7} =$

(5) $3 \cdot 4^2 - 16 =$

(6) $17 - 9 + 8 \cdot 4 \div 16 =$

Have the students key in the expressions and discuss their output. Why did they arrive at the answers they did? This short activity can act as an introduction to a discussion of the proper order of operations. A follow-up activity could then be introduced, as follows:

Each of the following equations is incorrect as written. Where should parentheses be added to correct the equation?

(1) $12 - 8 \cdot 1 + 7 = 32$

(2) $8 - 15 + 6 \div 3 = 1$

(3) $7 + 3^2 = 100$

(4) $20 \div 7 - 2 + 5^2 \cdot 3 = 79$

(5) $24 + 16 \div 8 - 4 = 1$

Further explorations should include how to use the memory keys, the correct key sequence for entering a fraction, and how to convert from fraction to decimal form. The proper sequence of keys can vary from calculator to calculator. Use the instruction booklet to discover how these operations work.

Students will sometimes mistakenly assume that the calculator should be used for every calculation. In order to dispel this misconception, you might try the following activity—the Great Calculator Mind Race. Inform the class that some of them will have calculators for this race and that others will not. Those using calculators must key in every number and symbol. That is, if they are to multiply 9×80, they must key in 9, ×, 8, 0, =. Students without calculators may use pencil and paper or do the problem mentally. Have each student take out a sheet of paper and write down numbers from 1 through 15. You then put the following fifteen race problems on an overhead transparency and have all students compute the answers. You should watch carefully to make certain that the students with calculators are actually punching in all numerals, symbols, and operation signs.

(1) $8 + 7 =$

(2) $40 \times 6 =$

(3) $101 - 1 =$

(4) $20 \div 5 =$

(5) $54 \times 10 =$

(6) $100 \times 54 =$

(7) $6.75 \times 10 =$

(8) $7,854 \times 10 =$

(9) $7,854 \times 100 =$

(10) $7,854 \times 1,000 =$

(11) $9 \times 9 =$

(12) $7,568,234 \times 0 =$

(13) $854 \div 1 =$

(14) $45 + 45 =$

(15) $86 \div 86 =$

Most of the students without the calculators should finish ahead of those using the calculators. Of course, you might then add a few more questions, such as the following, to show that there are times when the calculator is the tool of choice:

(16) $56,246 + 376 =$

(17) $857 - 435 =$

(18) $2,467 \times 16 =$

(19) $8,642 \div 42 =$

(20) $8.732 \times 16.5 =$

In some cases, problems can be solved either with or without the calculator. For example, consider the following lesson, which is designed to introduce the students to the idea of "casting out nines."

Using the digits 1, 2, 3, 5, and 7, construct a five-digit number. Then divide that number by 9 and write down the remainder. Repeat this again, using the digits to create another five-digit number. Again divide this number by 9 and record the remainder. What do you notice happening each time? Why do you think this happens? What is true about the sum of $1 + 2 + 3 + 5 + 7$? Does this play a role in what happens each time?

The students could do the division without using a calculator. However, this would take a great deal of time, since they could form more than a hundred five-digit numbers. The students would be concentrating on the division process instead of the remainders. A calculator permits them to focus on the casting-out-of-nines process and not the division algorithm.

Calculator Activities

The following are some activities to help students develop calculator skills.

Activity 1:   **The Range Game**
Skills: Estimation with whole numbers and decimals
Using the numbers 3, 4, 5, 6, 7, 8 *once only*
(1) Find a two-digit number and a one-digit number that yields
  (a) a product between 130 and 150.
  (b) a product between 200 and 300.
(2) Find a number of the form ___.___ (such as 3.4) and a two-digit number that yields a product between 231 and 251.
(3) Find a number of the form 0.___ ___ (such as 0.54) and a two-digit number that yields a product between 49 and 62.
(4) Find two numbers of the form ___.___ (such as 3.4) that yield a product between 20 and 29.

Activity 2:   **Target Number**
Skills: Estimating with whole numbers
(1) Given the numbers 2, 3, 5, 7, and 8. Choose any three digits from the given numbers. Multiply by 7. The target is 5,000. How close can you get?
(2) Given the numbers 0, 2, 4, 5, and 6. Choose any three digits from the given numbers. Multiply by 5. The target is 2,500. How close can you get?
(3) Given the numbers 0, 2, 4, 6, and 8. Choose any three digits from the given numbers. Multiply by 9. The target is 4,000. How close can you get?
(4) Given the numbers 1, 3, 5, 6, and 8. Choose any three digits from the given numbers. Multiply by 7. The target is 2,500. How close can you get?

Activity 3:   **Exploring with Fractions and Decimals**
Skills: Division, Patterns
All of the fractions below have repeating decimals. Determine the part after the decimal place that repeats. Can you predict which is the next fraction (with numerator = 1) that repeats?

$$\frac{1}{3} = \qquad \frac{1}{6} = \qquad \frac{1}{7} = \qquad \frac{1}{9} = \qquad \frac{1}{11} = \qquad \frac{1}{12} = \qquad \frac{1}{13} = \qquad \frac{1}{14} =$$

Activity 4:   Estimating Sums and Products
Skills: Estimation
Estimate the sum and product of the two numbers. Then perform the computation with your calculator. Find the difference between your estimate and the calculator result. (Always subtract the smallest from the largest so that the difference is a positive number.)

	Your Estimates	Check with Calculator	The Difference
(1) 38 + 51	_____ + _____ = _____	_____	_____
(2) 42 + 77	_____ + _____ = _____	_____	_____
(3) 39 + 9	_____ + _____ = _____	_____	_____
(4) 96 + 89	_____ + _____ = _____	_____	_____
(5) 51 + 41	_____ + _____ = _____	_____	_____
(6) 31 × 42	_____ × _____ = _____	_____	_____
(7) 21 × 21	_____ × _____ = _____	_____	_____
(8) 101 × 11	_____ × _____ = _____	_____	_____
(9) 99 × 4	_____ × _____ = _____	_____	_____
(10) 199 × 9	_____ × _____ = _____	_____	_____

(Add this column)

_____
Your Score

Which is better: A low score or a high score?

Activity 5:   Easier with or without the Calculator?
Skills: Determining when to use a calculator or not
Find the solution to each problem. Then check off whether it was easier with or without a calculator.

	Solution	Easier With	Easier Without
(1) 7 + 7 + 7 + 7 =	_____	___	___
4 + 4 + 4 + 4 + 4 + 4 =	_____	___	___
2 + 2 + 2 + 2 + 2 + 2 + 2 + 2 =	_____	___	___
10 + 10 + 10 =	_____	___	___
(2) 7 − 7 + 7 − 7 + 7 − 7 =	_____	___	___
4 + 4 + 4 − 4 − 4 − 4 + 4 =	_____	___	___
2 − 2 + 2 + 2 − 2 − 2 =	_____	___	___
100 − 100 − 100 + 100 =	_____	___	___
(3) 3 + 7 + 3 + 7 + 7 + 3 + 3 + 7 =	_____	___	___
4 + 6 + 4 + 4 + 6 + 6 =	_____	___	___
14 + 16 + 16 + 16 + 14 + 14 =	_____	___	___
125 + 125 + 75 + 75 =	_____	___	___
(4) 100 + 20 + 3 =	_____	___	___
200 + 300 + 20 + 4 =	_____	___	___
400 + 70 + 20 + 10 + 5 =	_____	___	___
800 + 100 + 10 =	_____	___	___
6 + 100 + 70 + 2,000 =	_____	___	___
(5) 2.5 + 3.5 =	_____	___	___
2.7 + 3.3 =	_____	___	___
3.5 + 2.7 =	_____	___	___
9.9 + 9.8 =	_____	___	___
(6) 1.5 × 10 =	_____	___	___
2.5 × 100 =	_____	___	___
10 × 3.75 =	_____	___	___
25 × 1.25 =	_____	___	___
1.2 × 2.3 =	_____	___	___

Activity 6: **Problem Solving with a Calculator**

Skill: Using the calculator as an aid to problem solving

A calculator that has fraction capabilities is required for this activity. Furthermore, a calculator without scientific notation will make the exercises more challenging.

(1) Find the largest number by which you can multiply 99 without causing your calculator to overflow. (Use a calculator without scientific notation.)

(2) Below is a pyramid of fractions that follow a pattern. Which fraction should occupy the top block of the pyramid?

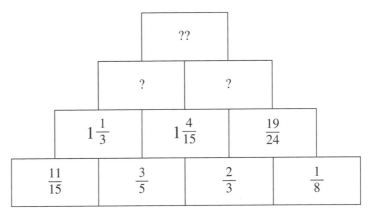

(3) The average life expectancy of an American born in 1990 is approximately 73 years. How many seconds is this?

(4) What is 35,000,052 × 3,570? Your answer must be exact. (Hint: How many zeros should be at the end?)

COMPUTERS

In many ways, the calculator and the computer are similar. Both are available to help remove the drudgery of computation, and both require intelligent use to obtain maximum efficiency. And neither can outthink the human mind. As calculators have become more complex in their design and capabilities (i.e., more programmable, more graphics, and so on), they have begun to take over some of the tasks that used to be associated with the computer. However, there are still many tasks that can be done with a computer and not with a calculator.

A computer can help you and your students in several ways. You can use your computer to produce handouts using word-processing tools and do your record keeping with spreadsheets. You can also construct and print graphs of different types, such as bar graphs, circle graphs, line graphs, and so on. The computer can be used to help you prepare presentations using software such as Hyperstudio. You can use the computer to communicate on the Internet.

The possibilities for student use appear to be limitless. There are many mathematics software programs available for all grade levels. Software utility programs afford the opportunity for students to use spreadsheets to analyze data, to graphically represent mathematical formulas, to test conjectures, and to run multiple simulations. Furthermore, computers allow students to make connections between the mathematics they are learning and the real world.

The amount of software available may seem overwhelming, and decisions to purchase software are not always at your discretion. Budgeting restrictions can limit your selections. However, it is important that you read the reviews of the latest software published in magazines and the NCTM journals, *Teaching Children Mathematics* and *Mathematics Teaching in the Middle Schools.* In general, before you decide to recommend or to purchase any software program, you should be certain that the software will do what you want it to do and that it is mathematically correct. Furthermore, before purchasing any software, be certain that the same goals cannot be achieved using other, less expensive aids such as drill cards, a math game, or other hands-on materials.

Internet Resources

Internet sites allow students to seek out homework help, ask questions, and quickly retrieve information such as biographical information on famous mathematicians. *Classroom Connect* (Housley, 1998) is a guide that provides information about the Internet and a list of useful Web sites. The following is a list of eighteen excellent Internet sites:

1. The Math Forum—http://www.mathforum.org
    Allows students to search for mathematics by browsing the Internet Mathematics Library, to ask Dr. Math questions, to join mathematical discussion groups, and to tackle problems of the week. Teachers can browse units and lessons and join a teacher-to-teacher discussion group.

2. Cool Math—http://www.coolmath.com/
    Built as an amusement park of mathematics, with games, puzzles, and activities for students and teachers alike. Many valuable links are available.

3. Math in Daily Life—http://www.learner.org/exhibits/dailymath/
    Explores how math can help in daily life by looking at the language of numbers in common situations, such as playing games, cooking, deciding to buy or lease a new car, or predicting retirement income using an interest calculator.

4. Math Forum Middle School Teachers' Place—http://mathforum.org/teachers/middle/
    Provides suggestions for lesson plans, activities and projects, and software for teachers of grades 6 through 8.

5. MathCounts—http://206.152.229.6/
    Provides information on the national math coaching and competition program for seventh- and eighth-grade students.

6. Teaching Pre-K–8 Idea Site—http://www.teachingk-8.com/
    Includes educator resources, a place for parents, and a teachers' lounge, where teachers interact by posting and answering questions.

7. Math Archives—http://archives.math.utk.edu
    Provides materials for teaching mathematics, such as software information, problem sets, lecture notes, and reports as well as links to electronic journals, grant information, and publishers of mathematical software and texts.

8. Eisenhower National Clearinghouse for Mathematics and Science Education—http://www.enc.org/

Offers information on such important issues as equity in education, the Third International Mathematics and Science Study (TIMSS), an extensive bibliography of journal articles, a guidebook of all federally sponsored K–12 mathematics and science programs, math standards and benchmarks, a professional development exchange, and reform links.

9. ERIC Clearinghouse for Science, Mathematics, and Environmental Education—http://www.ericse.org/
    Answers questions related to math, provides materials on request, and helps perform searches of the ERIC database; also provides information on digests, lessons, bulletins, organizations, and so on.

10. Math Central—http://mathCentral.uregina.ca/
    A comprehensive site out of Canada that includes a bulletin board where teachers can post questions, subscribe to Teacher Talk (an online teachers' forum), and search for resources in specific subject areas.

11. The Explorer (for math and science curricula)—http://unite.ukans.edu/
    Offers a collection of educational resources (instructional software, lab activities, curricula, lesson plans, student-created material) for K–12 mathematics and science education.

12. Interactive Mathematics Miscellany and Puzzles—http://www.cut-the-knot.com/content.html
    Contains interesting facts, challenging puzzles and brainteasers, activities in specific subject areas, engaging games, quotes, explanations, and stories. (Be sure to check out the Manifesto, which explains the beauty and importance of mathematics.)

13. SAMI (Science and Math Initiatives and the Teacher Help Service)—http://sami.lanl.gov
    A clearinghouse of resources, funding, and curriculum for rural math and science teachers.

14. The Role of Calculators in Math Education—http://education.ti.com/t3/therole.htm
    Outlines the benefits of calculator use in mathematics classrooms from kindergarten through the university level. Describes how calculators, when used appropriately, can aid in learning mathematics.

15. Math Archives Teaching Materials—http://archives.math.utk.edu/teaching.html
    Provides teaching materials, software, WWW links organized by mathematical topics, a searchable database, public domain and shareware software for Macintosh and Windows computers and for multi-platforms as well as links to other software sites.

16. Shack's Page of Math Problems—http://www.thewizardofodds.com/math/
    Includes 100+ math and logic problems, ranging from moderate to very difficult. All problems are challenging and require skills from nonmath-based reasoning to basic math to college level math. Each problem also comes with a difficulty rating from one to four stars.

17. Study WEB Math—http://www.studyweb.com/math
    A comprehensive index that provides fast and easy access for students and teachers to over 28,000 educational and reference Web sites, such as educational institutions, nonprofit organizations, and other research-oriented sites. Links are categorized by grade level and include a visual content rating.

18. National Council of Teachers of Mathematics—http://www.nctm.org

    The largest nonprofit professional association of mathematics educators dedicated to improving the teaching and learning of mathematics.

Professional Development

Professional organizations, such as the National Council of Teachers of Mathematics (NCTM), whose Web site is listed above, are often excellent places to find information about professional development, trends in mathematics education, conferences, and conventions. Each state also has an affiliated state group (e.g., Association of Mathematics Teachers of New Jersey). Finding your state's affiliated group should help in providing information about mathematics education happenings in your state. These state groups often publish yearbooks, journals, or monographs on the use of the computer that give examples donated by classroom teachers.

Computer Access

Computer use in the mathematics classroom varies from school to school. Many middle school classrooms have only a few or even just a single computer in the classroom. Other schools might have a complete computer laboratory available to your class. If you have a one-computer classroom, you can demonstrate computer programs or Internet sites (if access is available) using an appropriate computer projector or LCD panel. (If these are not available, you can have your students cluster about the computer in small groups and take turns running the program or watching the site.) Students can then work on their own in the computer lab at other times during the school day or after school. Many of your students may already have access to a personal computer at home and can continue their work there.

Software

Software falls into three categories: freeware (or public domain, no cost), shareware (minimal cost), and commercial software (cost varies). There are many commercially produced software products that can be used in your mathematics class. The Internet is an essential tool in finding and reviewing software of all three types. The following link provides all three categories of software to review:

   http://archives.math.utk.Ed/software/msdos/k-12/.html

The following link is a software preview guide for commercial software only. The user may enter grade level and curriculum area, and the link will generate a listing of titles, the distributor, and the cost for each.

   http://clearinghouse.k12.ca.us/c/@EKOeLze1866M6/search.html

Following is a list of Web site addresses for various types of software you may wish to examine:

1. *Shareware and Public Domain Software*

   http://shareware.cnet.com/

   http://www.macosarchives.com/education_-_math.html (on Macintosh only)

   http://www.edu-soft.org/library/index2.shtml#MATH

2. *Commercial Suppliers*

    http://www.edresources.com   (Educational Resources)

    http://www.learningco.com   (The Learning Company)

    http://www.stickybear.com   (Optimum Resources)

    http://www.scholastic.com   (Scholastic)

3. *Commercial Products*

"PrimeTime Math" by Tom Snyder Productions
    Students watch a video, record data, and then read, write, and calculate in a cooperative mode to solve real problems.

"The Cruncher" by Davidson
    Teaches students how to use spreadsheets for everyday life. Examples include applications from homework to family budgets.

"Math Blaster Pre-Algebra (or Algebra)" by Davidson
    Students journey through a mythical land, solving word problems and using ratios, proportions, percents, fractions, decimals, and more. The algebra version includes expressions, equations, plotting points, and polynomials.

"Carmen Sandiego Math Detective" by Broderbund
    Students can travel through twelve different missions, encountering hundreds of word problems involving fractions, decimals, computation skills, and problem-solving strategies.

"TesselMania! DELUXE" by MECC? The Learning Company
    Students use transformations and creativity to create tessellations in the manner of M. C. Escher.

"How the West Was Won + 3 × 4" by Sunburst
    Students get three random numbers and construct arithmetic equations using the proper order of operations. Skills involved include order of operations and negative integers.

"Math Arena" by Sunburst
    Students can resolve twenty different problem-solving activities.

"Geometer's Sketchpad" by Key Curriculum Press
    This dynamic geometry software permits the user to change the size and shape of geometric figures within a given problem. There is a free download available at www.keypress.com.

One last area of interest to mathematics teachers is often gradebook software programs, which are commercially available to help ease assessment concerns. Many programs offer versatile report formats and time-saving techniques. Student attendance can easily be tracked, information about each student can be recorded, and class sizes and class layouts or seating as well as student grades can be saved. Here are a few of the more popular gradebook programs.

"Grade Quick!" from Jackson Software

"Grade Machine Deluxe" from Misty City Software

"MicroGrade" from Chariot

"Easy Grade Pro" from Orbis Software

Evaluating Software

In deciding what software is appropriate for your own classroom, you should use some method of evaluation. You might have to decide what software to purchase for your school computer laboratory. In both cases, you will need some kind of evaluation form. Many appropriate forms can be found in the literature. The figure on the opposite page provides one such form. This basic evaluation form can be edited for many software types and grade levels. The form has three parts. Part I asks you to list background information about the program that can be easily found on the packaging or documentation. Part II asks you to evaluate (on a five-point scale) various parts of the program. Part III asks you to total the score and make comments on any strengths and/or weaknesses of the software.

Integrating Computer Technology into Your Teaching

The ways you can integrate computer technology into teaching are limitless. Here are two ways to do so.

To Medicate or Not? Software plays a vital role in the lesson "To Medicate or Not." This lesson provides a realistic problem for the students. A spreadsheet is used to resolve the situation. The spreadsheet greatly enhances the mathematics. (Try it without using the spreadsheet. It's virtually impossible.)

Problem: Doctors often have to plan the amount of medication given to a patient very carefully. If they administer too little, the medicine will have little effect. However, if the administration is too much, harmful effects may occur. Examine the following situation. A patient is instructed to take a drug every hour. Assume that there is no drug in the body before the initial dose. Each dose is sixty-four units. The body is able to get rid of half the drug every hour. Using the spreadsheet, calculate the amount of the drug in the body each hour.

	A	B	C
	Time in hours	Amount in body just before taking drug	Amount in body after taking drug
1			
2	0	0	64
3	1	= C2/2	= B3 + C2
4	2	= C3/2	= B4 + C2
5	3	= C4/2	= B5 + C2
6	4	= C5/2	= B6 + C2
7	5	= C6/2	= B7 + C2
8	6	= C7/2	= B8 + C2
9	7	= C8/2	= B9 + C2
10	8	= C9/2	= B10 + C2
11	9	= C10/2	= B11 + C2
12	10	= C11/2	= B12 + C2
13	11	= C12/2	= B13 + C2
14	12	= C13/2	= B14 + C2

PART I: Background Information
Evaluator:
Software Title:
Publisher:
Platform (type of computer and system requirements):
Does it come on a disk? CD-ROM?
Does package include anything in addition to the software and the documentation?
What computer did you evaluate it on?
Date reviewed:
List price (or price in discount stores):
Objectives:
Subject Area:
Software Type: lessons/tutorial   drill   review   simulation   testing   other

PART II: Evaluation
Rate the following twenty statements on a five-point scale:
5—excellent, 4—good, 3—satisfactory, 2—fair, 1—poor

1. Objectives are clearly stated.
2. Necessary technical documentation is included.
3. Materials for enrichment and remedial activities are provided.
4. Program is free of stereotypes.
5. Instruction matches objectives as stated in the documentation.
6. Instruction addresses various learning styles and intelligences.
7. Information is accurate.
8. Examples and illustrations are relevant.
9. Text is clear and printed in type suitable for target audience.
10. Spelling, punctuation, and grammar are correct.
11. Program includes remediation/enrichment when appropriate.
12. Reading level is appropriate for indicated grade level(s).
13. Required time is compatible with indicated grade level(s).
14. Appropriate amount of practice is provided to accomplish objectives.
15. Feedback is relevant to student responses.
16. Feedback gives help and/or remediation when needed.
17. Screen directions are easy to follow for grade level.
18. Help options are readily available.
19. User can control pace and sequence.
20. The graphics, audio, and visuals stimulate student interest and are of high quality.

PART III: Summary Evaluation
Out of 100 possible points, this software package scored _____.
Comments: Use your ratings above to comment on the strengths and weaknesses of the program.

Students can now play "What If?" by changing the initial dosage (C2):

- What if the initial dose was only 32 units? (Change C2 to 32)

- What if the amount in the body just before the initial dose was 32 units?

Internet Scavenger Hunt   Often, an Internet scavenger hunt can be used to have students explore ideas and find information about mathematics. Many of the Web sites listed earlier in this section can be used to answer most of the questions. Search engines such as Yahoo! and Excite are also valuable resources.

Problem:

(1) Find two perfect numbers. Explain what a perfect number is.

(2) Find a divisibility rule for 7.

(3) Find the approximate birth and death dates of Pythagoras. Also, find one significant accomplishment of Pythagoras.

(4) Find π to 100 decimal places.

(5) Find a prime number over 1,000,000.

Activities

1. Select a mathematics textbook for grade 7. Examine how technology is used throughout the book. Is technology integrated throughout the lessons? Or is it merely presented as an "add on" at the end of each chapter?

2. Identify two different calculators that could be used in a middle school mathematics classroom. Explain the functions of each one. Write a comparison of these two calculators and how each could be used.

3. Select a topic from a sixth-grade textbook. Prepare a lesson plan to teach this topic using a calculator in the lesson.

Bibliography

Bright, G., Waxman, H., and Williams, S. *Impact of Calculators on Mathematics Instruction.* Boston: University Press of America, 1994.

Dunham, P. "Looking for Trends: What's New in Graphing Calculator Research? " In G. Goodell (Ed.), *Proceedings of the Eighth Annual International Conference on Technology in Collegiate Mathematics.* pp. 120–124. Reading, MA: Addison Wesley Longman, 1997.

Harvey, J., Waits, B., and Demana, F. "The Influence of Technology on the Teaching and Learning of Algebra." *Journal of Mathematical Behavior* 14 (1995): 75–109.

Hiatt, Arthur A. "Activities for Calculators." *Arithmetic Teacher* (February 1987): 38–43.

Molnar, Andrew R. "The Next Great Crisis in American Education: Computer Literacy." *Journal of Educational Technology Systems* 7 (1978–1979): 275–283.

National Council of Teachers of Mathematics. *1995–1996 Handbook.* Reston, VA: Author, 1996.

National Council of Teachers of Mathematics. *Curriculum and Evaluation Standards for School Mathematics.* Reston, VA: Author, 1989.

Peck, Craig, Cuban, Larry, and Kirkpatrick, Heather. "Techno-Promoter Dream, Student Realities." *Phi Delta Kappan* 83, no. 6 (February 2002): 472–480.

Thompson, Carla J. "Integrating Computer Literacy into the Curriculum." *Mathematics for the Middle Grades.* (1982 Yearbook of the NCTM). Reston, VA: Virginia, 1982.

Thompson, Anthony D., and Sproule, Stephen L. "Deciding When to Use Calculators." *Mathematics Teaching in the Middle School* 6 (October, 2000): 126–129.

Williams, Susan E., and Copley, Juanita V. "Promoting Classroom Dialogue: Using Calculators to Discover Patterns in Dividing Decimals." *Mathematics Teaching in the Middle School* 1 (April 1994): 72–75.

Related Research

Becker, J. P. (1993). Current trends in mathematics education in the United States, with reference to computers and calculators. *Hiroshima Journal of Mathematics Education* 1: 37–50.

Dunham, P. H., & Dick, I P. (1994). Research on graphing calculators. *Mathematics Teacher* 87 (6), 440–445.

Fey, James. (Ed.). (1992). *Calculators in mathematics education.* 1992 yearbook of the NCTM. Reston, VA: National Council of Teachers of Mathematics.

Glasgow, B. (1998). The authority of the calculator in the minds of college students. *School Science and Mathematics* 98 (7): 383–388.

Gowland, D. (1998). Calculators: Help or hindrance? *Mathematics in School* 27 (1): 26–28.

Held, M. K. (1988). Calculators on tests: One giant step for mathematics education. *Mathematics Teacher* 81 (9): 710–713.

Held, M. K. (1997). The technological revolution and the reform of school mathematics. *American Journal of Education* 106: 5–61.

Hembree, Ray, & Dessart, Donald J. (1986). "Effects of hand-held calculators in precollege mathematics education: A metaanalysis." *Journal of Research in Mathematics Education* 17 (1): 83–99.

Rosner, M. A. (1998). *Teaching mathematics with the Internet.* El Segundo, CA: Classroom Connect.

Scherer, M. M. (Ed.). (1999). Integrating technology into the curriculum. *Educational Leadership,* 56 (5).

Taylor, Linda J. C., & Nichols, Jeri A. (1994). Graphing calculators aren't just for high school students. *Mathematics Teaching in the Middle School* 1 (3): 190–196.

Problem Solving, Reasoning, and Thinking: Make Them Use Their Heads

CHAPTER 7

Problem Solving and Reasoning

Reasoning is a major goal of all instruction. As teachers of mathematics, we have the opportunity to help middle school students develop their reasoning skills. No other subject offers a greater opportunity to incorporate practices that will help children think. In fact, *Standards 2000* includes problem-solving and reasoning as the first two process standards.

WHAT IS THINKING?

In this text, the terms *thinking* and *reasoning* are used synonymously. Thinking and reasoning are what separate us from other life forms. The thinking process goes on continually and can be divided into four categories, as shown in the figure below.

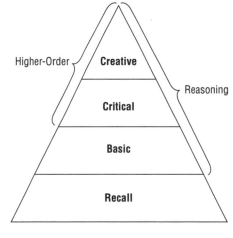

Hierarchy of Thinking

Recall thinking is the foundational level. This is thinking that, for adults, does not really require conscious thought. For example, if someone asks for the sum of 2 + 2, you do not really think; you automatically answer "4." This is basically memory. Remembering such things as your name, address, telephone number, and so on are all examples of recall thinking.

Basic thinking is the next level and is the most common form of thinking. Relatively fundamental or straightforward decisions are made in basic thinking. If someone wishes to buy four candy bars at 30¢ each, do they multiply or divide? The answer to this question is an example of basic thinking.

The next two levels, critical and creative thinking, are often referred to as higher-order thinking skills. In these levels U.S. students usually have not done well on most international tests. Middle school mathematics teachers must concentrate on developing these types of thinking.

Critical thinking is the ability to analyze a problem, determine if there is sufficient data to solve it, decide if there is any extra information in the problem, and analyze the situation. Such thinking includes recognizing consistent or inconsistent data, as well as contradictory data, and being able to draw conclusions from a set of data. Students should also be able to determine whether conclusions are valid or invalid.

There are multiple levels of *creative thinking*. Every time students approach a problem and solve it in a nonalgorithmic manner, they exhibit creative thinking. Students who provide an unusual, unique, or "different" solution to a problem exhibit another level of creative thinking. The results of this thinking are often totally different from what was expected. Highly creative students need not be the brightest students in your class (as measured by an IQ test). Creative students are often bored by the regular material in class and are often "off in a different world" of thinking. Don't be bothered or disturbed by the creative thinker. You should go out of your way to encourage creative thinking in your classroom. This will require a nonthreatening atmosphere in which students feel comfortable to put forth different and unusual ideas. You must insist that these ideas be respected and investigated, not merely shrugged off as irrelevant and off the topic. It is important to reward unusual ideas, accept them, and build on them. To stimulate creative thinking, you can provide stories about creative people. For example, the story about Gauss stimulates students' interest. As a child, Gauss's class was asked to find the sum of all the whole numbers from 1 through 100. Gauss was able to solve this in a few minutes. He placed the numbers in a row as follows:

$$1 + 2 + 3 + 4 + \ldots\ldots\ldots\ldots + 97 + 98 + 99 + 100$$

He then noticed that he had a series of number pairs that summed to 101:

$$1 + 100 = 101$$
$$2 + 99\ = 101$$
$$3 + 98\ = 101$$
$$4 + 97\ = 101$$

and so on. Thus the answer would simply be fifty pairs of numbers, each of whose sum was 101. The answer was $50 \times 101 = 5{,}050$.

In most cases, it is impossible to explain how our students arrive at some of their most creative ideas. Don't worry about it! Encourage it! Provide your students with the opportunity to be creative. And most of all, reward it!

WHY PROBLEM SOLVING?

We believe that there are two major reasons for teaching problem solving. First, solving problems is an everyday occurrence all students must face. Second, we feel that one way to teach children to think or reason is through the process of problem solving. Problem solving has long been recognized as one of the most important processes we can teach our students. In the NCTM's *Agenda for Action* (1980), the first item states that "problem solving be the focus of school mathematics in the 1980s." In the NCTM's 1989 Standards, the four strands or process standards carried throughout the curriculum stress mathematics as problem solving, reasoning, communication, and connections. The NCTM's *Standards 2000* includes problem solving as both a goal and a means of learning new mathematics, stating that:

> Instructional programs for prekindergarten through grade 12 should enable all students to
>
> • Build new mathematical knowledge through problem solving
>
> • Solve problems that arise in mathematics and other contexts
>
> • Apply and adapt a variety of appropriate strategies to problems
>
> • Monitor and reflect on the process of mathematical problem solving (p. 52)

Most educators now recognize problem solving and reasoning as major reasons for teaching mathematics. Problem solving is considered the process by which mathematics comes alive for the middle grade student.

In exploring why we should teach problem solving, we should first consider why we teach mathematics. Mathematics is fundamental in everyday life, but rarely can the problems students face be resolved by direct application of an algorithm or an arithmetic fact. The words "Solve me!" "Find my factors" or "Take my percent" don't appear in a store window or at a sale. Problem solving is the link between real-life problems and the skills learned in school. Students often wonder, "What good will this do me? When will I ever use it?" An emphasis on problem solving closes the apparent gap between the mathematics learned in the classroom and the mathematics needed to be a problem solver in the real world. Problem solving also helps connect the various topics learned in class each year. Problems are never solved in a vacuum; rather, they are related in some way to experiences encountered previously.

Middle school students face decision-making problems every day, such as "How do I save enough money to buy a baseball card I want?" or "How many people should I invite to my party?" or "What can I buy for lunch with the money I have?" These are all real-world problems for early adolescents. You can use these real-life situations in designing your lessons to help students become better reasoners and problem solvers.

Middle school students find this type of problem solving more exciting and interesting than merely repeating exercises using the same algorithmic approach. Problem solving requires students to think, which fosters a more positive attitude toward mathematics in general.

WHAT IS A PROBLEM?

If students are to become problem solvers and reasoners, they must first recognize what a problem is. "A problem is a situation, quantitative or otherwise, that confronts an individual or group of individuals, that requires resolution, and for which the individual sees no apparent path to obtaining the solution" (Krulik and Rudnick, 1998, p. 2).

For purposes here, we shall insist that a problem have a mathematical base. This may not be an arithmetic base. Many logic problems which do not involve numbers or computation are excellent vehicles for stimulating and improving the student's thinking abilities.

Notice the wording "and for which the individual sees no apparent path to obtaining a solution." This implies that the so-called word problems that often appear in textbooks do not necessarily involve problem solving. For the most part, word problems should be called "exercises." They have a distinct but different purpose—namely, to provide drill and practice in an algorithm or skill that has just been taught. The path to the solution obviously *is* known—it is to apply that very skill. We are not advocating that these exercises be removed from the textbook. On the contrary, they do serve a useful purpose. We are merely saying that they should be regarded as what they are—vehicles for practicing algorithms and skills, not to stimulate problem solving and reasoning. Furthermore, these word exercises, which appear after a skill has been taught, are usually of little interest to middle grade students. They have little or no desire to "solve" them. For example, a student in the fifth grade might be given a sheet of numbers to add:

$$\begin{array}{r} 851 \\ 427 \\ 615 \\ + \underline{739} \end{array} \qquad \begin{array}{r} 7321 \\ 6730 \\ 2111 \\ + \underline{5234} \end{array}$$

This cannot be considered a problem to solve. A word "problem" modification of this exercise is as follows:

There were 7,321 people at the school's first basketball game.

There were 6,730 people at the second basketball game.

There were 2,111 people at the third game.

There were 5,234 people at the fourth game.

What was the attendance at all four games?

Again, this requires calculation, not problem-solving, skills, and hence it is still an exercise. Compare the following, which does require problem-solving skills:

You are given the digits 3, 4, 5, 6, and 7.
(a) Write three different four-digit numbers and find their sum.
(b) What is the largest sum you can obtain?
(c) What is the smallest sum you can obtain?

This is a problem in the problem-solving sense. Now students must make some decisions while solving the problem—decisions that involve the concept of place value. At the same time, students get the required practice in addition of three- and four-place numbers.

A problem should be one that the learner finds interesting and wishes to resolve. If they refuse to attack the problem, then it can hardly be referred to as a problem. The problem must challenge the student. However, keep in mind that what is a problem for one student may not be a problem for another. You will need to be alert to how to provide challenging problems to solve for all the diverse learners in your class.

WHAT IS PROBLEM SOLVING?

Problem solving is a process. It is the means by which individuals take the skills and understandings they have developed previously and apply them to unfamiliar situations. This process begins with the initial confrontation of the problem and continues until an answer has been obtained and the learner has examined the solution process. The goal of teaching mathematics has two parts: (1) to help students learn facts, master skills, and obtain information; (2) to help students acquire the ability to use these facts, skills, and information in solving problems and developing their reasoning skills. This latter is most important: the skill of problem solving and reasoning.

Two words are used here that must be carefully considered: *answer* and *solution.* They are not interchangeable. The *solution* is the entire process from beginning to end. The *answer* is something that "drops out" along the way. If the truth be known, as far as the teacher is concerned, the answer is probably the least important part of the process. It is the solution—the analysis, strategy selection, and method of attack—that is critical if the learner is to become a problem solver and reasoner.

In his 1945 work, *How to Solve It,* George Polya introduced a set of *heuristics,* or strategies to follow in order to solve a problem. Polya's heuristics consist of the following four steps:

1. **Understand the problem.** What is the unknown? What are the data? What is the condition? Draw a figure, introduce suitable notation. Separate the various parts of the condition.

2. **Devise a plan.** Find the connection between the data and the unknown. Have you seen it before? Do you know a related problem?

3. **Carry out the plan.** Check each step. Can you see that each step is correct? Can you prove that it is correct?

4. **Look back.** Examine the answer obtained. Can you check the result? Can you check the argument? Can you derive the result differently? Can you see it at a glance? Can you use the result, or method, for some other problem?

Keep in mind that heuristics are merely a blueprint for a solution that can lead to an answer. Unlike an algorithm, which, if correctly chosen and applied, will guarantee a correct answer, heuristics can only provide a guide toward resolving the problem; they do not guarantee success.

Although these heuristics were derived by Polya more than fifty years ago, most current textbooks use some variation of these heuristics in their lessons on problem solving. In this book, the following set of heuristics is used:

1. **Read and explore.** Read the problem. Determine what it is all about. Decide what you are being asked to find. Determine if there is sufficient information. Is there excess information? Is something missing?

2. **Select a strategy.** Use one or more of the following strategies to solve a problem:

Look for a pattern	Draw a diagram
Guess and test	Use logical reasoning
Work backward	Write an equation
Reduce and expand	Solve a simpler problem
Act it out	Simulate or experiment
Make a table	Exhaustive listing

3. **Solve the problem.** Use your arithmetic, algebra, and other mathematics skills to carry out your plan and solve the problem. Find an answer.

4. **Look back and reflect.** Check your results. See if they are correct. Be certain that there are no computation errors. Have you have arrived at the answer in a correct manner? Can you use the method you used in solving this problem with other problems?

The figure below presents an elaboration of these heuristics in diagram form.

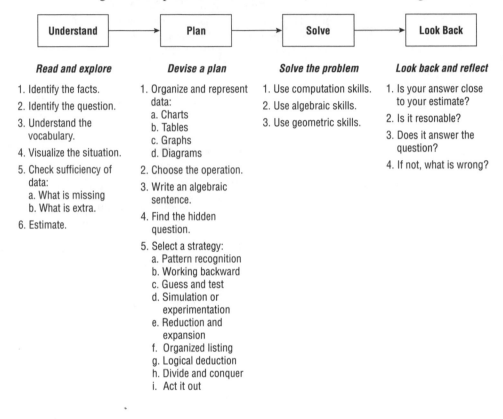

| Understand | Plan | Solve | Look Back |

Read and explore	*Devise a plan*	*Solve the problem*	*Look back and reflect*
1. Identify the facts.	1. Organize and represent data:	1. Use computation skills.	1. Is your answer close to your estimate?
2. Identify the question.	a. Charts	2. Use algebraic skills.	2. Is it resonable?
3. Understand the vocabulary.	b. Tables	3. Use geometric skills.	3. Does it answer the question?
4. Visualize the situation.	c. Graphs		4. If not, what is wrong?
5. Check sufficiency of data:	d. Diagrams		
a. What is missing	2. Choose the operation.		
b. What is extra.	3. Write an algebraic sentence.		
6. Estimate.	4. Find the hidden question.		
	5. Select a strategy:		
	a. Pattern recognition		
	b. Working backward		
	c. Guess and test		
	d. Simulation or experimentation		
	e. Reduction and expansion		
	f. Organized listing		
	g. Logical deduction		
	h. Divide and conquer		
	i. Act it out		

Read and Explore

In this first heuristic step, learners must gain an understanding of what is taking place in the problem, determine what they are being asked to find, and discover the appropriate information that will lead to the answer. Reading in mathematics is quite different from reading in other subjects. For one thing, there is no continuity of the characters. They change from problem to problem. Similarly, the situation or setting changes from problem to problem as well. You must teach your students how to read a mathematics problem. When presented with a problem, ask students to say what the problem is about in their own words. Also ask them to tell the class what the problem is asking them to find. If there are insufficient data, ask students to supply some data of their own that are reasonable. Also have students determine if there is any excess information.

Select a Strategy

This second heuristic, select a strategy, is the most critical step of the process and the one that is most unfamiliar to students. It also requires creativity. Each of the following strategies must be demonstrated with examples of problems and then discussed so that students will recognize the conditions that lead them to the appropriate strategy. Keep in mind that these strategies are rarely used alone; rather, several occur in conjunction.

Look for a Pattern   Many mathematicians feel that patterns are the entire basis for all mathematics. Indeed, patterns are to be found throughout the history of mathematics and have often led to discoveries that have furthered knowledge of mathematics. Students must be taught to look for patterns in arrays of numbers or figures.

Problem: If you will perform several tasks around the house for one month, your parents will pay you a certain amount of money. They offer you two ways to be paid. Plan A will give you $1 a day for each of the 30 days. Plan B will pay you 1¢ the first day, 2¢ the second day, 4¢ the third day, 8¢ the fourth day, and so on for the 30 days. Which plan would you select and why?

Approach: To resolve this problem, first compare the two payment plans: one is constant; one changes daily. Make a table for the first ten days and look for a pattern.

Day	Plan A	Plan B
1	$1	.01
2	$1	.02
3	$1	.04
4	$1	.08
5	$1	.16
6	$1	.32
7	$1	$1.28
9	$1	$2.56
10	$1	$5.12

It is easy to see that for thirty days, money earned in plan B will be far in excess of the money earned in plan A.

Draw a Diagram   Many students are visual learners. That is, they require a pictorial representation of a problem in order to see what is taking place. Many problems lend themselves to a drawing or diagram of the situation.

Problem: You get on an elevator at the first floor. You go up 7 floors, down 4 floors, up 8 floors, down 7 floors, up 5 floors, and down 3 floors. On what floor are you now?

Approach: A drawing or diagram of the action will enable students to see what is taking place. The drawing itself will show that the person would be on the sixth floor. This problem can also be solved by the use of integers. Up 7, up 8, and up 5 are all positive; down 4, down 7, and down 3 are negative. Be certain to start at the +1 floor.

Guess and Test   Some teachers feel that this strategy gives students an erroneous impression. That is, they will say to a student "Do you know or are you just guessing?" If students simply are asked a question such as "How many sides does an icosahedron have?" without any previous knowledge base, students will shout out guesses such as 5, 10, 12, 16, and so on. While guessing without basis is of little value, guessing in mathematics is rarely done in a vacuum. Each guess forms the basis for the next refinement of that guess. When using the guess-and-test strategy, a carefully constructed table is needed to keep track of your work.

Problem: A farmer has some pigs and some chickens. The animals have a total of 70 heads and 200 legs. How many of each kind of animal does the farmer have?

Approach: You can solve the problem algebraically by setting up a pair of equations in two variables and solving them simultaneously.

$$p + c = 70$$
$$4p + 2c = 200$$

However, your students may not have reached this level. So the problem can be solved using the guess-and-test strategy. Devise a table, as follows:

Pigs		Chickens		Total Legs	
H	L	H	L		
70	280	0	0	280	(Too many pigs)
50	200	20	40	240	(Still too many)
40	160	30	60	220	
35	140	35	70	210	
30	120	40	80	200	(This is it!)

Any problem that can be solved with a pair of equations in two variables solved simultaneously can also be solved by using the guess-and-test strategy.

Use Logical Reasoning

Some problems do not rely on numbers for their solution. While logic usually permeates all mathematical problem solving, there is a group of problems that can be solved by directly applying logical thinking.

Problem: Given a standard checkerboard and 32 dominoes, each of which covers exactly two squares, we can completely cover the checkerboard. (You can try this; it works!) Now, eliminate a square from one pair of opposite corners of the board and remove one domino. There are now 31 dominoes, and 62 squares. Can the dominoes completely cover the board as before? Demonstrate how to do it.

Approach: In the beginning, you might attempt to draw dominoes covering pairs of squares, either horizontally or vertically. You will probably give up rather quickly, since this can be a messy method of solution. You may wish to take a real checkerboard and cut out dominoes of the correct size so that each covers exactly two squares. Again, this is a rather cumbersome method and unlikely to yield a solution. Instead, try logical reasoning to solve the problem. The original checkerboard has 64 squares, 32 of them black and 32 of them white. If you look at a checkerboard, you will see that each time a domino is placed on the board, it covers two adjacent squares, one black and one white. Now look at what happened when the squares were cut from the opposite corners. We either removed two black squares or two white squares. There are now 30 of one color and 32 of the other. It is impossible to cover the board with 31 dominoes. The problem is resolved and the result is proved. "Solving the problem" in this case meant showing that it could not be done. Notice that using logic eliminated the necessity for actually getting a checkerboard and performing the experiment. This is an excellent example of the power of mathematics.

Work Backward

In some cases, working backward is the method for attacking a problem. The use of this strategy is easily recognizable, since the end situation is given and the starting situation is asked for.

Problem: Marci came to a ferryboat crossing the river and saw a sign stating that the cashier would double the amount of money she had in her pocket each time she crossed on board the ferry, but she would have to pay a fee of $2.40 per crossing. Marci decided she would take the ferry three times to see how the system worked. Sure enough, each time she rode the boat across, the cashier doubled the amount of money in her pocket and then took the $2.40 charge. Marci was quite surprised when, after the third crossing, she paid the $2.40 and found herself with no money. How much money had Marci started out with?

Approach: Set up a table to keep track of your work as you go through the trips in reverse (working backward).

Trip	Amount left after paying fee	Amount after doubling plus fee	Amount this crossing started with
3	0	$2.40	$1.20
2	$1.20	$3.60	$1.80
1	$1.80	$4.20	$2.10

Marci started with $2.10. Note that this problem could also be done with algebra.

Write an Equation Algebra is one of the most versatile mathematical skills. The ability to reduce a complicated problem situation to an equation provides us with a powerful tool. Students should never overlook the techniques of algebra they have learned, especially the skill of writing an equation.

Problem: On a string of 15 pearls, the center pearl is the largest and the most expensive. Starting from one end and including the center pearl, each pearl is worth $50 more than the previous one. Starting from the other end and including the center pearl, each pearl is worth $25 more than the previous one. The total value of the 15 pearls is $4,650. What is the value of the center pearl?

Approach: Let L = the value of the pearl at the top left and R = the value of the pearl at the top right. Then,

$$
\begin{array}{ll}
\text{L} & \text{R} \\
\quad \text{L} + 50 & \quad \text{R} + 25 \\
\quad\quad \text{L} + 100 & \quad\quad \text{R} + 50 \\
\quad\quad\quad \text{L} + 150 & \quad\quad\quad \text{R} + 75 \\
\quad\quad\quad\quad \text{L} + 200 & \quad\quad\quad\quad \text{R} + 100 \\
\quad\quad\quad\quad\quad \text{L} + 250 & \quad\quad\quad\quad\quad \text{R} + 125 \\
\quad\quad\quad\quad\quad\quad \text{L} + 300 & \quad\quad\quad\quad\quad\quad \text{R} + 150 \\
\quad\quad\quad\quad\quad\quad\quad \text{L} + 350 \\
\quad\quad\quad\quad\quad\quad\quad \text{R} + 175
\end{array}
$$

We now have two equations in two unknowns:

$8L + 1,400 + 7R + 525 = 4,650$ (only count the center pearl once)
$R + 175 = L + 350$

Solving these equations simultaneously reveals that the center pearl is worth $450.

Reduce and Expand In this strategy, you reduce the complexity of the problem by beginning with a reduced number of cases (preferably one or two) and gradually expand the number of items, observing what happens as the number increases. Hopefully, you will see a pattern emerging, a pattern you can apply to the actual number of cases asked for in the original problem.

Problem: The 12 members of the basketball team have a ritual they observe at the start of each game. After the players have been introduced, each player shakes hands with each of the other players. How many handshakes are exchanged?

Approach: If we begin with 2 players, we need 1 handshake. When we increase this number to 3 players, we now need 3 handshakes. Increasing the number to 4 players, we now need 6 handshakes. Five players will yield 10 handshakes. These numbers, 1, 3, 6, 10, . . . form a set of numbers known as the triangular numbers (due to the figure formed by arranging the appropriate number of dots for each number). The differences between these numbers are increasing by 1—for instance, a difference of 2 (between 1 and 3), a difference of 3 (between 3 and 6), a difference of 4 (between 6 and 10), and so on. Using this pattern, you can solve the problem. There will be 66 handshakes needed.

Solve a Simpler Problem

Sometimes a problem appears to be difficult because it contains large numbers, decimals, and/or fractions. These numbers tend to conceal the process and operations required for solving the problem. Using simpler numbers will usually reveal what has to be done. Solve the simpler problem and then follow the same steps using the original numbers.

Problem: Liu's class is studying colonial America. The class is going to make candles from beeswax, the way they were made more than two hundred years ago. They are going to make the candles in two shapes: 20 cubic candles and 15 cylindrical candles. For the cubic candles, they will use a total of $8\frac{1}{2}$ pounds of beeswax; for the cylindrical candles, they will use $6\frac{3}{4}$ pounds of the wax. In the storeroom they have two slabs of beeswax. The first one weighs 10 pounds, and the second weighs $7\frac{3}{4}$ pounds. How much wax will be left over once they make all the candles?

Approach: Substitute simpler numbers and solve the easier version. For the cubic candles, replace $8\frac{1}{2}$ by 9. For the cylindrical candles, replace $6\frac{3}{4}$ by 7. For the $7\frac{3}{4}$ pounds of wax, substitute 8 pounds.

	Simpler	*Original*	
Step 1:	$9 + 7 = 16$	$8\frac{1}{2} + 6\frac{3}{4} = 15\frac{1}{4}$	(Wax needed)
Step 2:	$10 + 8 = 18$	$10 + 7\frac{3}{4} = 17\frac{3}{4}$	(Wax available)
Step 3:	$18 - 16 = 2$	$17\frac{3}{4} - 15\frac{1}{4} = 2\frac{1}{2}$	(Wax left over)

There will be $2\frac{1}{2}$ pounds of the wax left over.

Act It Out

One method that ensures a problem can be solved is to actually act it out. If you can perform the action taking place, students can clearly see what is happening in the problem and resolve it.

Problem: A woman buys a horse for $60, sells it for $70, buys it back for $80, and then sells it again for $90. How much money did she gain or lose at the end of these transactions?

Approach: Have two students represent the people in the problem. Make $10 bills out of paper and have the students carry out the four transactions. Students might be surprised to find that the woman actually made a profit of $20 on the four transactions.

Simulate or Experiment

Sometimes it is awkward to actually act out a problem. It may be difficult to throw a chair out of a window to time its fall. It would be far better to simulate the action by examining the equation that represents the time it takes an object to fall. There are various levels of simulation. At the lowest level you can use manipulatives. The most sophisticated level is to simulate the action symbolically with an equation or a mathematical expression.

Problem: Emily has 12 animal cards, and her sister, Sarah, has 18. Their mother gives them a pack of 30 more cards and tells them to share them so that each girl will end up with the same number of cards. How many of the 30 cards will each girl take?

Approach: This problem can easily be simulated with concrete materials. You will need 60 chips or bottle caps. Put 12 in one pile and 18 in another. From the "new" 30, add 6 to the smaller pile to make them equal. Then divide the remaining 24 chips into two equal piles and place one pile with each of the original.

The problem can also be done algebraically. Let x = the number of animal cards that Emily will take. Then 30 – x equals the number of cards that Sarah will take. Now,

$$12 + x = 18 + (30 - x)$$

Make a Table   A table is an important way to organize data. The table helps present the information from the problem in a meaningful manner so that the data can easily be shown to reveal patterns. The key word here is *organize*. The data should not be listed haphazardly; rather, they must be organized in a manner most likely to reveal patterns.

Problem: How many ways can you make change for a dollar using only quarters, dimes, and nickels?

Approach: Make a table.

Quarters	Dimes	Nickels
4	0	0
3	2	1
3	1	3
3	0	5
2	5	0
2	4	2
2	3	4
2	2	6
2	1	8
2	0	10
1	7	1
1	6	3
1	5	5
1	4	7
1	3	9
1	2	11
1	1	13
1	0	15
0	10	0
0	9	2
0	8	4
0	7	6
0	6	8
0	5	10
0	4	12
0	3	14
0	2	16
0	1	18
0	0	20

There are 29 different ways to make change.

Solve the Problem   Now the student gets to apply the arithmetic, geometric, and algebraic skills learned in class. Once the appropriate strategy has been selected and applied to the given data, the student applies mathematics skills and finds the correct answer. Notice that this heuristic is only one-fourth of the entire process, yet many teachers spend most of their class time teaching the skills needed here.

Look Back and Reflect   Even though the answer has been found, there is a great deal that can be learned. Has the problem been correctly done? Is the answer reasonable? (A man who runs at a rate of 26 miles per hour hardly makes any sense; perhaps the answer was 2.6 miles per hour.) Finally, the student should ask, "What was there in the problem that made me approach it in the manner I did? What were the particular factors that led me to select that strategy? Can I use this strategy in other situations?"

TEACHING PROBLEM SOLVING

All students are capable of learning how to be problem solvers. Some teachers feel that low achievers should spend their time mastering the basic arithmetic algorithms first. This is definitely not the case. Problem-solving activities are not only appropriate for low achievers, but they may be the very thing that will encourage these students to become interested in mathematics and to master the subject. Current advances in technology enable all students to bypass the blockage caused by an inability to "do their fundamentals." Instead, by using a calculator for the fundamentals part of the solution process, every student can solve problems, if given the proper experiences.

Some people believe that having students do a lot of problems is, in itself, sufficient to make them problem solvers. Obviously, the more opportunities presented to practice the skills of problem solving, the better students will become at problem solving. However, problem solving must be taught. You need a plan that will enable you to teach students the process of problem solving. If you merely "show and tell" the solution to each problem, your students will never learn to be problem solvers but will simply learn how to solve specific problems. They will not grow in their thinking skills.

Putting It All Together

We have discussed all the heuristics of problem solving. There is another component to the final heuristic, namely, "extend"—or moving beyond the answer. The following example can demonstrate how a problem should be approached, resolved, and extended in your lesson.

Problem: Joanne and some of her friends are sitting around a circular table. Her mother brings in a tray of 25 cookies which the girls pass around. As the tray reaches each girl, she takes one cookie and passes the tray on to the next girl. Joanne takes the first cookie and passes the tray to the next girl, who takes a cookie and passes it on. This continues until all the cookies have been taken. Joanne got the first cookie and the last one as well. (She may also have taken some in between.) How many people are seated at the table?

Approach: There are basically two different approaches you can use. One is to divide the class into small groups of three or four students and have each group attempt to solve the problem. While they are working on the problem, you should move around the room and listen to the discussions taking place. You may find that some groups will want to use manipulatives. These should be available to them. You can work with individual groups, but be careful not to take over the discussion. When all the groups are done, have a representative from each present the group's solution. There will probably be more than one solution. Discuss the merits and deficiencies of each with the entire class. The results should be summarized and the strategies identified.

A second procedure would be for you to lead the discussion. This does not mean to solve the problem for the class as they watch. Rather, guide the discussion toward a solution and answer. Have one student read the problem aloud and describe the setting (i.e., what is going on in the problem). Have another student identify the important facts and write them on the overhead or chalkboard:

There were 25 cookies on the tray.

Joanne and her friends were seated at a round table.

Each took one cookie as the tray was passed.

Joanne took the first and the last cookies and perhaps some others.

Ask another student to tell what is being asked—namely, how many people were at the table. Then you can ask the student such questions as: How can we solve the problem? Can we simulate the action? Can we act it out? How many people are around the table? The direction the discussion takes depends on the answers students give to your questions. For example, the following discussion resulted from a student asking if there could be only one person at the table.

PAULA: Could there be one person at the table?

TEACHER (OR ANOTHER STUDENT): No. The problem says Joanne and her friends.

PAULA: Well, could there be two people?

MALCOLM: No. The problem said Joanne and her friends, plural. Could there be three people?

TEACHER: Let's see.

(The balance of the discussion takes the following course, with both teacher and students contributing.)

Let's put three people around the table and pass a tray of 25 "cookies" (or chips). Joanne receives cookies numbered 1, 4, 7, 10, 13, 16, 19, 22, 25. It works! There could be three people at the table, counting Joanne. We have found an answer. Should we stop now? No! Perhaps there are other answers.

Could there be four people? Let's see. Joanne would receive cookies 1, 5, 9, 13, 17, 21, 25. This works, too. There could be four people.

Could there be five people? Joanne would receive 1, 6, 11, 16, 21, 26—no! This does not work.

At this point, the students try six people, seven people, and so on and complete the solution. Do they see a pattern? What do the answers have in common? (The goal is to uncover the mathematics underlying the problem—namely, that all answers are the proper factors of 24. However, one and two have been ruled out by the conditions of the problem.) Then what is the greatest number of people that could be seated at the table? (Answer: 24.)

Now, extend the problem by asking how many people would there be at the table if there had been 40 cookies on the plate? 50 cookies? What about 24 cookies? (There would only be 23 people at the table, since as a prime number 23 has only two factors, itself and 1. It is a prime number.) For some students, you can extend this to a mathematical generalization that for n cookies there could be all the proper factors of $n - 1$, except for the one and two people seated at the table. This problem is an excellent example of the use of the simulation strategy.

More can be achieved in the "extend" part of the solution as we move beyond the original answer. First, a problem may have more than one correct answer. Second, the mathematical concepts of factors and primes were reviewed. In the process, students get additional drill and practice in their computational skills. The "extend" part of the heuristic plan is crucial in developing thinking.

Another problem can further illustrate the process of extension.

Problem: Laura has a new pet, a white rabbit named Ghost. She wants to teach Ghost to climb a flight of 10 steps. Ghost can hop up either 1 step or 2, and doesn't go back down. Each time he reaches the top step, Laura takes him back to the bottom. How many different ways can Ghost climb a flight of 10 steps?

Approach: Have a student read the problem aloud and discuss what is taking place. Give the students a few minutes to explore some different ways that Ghost can get to the top, such as 1-1-1-1-1-1-1-1-1-1, 2-2-2-2-2, 2-1-1-1-1-1-1-1-1, 1-2-1-1-1-1-1-1-1, and so on. The class should quickly realize that trying to write down all the possibilities in this haphazard manner won't work. At this point, you should step in and lead the discussion.

Lead the students to see that the 10 is completely arbitrary; another number could as easily be used. In fact, try the "reduce and expand" strategy. That is, reduce the number of steps to 1, then 2, then 3, then 4, and so on. Then look for a pattern. A carefully drawn table is a necessity. The completed table is shown here, but it should be developed by you and the students together.

Number of Steps	Number of Ways	Ways		
1	1	1		
2	2	1-1-2		
3	3	1-1-1	2-1	1-2
4	5	1-1-1-1	2-1-1	
			1-2-1	
		2-2	1-1-2	
5	8	1-1-1-1-1	2-1-1-1	1-2-2
			1-2-1-1	2-1-2
			1-1-2-1	2-2-1
			1-1-1-2	
6	13			
7	21			

Ask the students if they see a pattern in the sequence 1, 2, 3, 5, 8, 13, 21, . . . If not, lead them to recognize the Fibonacci sequence (i.e., each term is the sum of the two previous terms). Carry out the sequence to the final answer, or the tenth step, namely 89 ways.

Now extend the problem. Some of your students may be capable of understanding the argument that follows. If Ghost were on step 5, where would he have come from? Either from step 4 (jump 1) or from step 3 (jump 2). Thus, the number of ways he can get to step 5 is the number of ways he gets to step 3 plus the number of ways he gets to step 4. Thus, the Fibonacci sequence applies.

Creating Your Own Problem File

Many teachers feel that they cannot obtain sufficient problems for the courses they teach. As a result, teaching problem solving becomes an occasional and inconsistent undertaking. If you are systematic and a bit creative you can build a collection of problems in several ways. You can begin now to create a problem deck. Obtain a package of large file cards (such as 5" × 8" cards). Each time you see a problem that would be appropriate for middle grade students, copy it onto one of the cards. On the other side of the card, put one or more solutions to the problem, the name of the appropriate strategy, and the mathematical skill the problem requires or illustrates. You should also include the appropriate grade level.

You can find problem examples by looking through a variety of textbook series for the middle school grades. Most modern textbook series contain lessons on problem solving. They also have features that might contain some excellent problems. You can also examine some of the many collections of problem-solving materials that exist at all grade levels. Several are suggested in the bibliography at the end of this chapter. By carefully selecting those problems that are appropriate for your students, you begin to build your collection.

Attend mathematics conferences held in your city or region. At these conferences, listen carefully to speakers who present talks on problem solving. If you hear a good problem, add it to your collection. Look at the journals in mathematics. For example, *Teaching Mathematics in the Middle Schools* (a journal of the National Council of Teachers of Mathematics) has a column devoted to problem solving and a problem calendar that appears in each issue.

Extending Your Textbook

In addition to your problem file, your class textbook is a rich resource for problems. Just about every current mathematics textbook series has a sequence of problem-solving lessons that include sample problems. In addition, carefully examine the other problems in your textbook and use them. You will probably realize that many of these text "problems" are convergent—that is, they are intended only to give students practice in the skill that has just been introduced. However, with some slight modifications, these exercises can be extended into challenging problems to add to your file. The following examples provide ways you can extend the problems in your text:

1. What's Extra? Take a problem from your textbook. Add one or more pieces of information to serve as distractors. Have the students decide what's extra, remove it, and then solve the problem.

Textbook version: Maria has a collection of sports cards. She has 18 baseball player cards and $\frac{1}{3}$ as many hockey player cards. How many hockey player cards does she have?

Modified version: Maria has a collection of sports cards. She has 18 baseball player cards, 12 basketball player cards, and $\frac{1}{3}$ as many hockey player cards as baseball player ones. How many hockey player cards does she have?

2. What's Missing? Take a problem from your textbook. Remove a piece of significant data, making the problem unsolvable. Have the students identify what is missing and supply a reasonable piece of data.

Textbook version: Jack wants to buy a pair of roller blades that are on sale for $47 at the local store, reduced from $95. He counts the money he has saved and finds he has $28. He asks his father to lend him the rest. How much money does his father have to lend him to buy the skates?

Modified version: Jack wants to buy a pair of roller blades that are on sale for $47 at the local store, reduced from $95. He counts the money he has saved and asks his father to lend him the rest. How much money does his father have to lend him to buy the skates?

3. What If . . . ? Take a problem from your textbook. Have the students solve it. Now change one or more of the given conditions. Have the students solve the new problem and then discuss the impact of the "what if . . . ?"

Textbook version: Joanie hit the dartboard in the figure below with four darts. She landed on 31, 10, 11, and 9. What was her score?

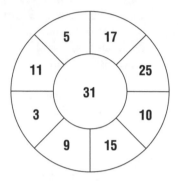

Modified version: Joanie hit the dartboard in the figure with four darts. If she scored 61, how did she do it? (There are many possible answers.)

Modified version #2: Cover up the 10 on the dartboard, leaving only the eight remaining numbers showing. What if Joanie hit the dartboard with exactly four darts and scored 61? How did she do it?

(This "What if . . . ?" leads to the answer "It cannot be done." This is because all the numbers that remain on the dartboard are odd numbers, and the sum of four odd numbers will always be even. Be sure to discuss this concept with your class.)

4. What's Wrong? Take a problem from your textbook. Either make an error in the solution or add something to the problem that makes it incorrect. The students must find the error, correct it, and then solve the problem.

Textbook version: Marsha had 21 fish in her collection, and her brother had 15. How many fish should she give her brother so that they have the same number?

Modified version: Marsha had 21 fish in her collection, and her brother had 15. "If you give me 6 fish, Marsha, then we will each have the same number of fish," said her brother. How many fish should she give her brother so that they have the same number?

5. What Questions Can You Answer? Take a problem from your textbook. Remove the question. Have the students make a list of as many questions as they can that are answerable from the given data.

Textbook version: Given rectangle ABCD with width BC = 5" and length DC = 12", what is the area of the rectangle?

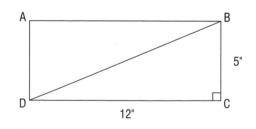

Modified version: Given rectangle ABCD with width BC = 5" and length DC = 12", what questions can you answer? Some possible questions might include:
(a) What is the perimeter of rectangle ABCD?
(b) What is the area of rectangle ABCD?
(c) What is the length of diagonal BD?
(d) What is the area of right triangle BCD?
(e) What is the perimeter of triangle BCD?

(The original question will usually appear on the list of questions that the students create.)

6. What's the Question if the Answer Is . . . ?

Take a problem from your textbook. Solve the problem yourself. Then remove the question from the problem. Give the students the answer. They must determine the question. When the problem has sufficient data, you can give them more than one "answer" and ask for the appropriate question.

Textbook version: Lucille bought a new bike. She rode 16.5 miles on Monday, 14.3 miles on Tuesday, and 15 miles on Wednesday. How many miles did she ride on the three days?

Modified version: Lucille bought a new bike. She rode 16.5 miles on Monday, 14.3 miles on Tuesday, and 15 miles on Wednesday.
(a) What's the question if the answer is 45.8 miles? (How far did she ride on all three days?)
(b) What's the question if the answer is 54.2 miles? (How much further must she ride to reach 100 miles?)
(c) What's the question if the answer is Tuesday? (On which day did she ride the fewest miles?)

7. What Number Makes Sense?

Take a problem from your textbook. Remove the numbers and list them in numerical order underneath the problem. Have the students place the numbers into the proper position and solve the problem.

Textbook version: Juanita noticed that the shoe store in the mall was having a big sale. For Saturday only, every pair of shoes in the store was reduced by 40 percent. The shoes she wanted usually sell for $68. If she bought them on Saturday, she would save $27.20. How much change did she receive from a $50 bill?

Modified version: Juanita noticed that the shoe store in the mall was having a big sale. For Saturday only, every pair of shoes in the store was reduced by _____ percent. The shoes she wanted usually sell for $_____. If she bought them on Saturday, she would save $_____ . How much change did she get from a $_____ bill?

27.20   40   50   68

Keys to Effective Teaching of Problem Solving

At the very beginning of this chapter, it was stated that reasoning is a major goal of all instruction in mathematics. In fact, one of the main purposes of teaching problem solving is to develop students' thinking and reasoning skills. The middle school is the ideal level for these skills to be developed. By this time, students have sufficient mastery of mathematics and the associated skills to be able to apply them to problem situations.

The teaching of reasoning skills depends on the teacher. The way you conduct your classroom, and especially the problem-solving activities, will determine the extent to which your students will develop thinking skills. *If you "show and tell" the solution to each problem, there will be no gain in thinking skills!* Following are some keys to help you become an effective teacher of problem solving and reasoning:

1. **Present problems often in your classes.** Problem solving should not be a "once a week" event. It is not an isolated topic to be taught whenever there is time left at the end of a class. Rather, make problem solving a frequent part of your mathematics classroom. Let it permeate what you teach and how you teach it.

2. **Pose a wide variety of problems.** Middle school students become bored when they must do the same thing repeatedly. This is one of the reasons that the middle school mathematics curriculum was such a wasteland; too much time is spent repeating the fundamentals of arithmetic that students have already learned. Once students have learned a particular strategy, move on. Pose problems that will continually challenge your students.

3. **Choose problems carefully.** Pay close attention to the settings of the problems and the difficulty level. Your students will not concentrate their efforts on problems they find boring, irrelevant, or too easy or difficult to solve. Often, students in one class can generate problems that can be posed in another class. Choose settings that involve the everyday lives of your students. Middle school students like problems relating to science fiction, rock concerts, athletic events, their own school, their classmates, CD collections, and so on.

4. **Pose problems so that students can understand what they are expected to do.** The instructions and the problems themselves must be stated clearly so that the students understand the task at hand. Ask students to repeat the directions in their own words to ensure understanding.

5. **Help the students identify what facts they are given and what they are asked to find.** Ask students to explain in their own words what is being asked for and what has been given. This should be done as a very first step in attempting to solve any problem.

6. **Put your students together to work in small groups.** Students show greater gains in problem-solving and reasoning skills when they work in small groups or pairs. Cooperative learning permits them to exchange ideas with one another. This helps them in deciding how best to attack a problem and which strategies to use. It also permits them to test their guesses and ideas and to make suggestions among themselves.

7. **Allow plenty of time to solve the problem.** Students need to reflect on their process each time they solve a problem. They need to discuss why they did what they did, their rationale, their various methods of attack, and so on. Allow them time for this sort of discussion, which is valuable to the process of developing metacognition.

8. **Provide opportunities for students to solve several problems using each new strategy.** If your students are to master the strategies, they must have practice applying them. By providing several problems using a new strategy, the students can see that the strategy can be applied in a wide range of different situations.

9. **Discuss with the class how a particular problem could have been solved differently.** A great deal of creative thinking takes place when students

attack problems in a variety of ways. Often, more than one strategy can be used as the primary method of attack. The selection of a particular strategy will depend on the individual student's learning style and preferences. Nevertheless, students should be aware of the variety of approaches that can be used to solve a particular problem. It is better to solve one problem in three different ways than to solve three different problems in one way.

10. **Model a positive attitude toward problem solving and reasoning for your students.** If you wish your students to feel the excitement and satisfaction that come with solving a problem, then you must demonstrate this feeling for them. Attack every problem with excitement, with an eagerness to solve it. Convey this to your students.

11. **Have your students explain and support their solutions in writing.** This procedure is supported by current research, practices, and testing. Most standardized tests either require or are considering requiring a narrative along with the solution to each problem. Insist that your students explain in writing how they solved the problem. This will enhance your middle school student's communication skills, something discussed extensively in NCTM's *Standards 2000.*

12. **Have your students think about their own thinking when they solve a problem.** In the teaching of problem solving, there are three major objectives you should strive to achieve. First, your students must be able to solve problems and find correct answers. Second, they must be able to explain their solutions both orally and in writing. Third, students should automatically reflect on the thought processes they used in the solution. This latter stage, thinking about one's own thinking, is referred to as "metacognition."

Problem solving should permeate all the teaching you do. Many of the arithmetic algorithms you will teach in class can be presented in a problem-solving setting. You must make a conscious effort to teach problem solving every day, not merely on occasion. Becoming a problem solver yourself is not easy; teaching your students to become problem solvers is even more difficult. Most of us become good problem solvers because we work at it. Your students will only learn to become problem solvers if they practice solving problems. Your job is to provide the necessary tools to learn these skills and then to provide students with practice using the skills. In this way they will become problem solvers.

Activities

1. Read George Polya's book *How to Solve It.* Select one of Polya's problem-solving strategies and discuss how you could apply it in your classroom.

2. Read one of the articles in the 1980 Yearbook of NCTM. Prepare a report on how this article applies to your own teaching.

3. Select one of the two problems below. Prepare a lesson plan you might use to help students solve the problem. Share your plan with another student in your class. See if your plan helps your partner solve the problem. Perhaps you might share your lesson with the entire class.

   a. Tennis balls come in a can of three, with the balls tangent to the top and bottom of the can as well as the sides. Is the can taller or larger around its circumference?

b. Joanna has eight coins in her pockets, some dimes and some quarters. Under what conditions will the value of the dimes exceed the value of the quarters?

4. Write a nine-digit number using the digits 1 through 9, so that the first two digits form a number exactly divisible by 2, the number formed by the first three digits is exactly divisible by 3, the number formed by the first four digits is exactly divisible by 4, and so on. (Answer: 381,654,729). Be prepared to explain how you approached the problem and your reasoning.

5. Discuss how the problem-solving strategies discussed in this chapter are different from the techniques you used when you solved word problems in school.

6. When students have learned a mathematical principle, one way to create a new problem is to show them a problem where the principle seems to apply but really cannot be used. For example, we know that $2\sqrt{2} \cdot 6\sqrt{8} = 12\sqrt{16}$. However, what does $2\sqrt{-2} \cdot 6\sqrt{-8} = ?$

7. Begin to build your own problem deck. Find at least one problem for each of the eleven strategies illustrated within this chapter.

8. Solve the following problem. Show as many different solutions as you can. Explain your reasoning in each solution.

Here is an array of numbers. If the sequence continues, where would the number 289 appear?

```
                               1
                         3           5
                     7       9      11
                 13      15      17      19
             21      23      25      27      29
         31      33      35      37      39      41
     43      45      47      49      51      53      55
 57      59      61      63      65      67      69      71
```

Bibliography

Charles, Randall A., Mason, Robert P., and White, Catherine A. "Problem Solving for All Students." *Mathematics for the Middle Grades* (1982 Yearbook of the NCTM). Reston, VA: National Council of Teachers of Mathematics, 1982.

DeYoung, Mary. "Challenge Problems: Love Them or Hate Them, but Learn from Them." *Mathematics Teaching in the Middle School* 6, no. 8 (April 2001): 484–488.

Krulik, S., and Rudnick, J. *Problem Solving: A Handbook for Elementary School Teachers.* Boston, MA: Allyn and Bacon, 1988.

Krulik, Stephen, and Rudnick, Jesse A. *A Handbook of Reasoning and Problem Solving for Junior and Senior High School.* Boston, MA: Allyn and Bacon, 1996.

Krulik, Stephen. (Ed.). *Problem Solving in School Mathematics* (1980 Yearbook of the NCTM). Reston VA: National Council of Teachers of Mathematics, 1980.

Krulik, Stephen, and Rudnick, Jesse A. *The New Sourcebook for Teaching Reasoning and Problem Solving in Junior and Senior High School.* Boston, MA: Allyn and Bacon, 1996.

Lindquist, Mary M. "Problem Solving with Five Easy Pieces." *Arithmetic Teacher* 25 (November 1977): 7–10.

Malloy, C. E., and Guild, D. B. "Problem Solving in the Middle Grades." *Mathematics Teaching in the Middle Grades* 6, no. 2 (October 2000): 105–108.

National Council of Teachers of Mathematics. *Principles and Standards for School Mathematics.* Reston, VA: Author, 2000.

Polya, George. *How to Solve It.* Princeton: Princeton University Press, 1945.

Posamentier, A., and Krulik, S. *Problem-Solving Strategies for Efficient and Elegant Solutions: A Resource for the Mathematics Teacher.* Thousand Oaks, CA: Corwin Press, 1998.

Stern, Frances. "Choosing Problems with Entry Points for All Students." *Mathematics Teaching in the Middle School* 6 (September 2000): 8–11.

Wheatley, Charlotte L. "Calculator Use and Problem-Solving Performance." *Journal for Research in Mathematics Education* 11 (November 1980): 323–334

Wickelgren, Wayne. *How to Solve Problems.* San Francisco: Freeman, 1974.

Related Research

Charles, Randall, Lester, Frank, & O'Daffer, Phares. (1987). *How to evaluate progress in problem solving.* Reston, VA: National Council of Teachers of Mathematics.

Day, R. P., & Scott, R. (1987). "For problem solving: Consider using a spreadsheet." *Math Times Journal* 1 (2): 20–28.

Meyer, C., & Sallee, T. (1983). *Make it simpler, a practical guide to problem solving in mathematics.* Menlo Park, CA: Addison-Wesley, 1983.

National Commission on Excellence in Education. (1983). *A nation at risk: The imperative for educational reform.* Washington, DC: U.S. Government Printing Office.

National Council of Teachers of Mathematics. (1980). *An agenda for action: Recommendations for school mathematics of the 1980s.* Reston, VA: Author.

National Council of Teachers of Mathematics. (1991). *Professional standards for teaching mathematics.* Reston, VA: Author.

National Council of Teachers of Mathematics. (1989). *Curriculum and evaluation standards for school mathematics.* Reston, VA: Author.

National Science Board Commission on Precollege Education in Mathematics, Science, and Technology. (1983). *Educating Americans for the twenty-first century. A plan of action for improving the mathematics, science, and technology education for all American elementary and secondary students so that their achievement is the best in the world by 1995.* Washington, DC: National Science Foundation.

Polya, George. (1980). On solving mathematical problems in high school. In Stephen Krulik (Ed.), *Problem solving in school mathematics* (1980 Yearbook of the NCTM). Reston, Va: Author.

Middle School Mathematics: Day-by-Day Teaching

CHAPTER 8

The First Five Minutes: Getting Started

When immigrants came to the United States at the start of the twentieth century, the Statue of Liberty was their first encounter with the New World. It was the initial sight that welcomed them to this country and lifted their spirits after a long, tedious, and often dangerous journey. It acted as a battery recharger, brought many out of the doldrums, and made them anxious to get started in their new lives.

In a similar manner, our students need a welcoming "signpost" when they arrive at their mathematics class each day. Too many of our students regard the beginning of the class as a time when little of importance gets done. Too many management details take place at this time, such as students entering and leaving the room and the teacher checking attendance, making announcements, and collecting homework. Students feel little is missed if they arrive five or ten minutes late. As a result, you may have a parade of latecomers, disrupting your class as they straggle in one at a time and take their seats.

It's a well-known axiom of teaching that you cannot teach students who aren't present. So often students are absent either physically or mentally. They have learned to "tune us out" until we get to the "really important stuff." Those first five to ten minutes of each mathematics class can easily become that wasteland, where students learn virtually nothing. And so, why should they bother coming to class on time?

These opening minutes provide an excellent opportunity for you to engage students in some much-needed review work. Rather than spend a large block of class time at the beginning of the semester trying to remediate weaknesses in arithmetic skills, you can select class openers that will provide the same practice, but without calling attention to this purpose.

The opening five minutes of every mathematics class are critical in the attempt to involve students in mathematics. The opening minutes set the tone for the entire class period that follows. You should use that time to involve students in activities that will "grab" their interest, make them want to come into class. As the old vaudeville theater managers used to say, you need a "hook" to get them into their seats. And you need to make the hook mathematically based.

This section deals with providing "hook" activities that can be used to gain students' interest and to make the students curious enough to want to come to class on time to find out what they will be doing that day and to see what the activity of the day will be. These five-minute openers may or may not have anything to do with the lesson of the day. All that is necessary is that (1) they should be based in mathematics, (2) they should be fun and interesting enough to make the students want to come to class to participate, and (3) they should take no more than five to ten minutes to complete. A word of caution: You cannot just copy and use the activities shown in this section. Rather, each activity is intended to serve as a model for similar activities that are specifically designed at your own students' level.

1. Which Doesn't Belong?   The ability to classify objects, to recognize common attributes, and to decide set membership are all skills that middle school students must master. In many cases, these skills have been overlooked in the lower elementary school grades and must be taught or at least reinforced in the middle school.

In this activity, the students are presented with a group of four items. In some way, one of the items is different from the others. The students must examine the choices and select the one that doesn't belong. They must be able to explain why they selected the item they did. In many cases, there may be more than one "correct" selection, depending on the student's explanation. (Not all items have to do with mathematics. Who says there can't be a little fun in math class?)

Directions: Select the one item in each set that is different from the other three and doesn't belong. Explain why you selected the item you did.

(a) 3	5	15	36
(b) 1	2	5	7
(c) $\sqrt{4}$	$\sqrt{9}$	$\sqrt{17}$	$\sqrt{25}$
(d) Red Sox	Jets	Eagles	Celtics
(e) right	acute	obtuse	left
(f) 121	19,391	1,933	24,642
(g) 81	8	1,000	1
(h) pro	centi	kilo	milli
(i) 1 yard 4"	40"	2' 10"	3' 4"
(j) I	V	X	A

Possible Selections:

(a) Some students may select 5 as the different one, since 3, 18, and 36 are all divisible by 3. Others may select 36, since it is the only number not a factor of 15. Others may select 36, since it is the only even number among the four choices.

(b) Some students may select 2, as the only even number among the choices. Others may select 1, since it is the only one of the choices that is not a prime number.

(c) Some students may select $\sqrt{17}$, since this is the only one with an irrational answer. Others may select $\sqrt{4}$, since 4 is the only even number under the radical sign.

(d) Some students may select the Red Sox, since they are the only team of the four whose basic uniform color is not green. Students who do not follow sports may not know this. However, they may also select the Red Sox, since this is the only team name that does not end in the letter *s*. (Although this one may not seem to be mathematical in nature, the students must continue to use their reasoning powers to examine the attributes of each item in order to decide which one to select as different.)

(e) Most students select "left," since the other choices describe angles in geometry.

(f) Some students may select 24,642, since it is the only even number among the four choices. Others may select 1,933, if they recognize that 121, 19,391, and 24,642 are examples of a palindrome—that is, a number that reads the same both forward and backward.

(g) Students may select 81, since it is the only one of the four that is not a perfect cube.

(h) *Pro* is the only selection that is not a prefix in the metric system.

(i) The only selection that does not equal 40 inches is 2 feet 10 inches.

(j) Some may select A, since it is the only one of the four that is not a Roman numeral. Others may select I, since it is the only one that does not come to a "point".

2. Solve These "Equations"

Directions: Have students solve these equations. Provide them with a model (i.e., 365 = <u>D</u>ays in a <u>Y</u>ear) so they will know what is expected.

(a) 365 = D_____ in a Y_____
(b) 60 = M_____ in an H_____
(c) 1,000 = G_____ in a K_____
(d) 20 = N_____ in a D_____
(e) 7 = D_____ in a W_____
(f) 2 = H_____ in a W_____
(g) 10 = D_____ in our N_____ S_____
(h) 36 = I_____ in a Y_____

Possible Answers:

(a) 365 = <u>Da</u>ys in a <u>Y</u>ear
(b) 60 = <u>Mi</u>nutes in an <u>H</u>our
(c) 1,000 = <u>Gra</u>ms in a <u>Ki</u>logram
(d) 20 = <u>Ni</u>ckels in a <u>D</u>ollar
(e) 7 = <u>Da</u>ys in a <u>W</u>eek
(f) 2 = <u>Ha</u>lves in a <u>W</u>hole
(g) 10 = <u>Di</u>gits in our <u>Nu</u>mber <u>Sy</u>stem
(h) 36 = <u>In</u>ches in a <u>Y</u>ard

3. Calendar Magic

OCTOBER 2000

SUN	MON	TUES	WED	THURS	FRI	SAT
1	2	3	4	5	6	7
8	9	10	11	12	13	14
15	16	17	18	19	20	21
22	23	24	25	26	27	28
29	30	31				

Directions:

(a) Take a calendar page for any month.
(b) Put a square around any nine numbers.
   (For example, 9–10–11, 16–17–18, 23–24–25, as shown)
(c) Add 8 to the smallest number in the square.
   (9 + 8 = 17)
(d) Multiply this number by 9.
   (17 × 9 = 153)
(e) Use a calculator to add all nine numbers.
   (9 + 10 + 11 + 16 + 17 + 18 + 23 + 24 + 25 = 153)
(f) Next add the three numbers in the middle row and multiply by 3.
   (16 + 17 + 18 = 51; 51 × 3 = 153)
(g) Find the arithmetic mean for the nine numbers. (17)

4. Number Magic

Directions:

(a) Using the digits 1 through 9, have your students select any three-digit number in the form abc. Have them write it twice, in the form abcabc.
(b) Tell one student that the number on the paper is divisible by 13. Have her check using a calculator if she wishes.
(c) Call on another student. Tell this student that the number on his paper is divisible by 7. Have him check.

(d) Call on a third student. Tell her that her number is divisible by 11.

(e) Call on yet another student. Tell this student his number is divisible by 141. Have him check, using a calculator.

(f) Now ask all your students to divide their numbers by 13, 11, and 7. The result will always be the number they started with.

Example:

(a) Select any three-digit number from the digits 1 through 9 (e.g., 275)

(b) Enter the number into your calculator twice, but with no operations. (275275)

(c) Divide by 13 (21175)

(d) Divide by 11 (1925)

(e) Divide by 7 (275)

Extending the Exercise: Ask your students what one operation could replace steps c, d, and e. If you multiply $13 \times 11 \times 7$, you obtain 1001. When you write your number twice with no operation, you are actually multiplying it by 1001.

If you have some insightful students in your algebra class, you can offer the following proof of why this works:

(a) The six-digit number the students selected can be written as:
$$100{,}000a + 10{,}000b + 1{,}000c + 100a + 10b + c$$

(b) This can be simplified to obtain $100{,}100a + 10{,}010b + 1{,}001c$.

(c) Now factor out 1001:
$$1001(100a + 10b + c)$$

(d) But 1001 is (13)(11)(7). This indicates that all numbers of the form abcabc have as factors 7, 11, 13, 77, 91, 143, and 1001.

5. Gray Elephants in Denmark

Directions: Give the class the following directions, one at a time, as they carry them out.

(a) Select any digit from 2 through 9. (Example: 6)

(b) Multiply the number by 9. (54)

(c) Add the digits in the number. ($5 + 4 = 9$)

(d) Subtract 5 from this sum. ($9 - 5 = 4$)

(e) If $A = 1$, $B = 2$, $C = 3$, and so on, select the letter that corresponds to the number. (i.e., $4 = D$)

(f) Pick a country whose name begins with this letter. (i.e., Denmark)

(g) Pick an animal whose name begins with the second letter of the country's name. (i.e., E = elephant)

(h) Think of the color of that animal.

(i) Now, amaze the class by announcing "There are no gray elephants in Denmark."

Explanation: This activity works because the students must always arrive at the number 4 in step (d). This corresponds to the letter D. There are very few countries that begin with the letter D. Most students will select Denmark. Similarly, there are few animals that begin with the letter E other than elephant (elk and emu are two rarely chosen), and most elephants are gray.

6. Memorizing the Dictionary

Directions: Announce to your class that you have memorized the dictionary over this past weekend. You are going to prove it to them. Select one student to go to the board. Blindfold yourself or turn your back to the board. Give the student the following directions. Have the class check his work.

(a) Select any three-digit number with three nonzero digits. (e.g., 257)

(b) Reverse the digits, put the larger number on top, and subtract.
Example: 752
            − 257
            ─────
             495

(c) Look on that page in the dictionary.
(d) Use the unit's digit to find the word in the left-hand column. (In this case, the fifth word in the left-hand column on page 495)
(e) Have the student tell you the first letter of the word and write the word on the board.
(f) You now tell the class the word without turning around.

Explanation: The reason this works is due to our number system, base 10. When the student reverses the number and subtracts, there are only nine possible differences:

198 297 396 495 594 693 792 891 990

In each case, the middle digit is 9, and the sum of the two outer digits is also 9. You can easily look on these nine pages, find the word that is required, and memorize it. In a standard dictionary, the pages are usually far enough apart so that each page shown will begin with a different letter. As soon as you are given the first letter of the word, you can write the entire word down.

7. Making Change *Directions:* Give students the following word problem:

Arnoldo is the cashier at the local game arcade. His job is to make change for the customers, and he is trying to find lots of possible ways he can make change for $1. He tries to make change for $1 with two coins, with three coins, with four coins, and so on.

Have students find all the possible ways to make change for a dollar with from two through twenty coins. Start the list for them. (Show the class the table filled in from 2 through 6; do not fill in the numbers enclosed in parentheses here. Be certain that your students describe the pattern they see beginning with ten coins.)

Number of coins	50¢	25¢	10¢	5¢
2	2	0	0	0
3	1	2	0	0
4	1	1	2	1
5	1	1	1	3
6	1	1	1	3
7	(1)	(1)	(0)	(5)
8	(0)	(3)	(0)	(5)
9	(0)	(2)	(3)	(4)
10	(0)	(0)	(10)	(0)
11	(0)	(0)	(9)	(2)
12	(0)	(0)	(8)	(4)
13	(0)	(0)	(7)	(6)
14	(0)	(0)	(6)	(8)
15	(0)	(0)	(5)	(10)
16	(0)	(0)	(4)	(12)
17	(0)	(0)	(3)	(14)
18	(0)	(0)	(2)	(16)
19	(0)	(0)	(1)	(18)
20	(0)	(0)	(0)	(20)

9. Magic Addition Strips *Directions:* Prepare the following twelve strips to project on the overhead projector:

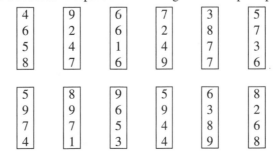

Ask one student to come to the front of the room and select any four of the strips. Place these four strips on the overhead projector, side by side. This forms a 4-by-4 number array. Ask the student to add them. As he begins, you write the answer as follows: Take the third horizontal number and subtract 2 from the fourth (units) digit. Place the 2 in front of the number. This is the answer the student will obtain. For example, suppose he has chosen the first four strips and placed them to form the following array:

4	9	6	7
6	2	6	2
5	4	1	4
8	7	6	9

While the student is adding these numbers, you take the third one (5414), subtract 2 (5412), and place the 2 in front. The sum is 25412.

If you carefully examine each of the strips, you will notice that the sum of the three numbers other than the third one is always 18. "Casting out the nines" (or in this case, two nines or eighteen), the result is the same as if there had been no numerals present other than the one in the third row. The 2 in front comes from adding the 18 to the units number and obtaining a result greater than 20.

10. Unusual Operations   *Directions:* Sometimes students enjoy doing the usual computation in an unusual manner. Ask the class to use the four digits 1, 3, 5, and 7 together with any operations they wish and make the numbers from 1 to 20.

Possible Answers:

$1 = (7 + 1) \div (3 + 5)$	$11 = 7 + 5 - 1^3$
$2 = (5 + 3 + 1) - 7$	$12 = (7 \cdot 5 + 1) \div 3$
$3 = (7 + 5) \div (1 + 3)$	$13 = 7 + 5 + 1^3$
$4 = 7 + 3 - 5 - 1$	$14 = 7 + 5 + 3 - 1$
$5 = 7 - [(5 + 1) \div 3]$	$15 = (7 + 5 + 3) \div 1$
$6 = 7 + 3 + 1 - 5$	$16 = 7 + 3 + 5 + 1$
$7 = 7 \div (5 - 3 - 1)$	$17 = (7 \cdot 3) + 1 - 5$
$8 = 7 + 5 - 3 - 1$	$18 = (5^3 + 1) \div 7$
$9 = 7 + [(5 + 1) \div 3]$	$19 = 7 + 3(5 - 1)$
$10 = 7 + 5 + 1 - 3$	$20 = (5 \cdot 1)(7 - 3)$

11. Adding to 50   Using the numbers 3, 9, 15, 21, and 39 only, add to get exactly 50. You may use any of the numbers more than once and you do not have to use all the numbers. (*Note to the teacher:* Since the five numbers given are all multiples of 3, there is no way that their sum can ever exactly reach 50.)

12. Which Is Greater?   Which is greater?
(a) the sum of the odd numbers from 1 through 99, inclusive? or
(b) the sum of the even numbers from 2 through 98, inclusive?

13. Under or Over   This game helps students sharpen their estimation skills.
For each of the sums listed, select the best estimate. Explain your reasoning.

(a) $\frac{3}{8} + \frac{14}{15} + \frac{5}{11}$ Over 2 or Under 2?

(b) $\frac{22}{15} + \frac{3}{4} + \frac{13}{9}$ Over 4 or Under 4?

(c) $3\frac{16}{17} + 2\frac{5}{9} + 1\frac{1}{2}$ Over 8 or Under 8?

(d) $\frac{7}{15} + \frac{2}{4} + \frac{1}{2} + \frac{4}{9}$ Over 2 or Under 2?

14. Pick the Largest Area   Which of the five figures shown below has the largest area? (The actual areas are given for your edification.)

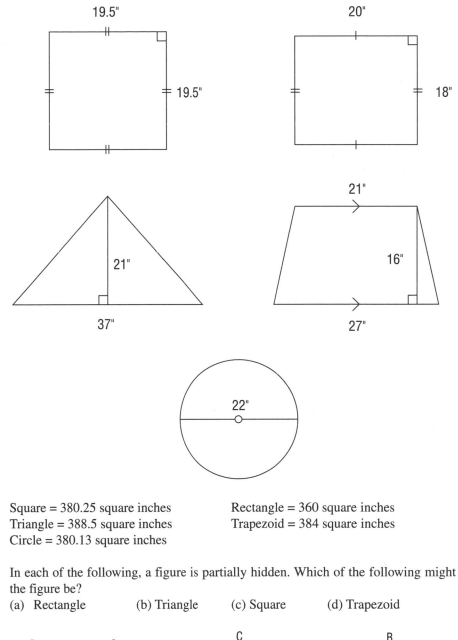

Square = 380.25 square inches	Rectangle = 360 square inches
Triangle = 388.5 square inches	Trapezoid = 384 square inches
Circle = 380.13 square inches	

15. Find the Hidden Figure   In each of the following, a figure is partially hidden. Which of the following might the figure be?

(a) Rectangle   (b) Triangle   (c) Square   (d) Trapezoid

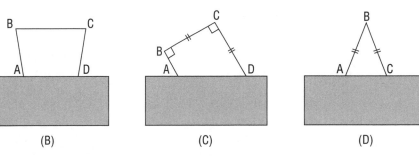

Answers: Figure A: a, d; Figure B: b, d; Figure C: a, c, d; Figure D: b, d

16. The Array *Directions:* Ask your students to examine the following array:

1	2	3	4	5	6	7	8	9	10
11	12	13	14	15	16	17	18	19	20
21	22	23	24	25	26	27	28	29	30
31	32	33	34	35	36	37	38	39	40
41	42	43	44	45	46	47	48	49	50
51	52	53	54	55	56	57	58	59	60
61	62	63	64	65	66	67	68	69	70
71	72	73	74	75	76	77	78	79	80
81	82	83	84	85	86	87	88	89	90
91	92	93	94	95	96	97	98	99	100

(a) Have one student circle any three consecutive numbers. Then have the student multiply the first and third numbers and square the second number. What do you notice?
Example: 13, 14, 15 $13 \times 15 = 195$, while $14^2 = 196$

(b) Try it again. Pick any three other consecutive numbers. Multiply the first and third numbers and square the second number. What do you notice?
Example: 45, 46, 47 $45 \times 47 = 2115$, while $46^2 = 2116$

(c) Try it a third and fourth time. Have students put your results in the following table:

Three Consecutive Numbers	*Product of First and Third*	*Square of Second*
13, 14, 15	195	196
45, 46, 47	2,115	2,116

Answer: In each case, the product of the first and third numbers is one less than the square of the second number. Ask a student to demonstrate why this is so. The reasoning is as follows:

(a) Let the three numbers be $n - 1$, n, $n + 1$
(b) Then the product of the first and third will always be $(n - 1)(n + 1) = n^2 - 1$
(c) The square of the second number will always be n^2.

17. Pyramid of Numbers Each of the integers in this pyramid is the sum of the two integers in the circles immediately below it. Have students fill in the rest of the missing numbers. (*Hint:* Work from the top of the pyramid to the bottom.)

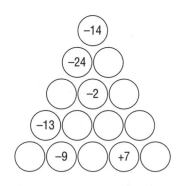

Answers:

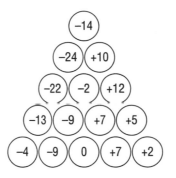

18. What Would You Do with the Remainder?

This set of four problems requires interpretation of the remainder.

(1) You wish to send 66 members of the school band to an away game. Each mini-van you order can hold 7 band members. How many minivans should you order? What would you do with the remainder?
  (a) Round up   (b) Round down   (c) Do nothing and list the remainder as is
  Answer: _____ minivans

(2) Five people went to dinner at a local restaurant. The bill was $48, including tax and tip. How much should each person pay if they share the bill equally? What would you do with the remainder?
  (a) Round up   (b) Round down   (c) Do nothing and list the remainder as is
  Answer: $_____

(3) Mrs. Lee wants to order large pizzas for her class party. She has $65, and each pizza costs $7. How many pizzas can she order?
  What would you do with the remainder?
  (a) Round up   (b) Round down   (c) Do nothing and list the remainder as is
  Answer: _____ pizzas

(4) There are 268 homes in the new complex. Three workers are sent in to connect each house to the cable TV. How many houses should each worker connect? What would you do with the remainder?
  (a) Round up   (b) Round down   (c) Do nothing and list the remainder as is
  Answer: _____ houses

19. What's My Rule?

In each of the following, state what the rule is and find the missing items in the table.

(a) *What's My Rule?*

x	y
$\frac{1}{2}$	$\frac{3}{10}$
2	$\frac{6}{5}$
$\frac{4}{5}$	$\frac{12}{25}$
$\frac{3}{4}$	?

The rule is: _____

(b) *What's My Rule?*

a	b
8	2
6	$1\frac{1}{2}$
$\frac{2}{3}$	$\frac{1}{6}$
$\frac{1}{5}$	?

The rule is: _____

(c) *What's My Rule?*

s	t
$\frac{2}{3}$	$\frac{8}{3}$
$\frac{1}{2}$	2
3	12
$\frac{1}{8}$	?

The rule is: _____

(d) *What's My Rule?*   (e) *What's My Rule?*   (f) *What's My Rule?*

m	p
3	8
16	21
$\frac{1}{2}$	$\frac{11}{2}$
$\frac{1}{3}$	?

The rule is: _____

x	y
7	4.5
4.5	2.0
13.75	11.25
8	?

The rule is: _____

c	d
8	4
7	3.5
4.62	2.31
2.82	?

The rule is: _____

Answers:
(a) The rule is: $y = (\frac{3}{5})x$ The missing term is $\frac{9}{20}$
(b) The rule is: $b = a \div 4$ The missing term is $\frac{1}{20}$
(c) The rule is: $s = 4t$ The missing term is $\frac{1}{2}$
(d) The rule is: $p = m + 5$ The missing term is $\frac{16}{3}$
(e) The rule is: $y = x - 2.5$ The missing term is 5.5
(f) The rule is: $d = .5c$ The missing term is 1.41

20. What's the Error Pattern?   In each of the following calculations, a student has made a consistent error. Describe the error pattern.

(a)

352	514	502	641
− 246	− 302	− 357	− 388
114	212	255	347

(b)

43	44	
52	20	853
+ 27	+ 28	+ 169
1112	812	91112

Answer: In a, the student always subtracts the smaller number from the larger, regardless of its position in the problem. In b, the student does not carry into the next column but simply writes the entire sum into the answer.

21. Credit Card Digits   There are 12 digits in Maria's credit card number. The digits were written in the 12 boxes shown below. The sum of any three consecutive digits is always 18. What is Maria's credit card number?

		5							7		5

Answer: Her number is 765,765,765,765. The leftmost 5 was put in simply to serve as a check.

Suppose the sum of any three consecutive digits had been 20. What would the number be now? (785,785,785,785)

22. Monomial Terms   Here is a simple opening activity for your students that will help them find the degree of any monomial term. Present the class with the following table:

Monomial	Whole Number Associated
$5x^2$	2
$-7xy$	2
17	0
$7x^2y^3$	5
7^2x^3	3
$10x^2y^2$	? (Answer: 4)
xyz^3	? (Answer: 5)
-5^3x	? (Answer: 1)

Now ask a student to tell what is happening here. Then extend this to the degree of the monomial.

23. Fraction Forms   Many middle school students have a great deal of trouble making the connection between fractions in decimal form, fraction form, and percent-equivalent form. This five-minute activity helps students make this connection in a game setting.

Prepare a sufficient number of slips of paper so that each student will receive one. On each slip of paper, put a fraction, decimal, or percent number, some of which may be equal but written in a different form. As students enter the room, they reach into the box of slips of paper and take one. The students are required to form a line such that they will be arranged in ascending order from smallest to greatest. After the allotted time, check the results with the class. Be certain to discuss any errors that occur. Some of the numbers that might appear on the slips of paper include:

.5	.49	.4	.04	.39	.43
$\dfrac{1}{2}$	$\dfrac{1}{4}$	$\dfrac{1}{8}$	$\dfrac{1}{10}$	$\dfrac{5}{12}$	$\dfrac{1}{5}$
4%	40%	39%	25%	400%	42%

24. Whole Numbers Sets   Given that a, b, and c represent three different whole numbers, none of them 0. Furthermore, a > b > c. Have each student select a set of possible values for a, b, and c, and then answer the following five questions:
(1) What can you say about a/c?
(2) What can you say about a/b?
(3) What can you say about b/c?
(4) Which is smaller, a/c or a/b?
(5) Which is larger, a/a, a/b, or b/a?

Have the students select another set of three numbers and repeat the activity. Call on several students to demonstrate their answers using their own set of numbers.

25. Find the Unequal Number   In each row, three of the numbers are equivalent. Find the number that is not equivalent to the other three. (The correct answer is in bold type.)

(a) $\frac{1}{2}$	.5	**.05**	50%
(b) 2.75	275%	$2\frac{3}{4}$	**.275**
(c) 10% of 20	20% of 10	2	**1**
(d) 25 cents	$(\frac{1}{4})$ of \$1	$(\frac{1}{2})$ of 50¢	**2 quarters**
(e) $\frac{2}{6}$	$\frac{30}{90}$	**$\frac{2}{3}$**	$33\frac{1}{3}\%$
(f) **5% of \$100**	\$10	20% of \$50	$(\frac{1}{2})$ of \$20
(g) $\frac{1}{6}$	$\frac{1}{2}-\frac{1}{3}$	**.06**	$\frac{1}{2} \times \frac{1}{3}$

26. Using Digits Once   Have students answer each of the following questions. In each set, the answers should include the digits from 0 through 9 used only once.

(1) (a) What is 9^2?
   (b) How many inches are there in one yard?
   (c) What would you pay for a jacket that costs $18 but is on sale for 50% off?
   (d) What is the product of 9 and 6?
   (e) What is the quotient of 49 and 7?
   (f) Change the improper fraction $\frac{8}{4}$ to a whole number.
   (g) Any number multiplied by 0 always equals what number?

(2) (a) What is $\frac{1}{2}$ the product of 12×8?
   (b) How many inches are there in $\frac{1}{3}$ of a foot and a half?
   (c) What is the sum in cents of 2 dimes, 5 nickels, and 5 pennies?
   (d) What is the largest prime number less than 80?
   (e) What is the product of 7 and 3?
   (f) Find the square root of 9?

(3) (a) What is the hundredths digit of the decimal approximation for π?
   (b) How much is 9^0?
   (c) How many square feet are there in a square yard?
   (d) What is $\sqrt{625}$?
   (e) How much is $9^2 - 3^1$?
   (f) How many degrees are there in a circle?

(4) (a) What is the second multiple of 15?
   (b) How many degrees are there in one-half of a right angle?
   (c) What is the common denominator for $\frac{1}{4}$ and $\frac{2}{3}$?
   (d) How much is twice 38?
   (e) What is 11 less than 100?

27. Math Sleuthing   In each of the following, read the clues to the class one at a time. Allow time for the students to work out the numbers in each clue.

(1) What are the lengths of the sides of this triangle?
   (a) The triangle is a right triangle.
   (b) The lengths of the three sides are even numbers.
   (c) The lengths of the sides form a pattern.
   (d) The perimeter of the triangle is less than 100.
   (e) The perimeter of the triangle is greater than 70.
   Answer: 18, 24, 30

(2) What's My Number?
   (a) I am between 10 and 40.
   (b) I am less than the value, in cents, of a quarter.
   (c) I am not even.
   (d) My number contains only digits less than 6.
   (e) My tens digit is less than my ones digit.
   (f) The digit in my tens place is an even number.
   Answer: 23

(3) Name the Numbers
   (a) I am thinking of five numbers.
   (b) The numbers are whole numbers.
   (c) The smallest number is 10.
   (d) The largest number is 30.
   (e) The average of the numbers is 20.
   Answer: There are many sequences that satisfy these clues. Since the average of the five numbers is 20, their sum is 100. If the first number is 10 and the last number is 30, the remaining three numbers must have a sum of 60. The numbers might be

10, 20, 20, 20, 30
10, 19, 20, 21, 30
10, 18, 20, 22, 30
and so on.

28. The Number Line The letters A, B, C, and D represent fractions on the number line, as shown in the figure.

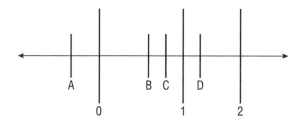

Select appropriate values for each of the letters, and then answer the following questions.
(a) $A \times B = ?$
(b) $B \times C = ?$
(c) Which is bigger, C/D or D/C?
(d) $10 \times A = ?$
(e) $B \times 2 = ?$
(f) Which letter is closest to $A \times C$?
(g) Which letter is closest to $B \times C$?

29. Wrong Reasoning What is wrong with the following reasoning?
How many days do you go to school?

Saturdays and Sundays in one year	= 104 days
Sleep (8 hours per day for 365 days)	= 122 days
Summer vacation (2 months)	= 60 days
Eating 3 meals daily (3 hours per day)	= 45 days
Allowing for holidays	= 15 days
	346 days
Days in school	= 365 − 346 = 19

30. Negative Expressions Let's examine the meanings of negative expressions. Complete the following table.

Expression	Value of x	Greater than 0	Equal to 0	Less than 0
x	$x < 0$			
x	$x > 0$			
x^2	$x < 0$			
x^3	$x < 0$			
x^3	$x > 0$			
$x^2 + 6$	$x < 0$			
$x^2 + 6$	$x = 0$			
$-5x$	$x > 0$			
$-5x$	$x < 0$			
$(x - 7)^2$	$x > 0$			
$(x - 7)^2$	$x = 0$			
$(x - 7)^2$	$x < 0$			

CHAPTER 9

The Next Fifteen Minutes: Unusual Ways of Presenting Usual Topics

It is a well-known axiom of teaching that knowledge of subject matter does not necessarily imply knowledge of how to teach that content. To teach mathematics, you must have a mastery of mathematics far beyond what you will be called on to teach. This is a "given." You must not only know the facts and principles of mathematics but also how to use these facts and principles to create new mathematics. Your extensive background in mathematics should give you this ability.

However, being able to convey your subject to middle grade students is just as important as how much you know. You must know the best and most appropriate ways to present material to your students. You will have to consider how your students learn and the best way to meld their learning styles with the material you wish to teach. You must know which parts of new concepts will be most likely to cause difficulties and the kinds of prior knowledge your students bring to the learning of mathematics. In other words, you must determine how to match content and learning. (Much of this is discussed in Chapter 4 on planning.)

One of the most difficult challenges you will face when teaching middle school mathematics is finding interesting ways to introduce new topics or develop a new concept with your class. There are a wide variety of ways for you to discover new approaches to teaching topics in your class. You might consider a historical event to introduce the topic, use a physical model to make a concept more concrete, use some form of recreational mathematics to challenge students, or delve into mathematics texts to come up with some unusual approaches to common topics. You must accumulate a wide array of available materials to interest your learners. Among these are hands-on models, textbook series (other than the one your class is using), videotapes, calculators, and up-to-date computer software.

Do not consider pedagogical knowledge as simply a bag of tricks to be used when the situation presents itself. Rather, this knowledge is a vast collection of instructional techniques, information on student backgrounds, learning theory, and above all, a way of addressing the many problems that will arise every day. Your collection should continue to grow as you gain experience in teaching mathematics.

English teachers are seen to be derelict in their responsibility if they do not read new books regularly. A social studies teacher must keep abreast of continuously changing world events. A science teacher must be aware of new developments in the various fields of science. Where does the responsibility of the mathematics teacher lie? New developments in the field of mathematics, such as the proof of Fermat's

Last Theorem or the resolution of the Four Color Problem, have technical aspects far beyond the middle school student. Yet, the mathematics teacher does have a responsibility to read professional journals and attend professional meetings to discover materials that might yield new and exciting ways to teach mathematics.

Many mathematics teachers feel that by the time students reach middle school, they should no longer need physical models to illustrate a concept and that pencil-and-paper simulations should suffice. Learning theorists have found that this is not true. Chronological age does not necessarily match mental maturity. Many preadolescents need the awareness and comfort of a physical model.

In this chapter, many ideas for lessons on number sense, algebra, geometry, probability and statistics, and discrete mathematics are presented. You can adapt these lessons to your and your students' needs. These lessons can serve as models for your lessons, which will be designed to take into account your students' knowledge and abilities. These model lessons employ technology, homemade materials, and a wide variety of techniques that the middle school mathematics teacher can employ in designing an effective middle school mathematics curriculum.

Each lesson follows the lesson plan format discussed in Chapter 4. Lessons begin with the Objective (which gives the topic being presented), followed by Materials (if any), the Introduction (which offers an interesting way to begin discussing the topic), the Development section (in which the topic is presented and carried through), and finally the Discussion and Summary of the lesson. A section on Practice is also included, if appropriate to the lesson.

Lesson 1: Basic Concepts of Probability

Objective: To introduce the basic concepts of probability

Introduction: Are you a good guesser? When should you guess? If you aren't sure of an answer, should you guess? If there are only two possible outcomes, does it pay to guess? What if there were five different possible outcomes? Let's do an experiment that will help you answer these questions.

Development:

(1) Have each student take out a sheet of paper and number it from 1 to 20 for a true-false quiz.

(2) Announce: "This will be a test and you will not know the questions. Simply mark True or False for each number on your paper. This will be your answer."

(3) When they have finished, tell them that you will now read the correct answers. They are to mark their own papers.

(4) Here are the answers. They were obtained by tossing a fair coin twenty times. Notice that although you would have expected 10 heads and 10 tails, the results actually were 12 and 8. The more times you toss the coin, the closer it would come to 50–50.

Answers:

1. F	6. T	11. F	16. F
2. F	7. F	12. T	17. F
3. T	8. F	13. T	18. F
4. F	9. T	14. F	19. T
5. T	10. F	15. T	20. F

(5) Have each student report the number of correct responses and the number of incorrect responses. How close were they to 50–50? Now total the responses for the entire class and place the results on the chalkboard or overhead projector. Did they come close to 50–50? Discuss these findings with your class. Be certain the

students understand that the expected probability is more closely approached when the number of cases is increased.

Discussion: Discuss the following ideas with the students:

(1) What would you expect the probability to be? (It should be about 10 heads and 10 tails.)

(2) Why did it come out with 12 false and 8 true? (Not enough tosses of the coin. You need many more. The more tosses, the closer it comes to 50 percent.)

(3) What would be the probability of getting neither a head nor a tail on one toss of the coin? (0 percent)

(4) What would be the probability that you got either a head or a tail on one toss of the coin? (100 percent or 1)

(5) Can you think of another situation where the probability of the event taking place is 0? (two birthdays in the same year; having snow fall when the outside temperature is 100°)

(6) Can you think of another situation where the probability of the event taking place is 100 percent? (Having a birthday this year; the sun will rise in the east and set in the west)

(7) What is the probability of getting two heads when you toss a coin three times? Discuss the concept of a sample space, which is the representation of all the possible outcomes. The sample space for tossing two coins is: H-T H-H T-H T-T (The probability of getting two heads is $\frac{1}{4}$.)

Summary: In this lesson, students are introduced to some basic ideas and vocabulary of probability. The notions of certainty (100 percent probability) and impossibility (0 percent probability) are illustrated, as are the ideas of theoretical and experimental probability. The tossing of a coin and the responses on a true-false test illustrate the probability of $\frac{1}{2}$. Finally, a very important concept of sample space, which indicates all possible outcomes for a given experiment, is presented.

Lesson 2: Angles of a Triangle

Objective: To develop the theorem that the sum of the measures of the interior angles of a triangle is 180°.

Materials: A series of triangles that have been cut from paper. (These either can be prepared in advance, or you can have the students draw and cut out any kind of triangle they wish.) Also, a protractor for each student.

Introduction: Have each student or group of students either select any one of a variety of previously prepared triangles, or have them draw and cut out a triangle of their own choice. If you prepare them in advance, be certain that some of the triangles are acute, obtuse, right, scalene, equilateral, and so on.

Development: (1) Have students mark the three angles of their triangle A, B, and C, as shown in the figure.

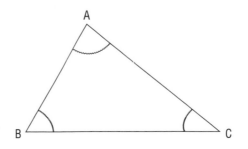

(2) Cut or tear off the three angles as shown.

(3) Now place the angles so that their sides are adjacent and they meet at a common point.

(4) Ask if a student can suggest a theorem about the sum of the measures of the angles of the triangle.

Discussion: Be certain that the students are trying several different kind of triangles, including a right triangle, a scalene triangle, an equilateral triangle, and so on. In all cases, their results should be the same. At this time, it might be appropriate to have the students use their protractors to measure the three interior angles of several triangles. They will, of course, find that the sum is 180°, which will confirm what they found in their experiment. It will also give them some much-needed practice in using the protractor.

Practice: Give several problems in which the measures of two angles of a triangle are given and students must find the measure of the third angle.

(a) $\angle A = 40°$ (b) $\angle R = 25°$ (c) $\angle A = \angle B = ?$
   $\angle B = 30°$ $\angle S = 25°$ $\angle C = 100°$
   $\angle C = ?$ $\angle T = ?$

Summary: This lesson provides students with a paper-and-pencil activity that allows them to discover that the sum of the measures of the interior angles of *any* triangle is 180°. This is a fundamental theorem of Euclidian geometry. The activity also reviews the fact that the sum of the measures of adjacent angles about a point and on one side of a straight line is equal to 180°. Opportunity for practicing the use of the protractor is also provided.

Lesson 3: Prime Numbers

Objective: To locate the prime numbers between 2 and 100

Material: A chart showing all the numbers from 2 through 100 (If possible, prepare one chart for each student.)

	2	3	4	5	6	7	8	9	10
11	12	13	14	15	16	17	18	19	20
21	22	23	24	25	26	27	28	29	30
31	32	33	34	35	36	37	38	39	40
41	42	43	44	45	46	47	48	49	50
51	52	53	54	55	56	57	58	59	60
61	62	63	64	65	66	67	68	69	70
71	72	73	74	75	76	77	78	79	80
81	82	83	84	85	86	87	88	89	90
91	92	93	94	95	96	97	98	99	100

Sieve of Eratosthenes

Development: (1) Begin by asking students to define a prime number and a composite number. They should understand that a prime number has no factors other than itself and 1.

(2) Tell students they will be using a method devised by the ancient Greek mathematician Eratosthenes to find the prime numbers between 2 and 100.

(3) The first prime number on the chart is 2. Have students put a circle around the number 2 and then cross out all the numbers that contain 2 as a factor (i.e., all the even numbers).

(4) The next prime number on the chart is 3. Have them put a circle around 3 and then cross out all the numbers that contain 3 as a factor (i.e., 3, 6, 9, . . .) Be certain that the students realize that some of these numbers have already been crossed out.

(5) The next number on the chart that is not crossed out is 5, another prime. Put a circle around 5 and then cross out all numbers that are multiples of 5. (Notice that this is another way to say "all the numbers that contain 5 as a factor").

(6) The next number not crossed out is 7. Put a circle around 7. Cross out all the multiples of 7 that remain.

(7) Have the students put a circle around all the remaining numbers that have not been crossed out.

(8) All the numbers that have been circled are prime numbers. Have the students make a list of these numbers on the board. They can then use their calculators to determine whether or not each number has a divisor other than 1 and itself.

Discussion:

(1) The prime numbers are important in learning about factorization. The *prime factorization theorem* states that every composite number can be represented as a product of prime factors in only one way. Discuss with the students the factoring of some numbers. For example, $4 = 2 \times 2$; $6 = 2 \times 3$; $8 = 2 \times 2 \times 2$; $10 = 2 \times 5$; $12 = 2 \times 2 \times 3$; $18 = 2 \times 3 \times 3$. Have students practice representing several more complicated composite numbers as the product of primes.

(2) When two prime numbers differ by exactly 2 (such as 3 and 5, 11 and 13, 17 and 19, 29 and 31, and so on) we refer to them as "twin primes." Have students find as many sets of twin primes on their list as they can. How many more can they find above 100?

(3) The numbers 3, 5, and 7 are called "prime triples." Can students find any more prime triples?

(4) Would there be more prime numbers between 2 and 100 or between 101 and 200?

Summary:

This lesson uses the Sieve of Eratosthenes to find all the prime numbers between 2 and 100. Prime numbers, the numbers that have no factors other than themselves and 1, play a significant role in mathematics, particularly in the area of factorization. The prime factorization theorem is an important part of the subject of number theory.

Lesson 4: Nonlinear Number Sets

Objective: To introduce a nonlinear data set (exponential function)

Materials: A ream of $8\frac{1}{2}" \times 11"$ paper; a ruler for each student

Introduction: Present the class with the following problem:

The Empire State Building is approximately 1,250 feet tall. Suppose you were to take a single sheet of paper and fold it in half. Then fold it again. Do it again! And again! How many times would you have to fold the sheet of paper to reach higher than the Empire State Building? (Have the students fold and refold a sheet of paper until they can no longer fold it.)

Development:

(1) Have the students fold a single sheet of paper in half several times and discuss what is happening. They should note that the thickness is doubling each time.

(2)   Ask them "How thick is a single sheet of paper?" (Find out by having the students measure the thickness of the ream of paper and divide by 500. Then have them convert this to feet.)

(3)   On the board, make a table with two columns. One column is the number of folds; the other is the thickness of the paper after the fold has been made.

(4)   Ask students when they think the thickness will reach 1,250 feet. (after only 22 folds)

(5)   Have students draw a set of axes on a sheet of paper. On the x axis, have them plot the number of folds. On the y axis, have them plot the thickness. Make a graph of the values in the table. Connect the points as well as you can. Have a student tell what the graph looks like.

Discussion: (1)   Ask the students: Why can't we physically fold the paper in half 22 times? (because the folds become too thick)

(2)   Why did the thickness of the paper reach the height of the Empire State Building in only 22 folds? (because the doubling process expands rapidly)

(3)   What is meant by an exponential function? Why was our folding experiment "exponential"? (a doubling process was used, giving the powers of 2)

Summary: This lesson provides an opportunity to see the power of an exponential function.

Lesson 5: The Pigeonhole Principle

Objective: To introduce the concept of the "pigeonhole principle" in discrete mathematics

Materials: An egg carton with 12 cups, or 12 paper cups; markers such as beans or chips

Introduction: Begin by asking the class the following question: "How many people must I ask to be certain that at least two have their birthdays in the same month?" Discuss their guesses.

Development: (1)   Let's do an experiment. We'll label each compartment of the egg box with the name of a month. Let's see how many people we must actually ask before we get two of the students with their birthdays in the same month. Ask students the month of their birthday. Each time a month is given, place a marker in the appropriate cup of the egg carton. As soon as there are two markers in one compartment, stop. How many people did we ask? Is this the number we *must* ask?

(2)   Let's look at a worst-case scenario. What might happen when we ask the first student? (Answer: My birthday is in January.) Let's put a marker in "January."

(3)   What might happen when we ask the next student? (Answer: My birthday comes in February.) Let's put a marker in "February."

(4)   Continue in a similar manner. How many people must we ask to be *absolutely certain* we have two birthdays in the same month? (Answer: 13. After twelve months, the next one puts two in one month.)

(5)   There may be fewer; but, if we ask 13 people, we are certain that two have a birthday in the same month.

Discussion: (1)   How many people would we have to ask to be certain that there are three students who have birthdays in the same month? (Answer: 25 students. After 24, we could have two in each month. The twenty-fifth assures us of three in a month.)

(2) How about if we wanted four birthdays in the same month? Five birthdays? Let's make a table of our results:

Number of people with a birthday in the same month	Number we must ask to be certain
2	13
3	25
4	37
5	49
•	•
•	•
•	•
n	$12(n-1)+1$

(3) How many people would we have to ask to be sure that we had two people who celebrate their birthdays on the same day of the year? (Answer: 366; 367 in a leap year)

(4) How many people would we have to ask to be sure that at least two celebrate their birthdays in May? (Theoretically, it could be an infinite number of people.)

Extensions: (1) Suppose we want to determine how many people to ask if we wish to find two with their birthdays on the same day of the week? (Answer: $7 + 1 = 8$)

(2) Suppose I have a drawer with black socks and white socks in it. How many socks must I take from the drawer without looking to be certain I have a pair of the same color? (Answer: $2 + 1 = 3$)

(3) I have a bank with some pennies, nickels, dimes, and quarters in it. How many coins must I select to be certain I have four of the same kind? (Answer: $12 + 1 = 13$)

Summary: This lesson introduces students to the "pigeonhole principle," and provides an opportunity for students to develop their logical and critical thinking skills. Students discover that you must ask thirteen people for their month of birth to guarantee that at least two of them were born in the same month. This can be proved, as was shown, using an egg carton and marker chips. The lesson also requires that students generalize their findings with an algebraic formula.

Lesson 6: Graphing Continuous Data

Objectives: To record continuous data and draw a linear graph; to use the data to compute the mean and median

Materials: For each group of students, one marble, a tube from paper towels, a protractor, Scotch tape, and a meter stick

Development: (1) Divide the class into groups of four students. In each group, one student will drop the marble into the tube, one will hold the protractor and measure the angle the tube makes with the floor, one will measure the distance from the bottom of the tube that the marble rolls until it stops, and one student will record the data for each trial.

(2) Have students set up their materials as shown in the diagram.

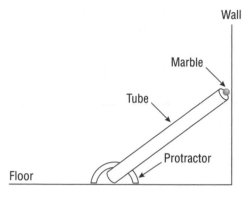

(3) Begin with the tube held vertically against the wall and the bottom resting on the floor. Drop the marble. How far did it roll before it stops? The angle it made with the floor was 90°. The marble rolls 0 centimeters. Enter this data in a table.

(4) Decrease the angle by 15°. The angle the tube now makes with the floor is 75°. Repeat the experiment. How far does the marble roll now until it stops? Record the data.

(5) Now that the class knows how to conduct the experiment, have each group perform it three times for each of the following angles: 90°, 75°, 60°, 45°, 30°, 15°, 0°. Have them record their findings.

(6) After students have completed the experiment, have each group use the data collected to find the mean distance for each angle.

(7) Use the data to compute a class mean for each angle.

(8) Have students plot the set of number pairs for the average distance measured against the angle (angle, distance). Connect the points and discuss the graph that results.

Discussion: Discuss the outcomes of the experiment with the class and the way in which mathematics was used to obtain the data and show the results. Ask the class why they think you had each group perform the experiment three times before calculating the class mean. (The more trials, the more reliable is the result.)

Summary: This lesson demonstrates the connection between the scientist and the mathematician. The scientist performs the experiment and then uses statistics to describe the results. Mathematics is often described as the language of the scientist. Statistics and graphing are chosen to present findings of the experiment. In this lesson, students performed the experiment, recorded their data, calculated the mean, and constructed the resulting graph.

Lesson 7: Area of a Circle

Objective: To develop and apply the formula for the area of a circle

Materials: For each group of students, a pair of scissors, a ruler, and a construction paper circle

Development: (This lesson can also be done as a demonstration on the overhead projector or chalkboard.)

(1) Divide the circle into a series of pie-shaped "wedges" that resemble triangles, as shown below:

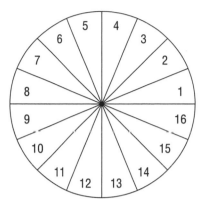

(2) Discuss the formula for the circumference of the circle ($C = 2\pi r$) in terms of the radius r.

(3) Now cut the circle into the triangles and rearrange them in alternating directions, as shown:

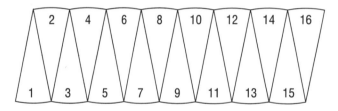

(4) The figure now resembles a parallelogram, whose area is $A = b \times h$. The base of the parallelogram is approximately one-half the circumference. The altitude is the same as the radius of the original circle, r. The formula for the area of the parallelogram is:

$A = bh$
$A = (\tfrac{1}{2})(C)(r)$
$A = (\tfrac{1}{2})(2\pi r)(r)$
$A = \pi r^2$

Discussion: The concept of approximating the area of a circle by dividing the circle into sectors, rearranging them to approximate a parallelogram, and then finding the area of the parallelogram is not an easy one for middle school students to grasp. You should demonstrate this notion to the students by first dividing the circle into four sectors and rearranging them. Increase the number of sectors, and the students will be able to see that the figure composed of sectors is beginning to resemble a parallelogram.

Extension: Have the class apply the formula, given the radius. For example, find the area of a circle whose diameter is 20 inches.

$A = \pi r^2$
$A = \pi \cdot 10^2$
$A = 100\pi = 100 \cdot 3.14 = 314$ square inches

Then have them reverse the formula—that is, find the radius, given the area.

Summary: This lesson reveals to students a physical way of obtaining the formula for the area of a circle. It also introduces the mathematical idea of a *limit*. The larger the number of sectors used, the closer the rearrangement approaches a parallelogram. The smaller the arcs, the closer they approach a straight line. The concept of a limit is one that permeates a significant amount of mathematics, particularly in calculus.

Lesson 8: Square Roots

Objectives: To determine the meaning of square root and how to take a square root

Materials: A calculator for each student or group of students

Introduction: Suppose the square root key on your calculator is broken. How would you find the square root of 19?

Development:
(1) Begin by asking the class what is meant by "the square of a number," and "a perfect square." Be certain that each student understands these two concepts. Ask for the square of some numbers, such as "4 squared," "11 squared," "17 squared," and so on. (Students can use their calculators.) Explain why 16 and 121 are called "perfect squares," while 7 and 35 are not perfect squares.
(2) By $\sqrt{19}$, what is it we wish to find? (a number that, when multiplied by itself, gives 19).
(3) Is 19 a perfect square? Why not?
(4) Can we locate it between two numbers that we know are perfect squares? What are they? (16 and 25)
(5) How much is $\sqrt{16}$? How much is $\sqrt{25}$? Then $\sqrt{19}$ is somewhere between 4 and 5.
(6) Is $\sqrt{19}$ closer to $\sqrt{16}$ or $\sqrt{25}$? Then $\sqrt{19}$ will be closer to 4 than to 5.
(7) Use your calculator to find $(4.1)^2$. Did you get 16.81? Try $(4.2)^2$. You should get 17.64. Continue until you find a number that, when squared, goes past 19.
(8) The class should find that $(4.3)^2 = 18.49$, while $(4.4)^2 = 19.36$. Thus, $\sqrt{19}$ is slightly more than $(4.3)^2$.
(9) The class can now continue in this manner, squaring 4.31, 4.32, and so on until they arrive at 4.36.
(10) Have the class check by using the square root key on their calculators. Check to see how close they have actually come.

Discussion: In this lesson, squares and square roots are treated as numbers—that is, factors and products. You might want to add the geometric concept of squares and square roots. That is, 36 square inches is the area of a square whose side is 6 inches. Thus, the area of a square is the square of its side, and a side of a square is the square root of its area.

Summary: This lesson provides students with a method of finding a square root without referring to tables or a calculator. Practically, the need to use this method will rarely arise, but the method is embedded in the history of mathematics, since such a method was developed by a mathematician named Horner. The lesson also provides drill and practice in multiplication of decimals.

Lesson 9: Number Patterns in an Array

Objectives: To build students' ability to discover number patterns in an array; to build students' ability to communicate the pattern rules using words and algebraic expressions

Materials: 100-triangle sheet for each student, as shown in the figure

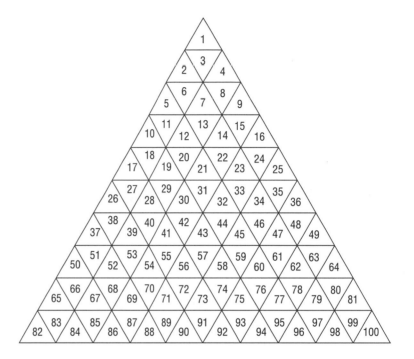

Development: Ask students to carefully examine their 100-triangle sheet to discover as many number patterns as they can. You might have to help them discover some patterns by asking questions such as the following:

(a) Can you find the square numbers? (down the right-hand side of the triangle)

(b) Starting from the top of the triangle, how many triangles are in each row? (1, 3, 5, 7, . . .)

(c) What are the differences between successive numbers in the left-hand side of the triangle? (1, 3, 5, 7, . . .)

(d) What are the differences between successive numbers in the middle column of numbers? (2, 4, 6, 8, . . .)

(e) What is the sum of the numbers in any row? (the middle number of that row × the number of that row)

(f) Look at the center "diamonds" (formed by two triangles—one from each of two consecutive rows). What can you tell about them? (1 + 3 = 4; 7 + 13 = 20; 21 + 31 = 52; 43 + 57 = 100. They differ by multiples of 16.)

Discussion: The triangle is a feast of number patterns and relationships. The even-number sequence 2, 4, 6, 8, . . . and the odd-number sequence 1, 3, 5, 7, . . . are prominent throughout the triangle. Challenge the students to find as many patterns as they can and share these with the rest of the class. Discuss each pattern and have students attempt to write the pattern rule. Have them see how many different patterns they can find.

Summary: The focus of this lesson is on the discovery of number patterns. Mathematicians are constantly looking for patterns and formulate them to generalize their findings. The lesson also provides the students with drill and practice in their basic skills and number facts.

Lesson 10: The Calendar, Algebra, and Number Relationships

Objectives: To examine number patterns in a calendar; to use algebra to prove some number properties

Materials: A calendar showing one month, as shown in the figure

S	M	T	W	Th	F	S
					1	2
3	4	5	6	7	8	9
10	11	12	13	14	15	16
17	18	19	20	21	22	23
24	25	26	27	28	29	30
31						

Development: (1)   Distribute a calendar month to each student or group of students. Ask them to draw a square around any nine numbers on their calendar. *Example:* a square has been drawn around the following nine numbers:

4	5	6
11	12	13
18	19	20

(2)   Ask students to find the sum of their nine numbers. (108)

(3)   Then find the arithmetic mean of the nine numbers. (12. Their mean should be the middle number in their square arrays.)

(4)   Ask the class to prove or disprove that this will always work. The proof is relatively straightforward.

m	m + 1	m + 2
m + 7	m + 8	m + 9
m + 14	m + 15	m + 16

The sum $= 9m + 72 = 9(m + 8)$. Dividing by 9 gives the arithmetic mean, $m + 8$.

(5)   Other patterns they might find include:
• The sum of the three numbers in each diagonal is the same (36)
• The sum of the numbers in the middle row and middle column is the same as the sum of the numbers in each diagonal (36)

(6)   Again, ask students to prove/disprove these statements:
Diagonal: $m+14 + m+8 + m+2 = 3m + 24$
Diagonal: $m+16 + m+8 + m = 3m + 24$
Middle row: $m+7 + m+8 + m+9 = 3m + 24$
Middle column: $m+1 + m+8 + m+15 = 3m + 24$

Discussion: In this lesson we have chosen to deal with a three-by-three matrix, which the findings were easier to work with. At this point, you might wish to expand the lesson and examine the numbers contained in a four-by-four matrix. Interesting relationships can be found and expressed, as they were using the three-by-three matrix.

Summary: This lesson provides students with another opportunity to discover number patterns and relationships. However, it goes farther; it asks students to express these relationships in algebraic terms and to show, algebraically, that the discovered relationships are valid.

Lesson 11: Reduction and Expansion

Objectives: To examine a nonlinear function; to use the problem-solving strategy of reduction and expansion; to practice algebraic thinking

Materials: Five pieces of poster board, each marked with a large T; five pieces of poster board each marked with a large F (You can also use slips of paper marked in the same manner.)

Introduction: Mrs. Yang decided to surprise her math class with a five-question, true-false quiz. Maria forgot to study, so she decided to just guess at all five answers. What is the probability that Maria got all five answers correct?

Development:
(1) What are some possible sets of answers Mrs. Yang might have chosen? Use your cards to show the possible set. (Place some of the possibilities on the board. Some might include: T T T T T, T T T T F, T T T F T, T T F T T, T F T T T, F T T T T, T T T F F, T T F T F and so on.)
(2) How many possible answer keys could she make?
(3) Use the reduction and expansion strategy. Suppose there was only one question. How many answer keys are possible? (2; T or F)
(4) Expand the number of questions to two. Now how many possible answer keys are there? (4: T T, T F, F T, F F)
(5) How about three questions? (8: T T T, T T F, T F T, F T T, T F F, F T F, F F T, F F F)
(6) Make a table of the data.

Number of questions	Number of answer keys
1	2
2	4
3	8
4	16
5	32
.	.
.	.
.	.
x	2^x

There are 32 possible answer keys for five questions. Since Maria could only guess one of these, her chance of guessing the correct one would be $\frac{1}{32}$.

(7) Have the class graph their data, as shown on the next page.

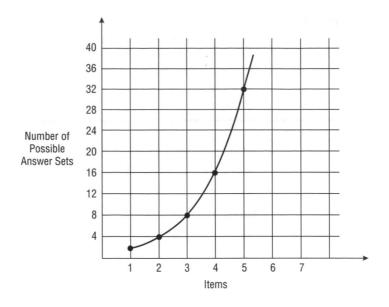

(8) Suppose the test Mrs. Yang gave had contained seven true-false questions. How many possible answer keys would there have been? (128)

(9) Suppose the test had been a multiple-choice test of five questions, each with four possible choices. Discuss how many possible answer keys there would have been for this test. ($4^5 = 1,024$)

Discussion: Note that the graph developed in this lesson is not linear. The plotted points do not lie on a straight line. Rather, it is the graph of the exponential function $y = 2^x$ (exponential since the exponent is a variable). It might be interesting at this time to graph other functions, such as $y = 2x$ (linear) and $y = x^2$ (quadratic). Discuss these concepts using probability theory, if students have been exposed to the fundamental ideas of probability. For example, if there are five events and the probability of success in each event is $\frac{1}{2}$, then the probability of success in all five events would be the product of the five probabilities, namely $(\frac{1}{2})(\frac{1}{2})(\frac{1}{2})(\frac{1}{2})(\frac{1}{2}) = \frac{1}{32}$. This same logic can be used with the number of possible answer keys. Since each response can occur in two ways (true or false), then five responses would occur in $2 \times 2 \times 2 \times 2 \times 2 = 32$ ways. A tree diagram would also be appropriate at this time.

Summary: This lesson contains several important mathematical concepts and skills. It looked at finding the number of ways a series of events could take place when one knows the number of possible outcomes for each event. Using the total number of outcomes as a sample space, it was possible to find the probability of a single outcome. The lesson also included the graphing of a nonlinear function. The students were given another opportunity to use the "reduction and expansion" problem-solving strategy.

Lesson 12: Unusual Number Properties

Objectives: To acquaint students with some unusual properties of our number system; to have students discover number patterns using their calculators

Materials: Calculators (any four-function calculator will suffice)

Introduction: Have students use their calculators to multiply 1089 by the consecutive integers 1 through 9. Have them arrange their results in tabular form and look for any interesting pattern they can find. Have them reverse the digits of the products and search for some additional patterns of interest.

Product	*Product with digits reversed*
$1 \times 1089 = 1089$	9801
$2 \times 1089 = 2178$	8712
$3 \times 1089 = 3267$	7623
$4 \times 1089 = 4356$	6534
$5 \times 1089 = 5445$	5445
$6 \times 1089 = 6534$	4356
$7 \times 1089 = 7623$	3267
$8 \times 1089 = 8712$	2178
$9 \times 1089 = 9801$	1089

Have students examine the products. What do they see about the units' digits in each array? The tens' digits? What do they notice about the first and second digits of the answers? What are the factors of 1089? (3, 3, 11, 11) What happened to the digits of 1089 when it was multiplied by 9? Can they find any other numbers to develop other unusual properties?

Development: Students should be encouraged to investigate other number patterns and predict the results. After showing them two or three of the elements in each of the following sets, have them continue the process.

(a) $4 \times 101 = 404$
$4 \times 10101 = 40404$
$4 \times 1010101 = 4040404$
$4 \times 101010101 = 404040404$

(b) $37 \times 3 = 111$
$37 \times 6 = 222$
$37 \times 9 = 333$
$37 \times 12 = 444$
$37 \times 15 = 555$
$37 \times 18 = 666$
$37 \times 21 = 777$
$37 \times 24 = 888$
$37 \times 27 = 999$

(c) $1 \times 8 + 1 = 9$
$12 \times 8 + 2 = 98$
$123 \times 8 + 3 = 987$
$1,234 \times 8 + 4 = 9,876$
$12,345 \times 8 + 5 = 98,765$
$123,456 \times 8 + 6 = 987,654$
$1,234,567 \times 8 + 7 = 9,876,543$
$12,345,678 \times 8 + 8 = 98,765,432$
$123,456,789 \times 8 + 8 = 987,654,321$

(d) $12,345,679 \times 9 = 111,111,111$
$12,345,679 \times 18 = 222,222,222$
$12,345,679 \times 27 = 333,333,333$
$12,345,679 \times 36 = 444,444,444$
$12,345,679 \times 45 = 555,555,555$
$12,345,679 \times 54 = 666,666,666$
$12,345,679 \times 63 = 777,777,777$
$12,345,679 \times 72 = 888,888,888$
$12,345,679 \times 81 = 999,999,999$

(e) $0 \times 9 + 1 = 1$
$1 \times 9 + 2 = 11$
$12 \times 9 + 3 = 111$
$123 \times 9 + 4 = 1,111$
$1234 \times 9 + 5 = 11,111$
$12345 \times 9 + 6 = 111,111$
$123456 \times 9 + 7 = 1,111,111$
$1234567 \times 9 + 8 = 11,111,111$
$12345678 \times 9 + 9 = 111,111,111$

(f) For each of the following pairs of numbers, have the students find the sum and the product. Then, in their own words, have them describe what is happening. Can they find other pairs of numbers that behave in a similar manner?

9, 9   3, 24   2, 47   2,497

Discussion: Number curiosities abound throughout our number system. As curiosities, they will probably pique the interest of many children, which might well lead them to further investigate numbers and other aspects of mathematics. Some might even attempt to find out what makes these curiosities occur. If time permits, this might be an ideal place to have students look at palindromes. A palindrome is a number that reads the same from left to right as it does from right to left. Some examples of palindromes are 12321, 1441, 28582. There is an interesting method for forming palindromes that will give students practice in addition, as follows:

(a) Pick any number.

(b) Reverse the digits and add the new number to the original number.

For example, suppose we select 38. Reverse the digits and get 83. Now add $83 + 38 = 121$, which is a palindrome.

Sometimes the palindrome does not occur on the first "reverse and add." If it doesn't, repeat the process with the new sum. You may have to "reverse and add" several times to reach a palindrome. For example, suppose we selected 86 as our original number.

$$86 + 68 = 154$$
$$154 + 451 = 605$$
$$605 + 506 = 1,111, \text{ which is a palindrome}$$

Summary: This lesson is really a fun lesson. Number curiosities often are presented as puzzles in school texts, and puzzle books are available in bookstores and libraries. These curiosities provide students with enjoyable drill and practice. Students enjoy puzzles, and this lesson takes advantage of that interest.

Lesson 13: Multiplying Negative Numbers

Objective: To present a model that illustrates that the product of two negative numbers is a positive number

Materials: None

Introduction: Students are usually willing to accept the fact that $(+a)(-b) = -ab$, since they can apply their knowledge of multiplication as repeated addition. Thus, $(+3)(-4) = (-4) + (-4) + (-4) = -12$. Similarly, the use of the commutative principle for multiplication permits them to accept the fact that $(-3)(+4) = (+4)(-3) = (-3) + (-3) + (-3)+(-3) = -12$. However, it is difficult to visualize the product of two negative numbers, since no model exists. This activity permits you to make the product of $(-3)(-4)$ seem reasonable to the class. Remember, *this is not a proof;* it is merely a way of making the algorithm meaningful to your students.

Development: (1) Begin with the following set of products:

$$(-3)(+5) = -15$$
$$(-3)(+4) = -12$$
$$(-3)(+3) = -9$$

(2) Now ask the students to explain what is happening to each factor and the product as we multiply. The first factor (-3) remains constant. The second factor *decreases* by 1 (i.e., +5, +4, +3, . . .). The product, however, *increases* by 3 (i.e., $-15, -12, -9, \ldots$).

(3) Let's continue this pattern and see what happens:

$$(-3)(+5) = -15$$
$$(-3)(+4) = -12$$
$$(-3)(+3) = -9$$
$$(-3)(+2) = -6$$
$$(-3)(+1) = -3$$
$$(-3)(0) = 0$$

(4) Ask the students to tell what happens as we continue the pattern. The factor -3 remains constant. The second factor decreases by 1 to -1. The product must now increase by 3 to ?

$$(-3)(+5) = -15$$
$$(-3)(+4) = -12$$
$$(-3)(+3) = -9$$
$$(-3)(+2) = -6$$
$$(-3)(+1) = -3$$
$$(-3)(0) = 0$$
$$(-3)(-1) = +3$$
$$(-3)(-2) = +6$$

(5) This demonstrates the reasonableness of $(-a)(-b) = +ab$.

(6) Your students should be familiar with the distributive principle of multiplication over addition. We know that $x(y + z) = xz + yz$. Let's examine $(-4)[(+3) + (-3)]$. The sum of $+3$ and -3 must equal 0. This makes the product 0, since $(-4)(0) = 0$. Now use the distributive principle:

$$(-4)[(+3) + (-3)] = (-4)(+3) + (-4)(-3)$$

Since $(-4)(+3) = -12$, and the value of the expression has already been shown to equal 0, therefore $(-12) + (-4)(-3)$ must equal 0. Thus, $(-4)(-3)$ must be $+12$. Again, we have demonstrated that $(-a)(-b) = +ab$.

Discussion: When you introduce students to negative numbers, you bring them into the realm of the mathematician. The mathematician Kronacher said that God gave us the natural numbers and that all the rest is the work of man. The integers are an extension of the natural numbers and have their own defined operations and properties. They are the beginning of abstraction (that is, not concrete). For ages, mathematics teachers have been attempting to find concrete models that can illustrate to young students the "laws of signs" for the integers. Some of them, such as the ones shown in this lesson, are plausible, while others are just silly. The truth of the matter is that in the operation of multiplication of integers, a negative times a negative is a positive number because the definition, rules, and properties require it. The integers are a postulational system, and $(-)(-) = +$ was required to make the system work. You should use the illustrations presented in this lesson, since students need help in understanding the system. Integers are a part of mathematics, and mathematics is a postulational system. Your students should learn how mathematics works. They are already familiar with the process of operating under arbitrary rules, since most athletic events are carried out according to arbitrary rules.

Summary: This lesson provides models that you can use to illustrate that $(-)(-) = +$. These models are not proofs but are intended to make the rules plausible and acceptable to the students.

Practice:　Find the following products:

$(+3)(-5) = ?$ $(-5)(-7) = ?$

$(-3)(+5) = ?$ $(-7)(-4)(+5) = ?$

$(-42)(-17) = ?$ $(-5)(-3)(-2) = ?$

$(-18)(+15)(-2) = ?$ $(-3x)(-2x)(-4x) = ?$

$(-2)(-2)(-2)(-2) = ?$ $(-3)(-3)(-3)(-3)(-3)(-3) = ?$

Extension:　Ask the students to formulate a rule if the number of negative factors is odd and if the number of negative factors is even. To further ensure students' understanding, ask them to complete the following multiplication table. Several calculations have been done for them. Be sure to discuss the patterns they find in the finished grid.

x	4	3	2	1	0	−1	−2	−3	−4
4	16	12	8	4	0			−12	
3	12	9	6	3	0				
2	8				0		−4		
1	4				0				
0	0	0	0	0	0	0	0	0	0
−1	−4				0				
−2	−8		−4		0				
−3	−12				0				
−4		−12			0				

Lesson 14: Volume of a Solid Figure

Objectives:　To explore the volume of a rectangular solid figure; to collect data and draw a representative graph

Materials:　Sheets of 8" × 10" paper, pairs of scissors, rulers, tape

Development:　(1)　Divide the class into groups of four students. Provide each group with a sheet of 8" × 10" paper, a pair of scissors, a ruler, and some tape.

(2)　Instruct the students that they are to cut small 1" × 1" squares from each of the four corners of the sheet of paper, as shown:

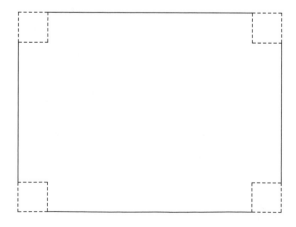

(3) Have them fold up the four sides and tape them together to form a rectangular open box.

(4) Ask each group to find the volume of the open box they have made.

(V = L × W × H)
(L × W × H = 8 × 6 × 1 = 48 cubic inches)

(5) Give each group another sheet of paper and have them cut a 2" × 2" square from each corner, fold the figure, and make another open rectangular box. Ask them how they think the volume of the new box will compare to the volume of the original. Have them use the formula and compute the volume of this second box. (It will be the same; 6 × 4 × 2 = 48 cubic inches.)

(6) Now that the students understand the procedure, have them calculate the volume for each box with the cutout size given below. Have them record their data in the table. (The volumes are filled in for each case.)

Size of cutout squares	Volume of open box
0.5"	9" × 7" × 0.5" = 31.5 cubic inches
1"	8" × 6" × 1" = 48 cubic inches
1.5"	7" × 5" × 1.5" = 52.5 cubic inches
2"	6" × 4" × 2" = 48 cubic inches
2.5"	5" × 3" × 2.5" = 37.5 cubic inches
3"	4" × 2" × 3"= 24 cubic inches
3.5"	3" × 1" × 3.5" = 10.5 cubic inches

(7) Of the cutouts shown, which produced the greatest volume? (1.5") What would happen if you cut out a 4" square from each corner?

(8) Now have the students graph their data. Their graph should look like the following graph:

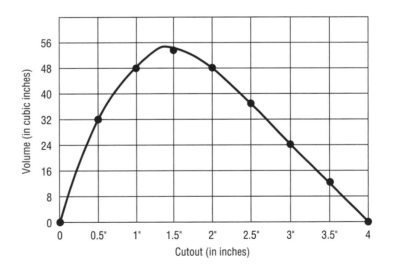

Discussion: The curve that is plotted reveals the size of the cutout that produces the maximum volume. This result is probably a new experience for most students and should be discussed. With some students, you might wish to plot a few more points closer to the maximum to find out, with greater accuracy, where the maximum point actually occurs. A calculator would be helpful in doing this. (Approximately 1.46")

Extension: Let's explore the surface area of each of the "boxes" we constructed. Which box has the largest surface area? Which has the smallest? (Note: The larger the square that is cut from each corner, the smaller the surface area will be. The formula for surface area is given as SA = 80 – 4x^2 where x = the length of the side of the square that was cut out.)

Summary: This lesson involved the students in finding the volume of an open rectangular box by using the formula V = L × W × H. The data obtained by varying the size of the square cutouts at the corners of a rectangular sheet of paper was used to construct a graph, and the size cutout that produced the maximum volume was determined.

Lesson 15: Linear Equations

Objective: To practice solving linear equations in a game setting

Materials: A pair of dice; 20 Equation Cards, 3" × 5" cards with one of the following equations on each:

12x = 12	x^2 = 4	g + 7 = 7	t/5 = 3
13d = 52	110 – y = 100	r + 5 = 20	m + 17 = 26
M + 23 = 29	t – 5 = 7	2 + r = 20	8n = 64
b/3 = 1	s + 12 = 12	7p = 49	y/7 = 1
5t = 25	6x = 18	12r = 24	m^3 = 1

Development: (1) Divide the class into groups of four or five students. Each group receives a set of the Equation Cards and a pair of dice.
(2) The Equation Cards are shuffled, and the pack is placed face down in the center of the group.
(3) Players roll a single die to determine which player goes first. The highest number goes first, and play proceeds around the group in a clockwise manner.
(4) The player whose turn it is turns the top Equation Card face up and rolls the pair of dice.
(5) Using the two numbers that land face up on the dice, the player must make a number that satisfies the equation on the Equation Card. For example, if the numbers are 5 and 4, the player can make a 9, a 1, or a 20. The equation card 12x = 12 is satisfied by x = 1.
(6) If the player makes a number that is the solution to the equation, the player receives a point. If not, the score for that round for that player is 0, and play proceeds to the next student. The Equation Card is placed on the bottom of the deck, face down.
(7) Play ends when any one player has scored four points.

Summary: This lesson provides students, in a game activity format, with the opportunity to practice the solution of simple linear equations. At the same time, it provides them with significant computational drill and practice.

Lesson 16: Multiplication Methods

Objective: To practice multiplication using three historical methods

Introduction: Ask the students to multiply 38 × 24 using their usual method. Students should be informed that people were able to do multiplication without knowing anything more than single-digit multiplication.

Development: (1) Begin by asking one student to come to the board and multiply 38 × 24. Most likely, the student will use the traditional multiplication algorithm:

$$
\begin{array}{r}
38 \\
\times\ 24 \\
\hline
152 \\
76\ \ \\
\hline
912
\end{array}
$$

A. Doubling Method

(2) Now inform the class that you will do the same problem, but unfortunately, you can only multiply by 2. Proceed by constructing a table, doubling as you go, as follows:

$$
\begin{array}{rcl}
1 \times 24 &=& 24 \\
2 \times 24 &=& 48 \\
4 \times 24 &=& 96 \\
8 \times 24 &=& 192 \\
16 \times 24 &=& 384 \\
32 \times 24 &=& 768
\end{array}
$$

(3) Select the numbers from the first column whose sum is 38 (the second factor in our problem)—that is, 32 + 4 + 2. Now add the corresponding products:

$$
\begin{array}{rcr}
32 \times 24 &=& 768 \\
4 \times 24 &=& 96 \\
+\ 2 \times 24 &=& 48 \\
\hline
38 \times 24 &=& 912
\end{array}
$$

(4) Why does this work? $24 \times 38 = 24(32 + 4 + 2) = 768 + 96 + 48 = 912$

Have your students try another two-digit by two-digit multiplication problem using the doubling method.

B. Russian Peasant Method

(5) This method again relies on the doubling process but adds another twist. To multiply these same numbers, 38 × 24, set up two columns. In one we will double; in the other, we will halve, discarding the remainder of 1 if it appears.

38	24	
19	48	
9	96	(discarding remainder of 1)
4	192	(discarding remainder of 1)
2	384	
1	768	

Now select the numbers from column 2 that correspond to the odd numbers in column 1:

19	48
9	96
1	768
	912

C. Lattice Multiplication (Gelosia)

(6) In the Middle Ages, multiplication was often done using a "sand board" (because there was little paper available at the time). A grate, or "gelosia," was drawn for

the numbers to be multiplied, and the two factors to be multiplied were written, as shown:

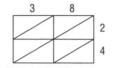

(7) Now do the single-digit multiplication as shown, writing the products in the appropriate cells of the grate:

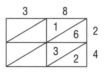

(8) Completing the grate, now add along the diagonals, obtaining the product (912), as shown:

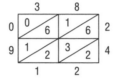

(9) Have students attempt some multiplication problems using the three methods shown. As a project, they might do some research to find some other methods of multiplying that are different from their own method.

Discussion: This lesson presents three historically significant methods of multiplying whole numbers. The history of the development of mathematics and the lives of mathematicians is something every mathematics teacher should include in classroom presentations. Students should know something of the development of mathematics, of the people who created and developed it, and some of its many applications. The common multiplication algorithm is not the only one ever used, as this lesson demonstrates. Be certain to review each of the models shown, including the commonly used algorithm. Students should be aware of what they are doing in addition to knowing how to do it.

Summary: This lesson provides students with computational drill and practice as well as the opportunity to examine various historical multiplication algorithms.

Lesson 17: Midpoints of Quadrilaterals

Objective: To discover what happens when the midpoints of consecutive sides of various quadrilaterals are joined

Materials: Paper, rulers, scissors

Development: (1) Divide the class into groups of four to five students. Provide each group with scissors, rulers, and paper for each student.
(2) Have each student in the group draw a quadrilateral of any shape and size and cut it out.
(3) Either by using their rulers or by paper folding, have students find the midpoints of each of the four sides of the quadrilateral.

(4) Connect the midpoints in order, using straight lines, as shown in the figure.

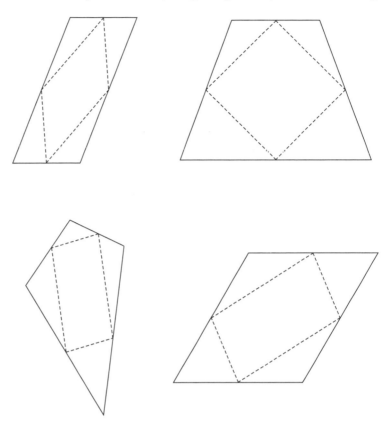

(5) Ask students to examine the figures formed in this manner. What conclusion(s) can they make?

(6) Have a spokesperson for each group tell what conclusions the group made.

(7) Note that the resulting figure will always be a parallelogram. In some cases, when the original quadrilateral was a parallelogram (or rectangle or square), the resulting figure may also exhibit special properties.

Discussion: This lesson provides students with an opportunity to discover, by careful measurement, the geometric fact that the line segments that connect consecutive midpoints of any quadrilateral form a parallelogram. The proof of this fact is beyond the scope of most middle school students, since it depends on the theorem that in any triangle the line segment that connects the midpoints of two sides is parallel to and equals one-half of the third side. Students will discover by measuring carefully that the opposite sides of the newly formed quadrilateral have the same length, making the figure a parallelogram. A quadrilateral is a parallelogram if and only if the opposite sides are equal in length. Discuss with the students that measurement is only approximate and as such does not constitute a proof. Measurement only establishes a basis for a conjecture, which in this case can be proven by applying some geometric facts that they will learn as they continue their study of mathematics.

Summary: This lesson provides students with the opportunity to practice linear measurement skills and leads them to discover the geometric fact that the figure formed by connecting consecutive midpoints of any quadrilateral is a parallelogram. It also provides students with the opportunity to review the properties of a parallelogram.

Lesson 18: Inscribed Angles

Objective: To use protractors to discover the relationship between the measure of inscribed angles and the central angles that subtend (or intercept) the same arc

Materials: For the class, protractors and $8\frac{1}{2}"\times 11"$ paper on which is drawn a large circle with a chord (representing a "goal cage"), and several points on the circumference, as shown in the figure.

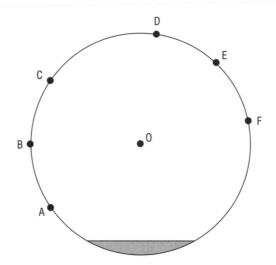

Introduction: Although it may appear otherwise, all inscribed angles that subtend the same arc have the same measure. In a formal geometry class, the students will prove that a central angle that subtends the same arc as an inscribed angle has twice the measure of the inscribed angle. Distribute the papers and protractors and pose the following problem:

The circle on the paper represents a circular swimming pool being used for a game of water polo. The chord and segment form the netted "cage" or "goal." From which of the points on the circle would you prefer to take a shot at the goal?

Development: (1) Divide the class into small groups or permit the students to work alone.

(2) After students have made their choices, have them draw the chords from the point they have selected to the ends of the net and measure the angle formed. These will be the inscribed angles.

(3) Collect the data from the class and record the results on the following table:

Angle	A	B	C	D	E	F	G
Measure							

(4) What conclusions can the students reach after examining the data in the table?

(5) Now have them draw the radii from the center of the circle to the endpoints of the goal cage and measure the central angle formed. What conclusion can they now reach?

Discussion: This lesson reveals the relationship between central and inscribed angles with the same intercepted arc, and also how mathematicians work. Students should discover that the number of degrees in the central angle is twice the number of degrees in the measure of the inscribed angle with the same intercepted arc. After their discovery, they then attempt to show that their discovery is true.

Extension: You can extend the lesson by using a half-circle (semicircle) and having the students draw chords from the points on the circle to the ends of the diameter and then measure the inscribed angles. They will discover that an angle inscribed in a semicircle is a right angle.

Summary: This lesson provides the students with the opportunity to use their protractors to verify some important theorems of Euclidian geometry. Students discover that a central angle has twice the measure of an an inscribed angle that intercepts the same arc. They also develop data from which conclusions are reached. They gain familiarity in working with a statistical tool—the table on which they record the data.

Lesson 19: Tower of Hanoi

Objective: To use an ancient Indian puzzle and the problem-solving strategy of reduction and expansion to discover and generalize a number pattern

Materials: The puzzle, known as the Tower of Hanoi or the Tower of Brahma, is available commercially. You can use materials readily available in your own classroom to make the puzzle. Cut six discs (or squares) for each group of students. Discs can be cut from posterboard and should be of increasing size, as shown in the diagram. Pegs are not necessary; the discs can be placed in piles or on three paper plates.

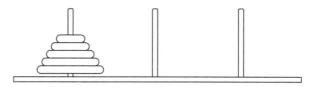

Introduction: An ancient legend from India says that at the creation, God put 64 golden discs of increasing size on one of the three pegs in the temple. The priests were supposed to move all the discs to one of the other pegs so that they would be in exactly the same order. The rules for the moving of the discs were simple:

1. Only one disc can be moved at a time.

2. Each disc must be moved onto a peg.

3. At no time can a disc be placed on top of a disc that is smaller than the disc being moved.

The legend has it that when all 64 discs have been successfully moved to another peg, the world will disappear.

Development: (1) Discuss the problem with the entire class. Lead them to see that attempting to solve the problem with 64 discs would be unwieldy. The solution calls for using the reduction and expansion strategy.

(2) Divide the class into groups of three to four students. Give each group of students three paper plates and a set of 6 discs.

(3) Go through the first two situations with the class, using a model or the overhead projector. With only 1 disc, only one move is required. With two discs, three moves are required, as shown in the diagrams on the next page.

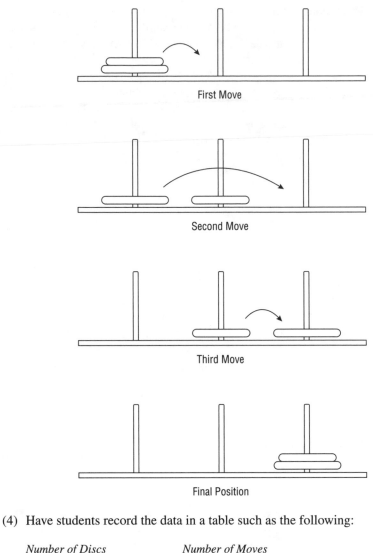

First Move

Second Move

Third Move

Final Position

(4)   Have students record the data in a table such as the following:

Number of Discs	Number of Moves
1	1
2	3
3	
4	
5	
6	

(5)   Have students continue the problem using 3 discs (7 moves), 4 discs (15 moves), 5 discs (31 moves). Ask the class to predict how many moves are needed for 6 discs (63 moves).

(6)   Now examine the sequence of moves: 1, 3, 7, 15, 31

(7)   This is not an obvious or familiar sequence, so the class may need a hint. Have them compare this sequence with the sequence: 1, 4, 8, 16, 32. This is the sequence 2^n. More than likely, someone will see that the sequence they have discovered is generalized as $2^n - 1$.

Discussion: Now that the formula has been established, it is fairly easy to determine the number of moves for any number of discs n. For example, for 10 discs, it would take $2^{10} - 1$, or 1,023 moves. For the number of moves for 64 discs, it would take $2^{64} - 1$, which is a 20-digit number. If the ancient priests were to move one disc per second, it would take more than 575 billion years to complete their task. The world would still have many years to go before it would disappear. (*Note:* This is a good time to make use of technology; paper-and-pencil calculations are not appropriate.)

Summary: This lesson provides students with an example of the power of the reduction and expansion strategy in mathematics. Pattern identification and the creation of an algebraic expression to represent the pattern is another skill students develop. The lesson also brings up the topic of number explosions. The powers of 2 expand quickly, as the problem shows.

Lesson 20: Bisecting an Angle

Objective: To bisect a given angle, given a ruler and the properties of the rhombus

Materials: A protractor and ordinary two-edged ruler for each student

Introduction: Bisecting an angle is a traditional construction problem that students can perform using only a straightedge and compasses. Most students can easily learn how to do the construction, but few understand why it works. This lesson provides the opportunity for the students to see the why.

Development: (1) Have students draw an angle of any given size on a sheet of blank paper and also draw an estimate of where they think the angle bisector will fall.
(2) Have them place the ruler so that one edge of the ruler lies on side BC of the angle. Trace the other edge of the ruler. (See position 1 of the figure.)
(3) Have the students now position their rulers so that one edge lies along side BA of the angle and trace the other edge of the ruler. (See position 2 of the figure.)
(4) Have students label the intersection of the two traced lines as D. Line BD is the angle bisector of angle ABC. Have students use their protractors to verify that BD is actually the angle bisector. Have them compare line BD with their estimate of where they thought the angle bisector would fall.

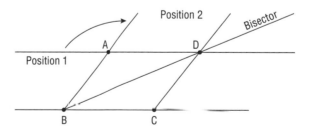

Discussion: Why does this construction work? The opposite edges of the ruler are parallel, and ABCD is a parallelogram. Since the length of each side of the parallelogram is the width of the ruler, all four sides of the parallelogram are equal and the parallelogram is a rhombus. One of the properties of the rhombus is that the diagonal bisects the angles through which it is drawn; thus, BD bisects angle B. Review the properties of the rhombus with the class and discuss how the rhombus differs from a square and an ordinary parallelogram.

Summary: This lesson gives students the opportunity to review the properties of the rhombus and how to use these properties to construct an angle bisector. Students also get practice in measuring with a protractor.

Lesson 21: Bisecting a Line Segment

Objective: To use an ordinary ruler and the properties of a parallelogram to bisect a line segment

Materials: A two-edged ruler or straightedge

Introduction: Bisecting a line segment is a traditional geometric construction that students learn to do with a pair of compasses and a straight edge. Most students can easily learn to do this, but few understand why it works. Since virtually all students know that the diagonals of a parallelogram bisect each other, this technique is a real learning experience.

Development: (1) Have each student draw a line segment AB of any length in the middle of a blank sheet of paper. Have them place a point where they estimate the midpoint to be.
(2) Have them place the ruler so that the upper edge passes through point A and the lower edge passes through point B. Trace both edges of the ruler in this position (Position 1 in the figure).
(3) Have students turn their rulers so that the opposite edges pass through points A and B. Again, trace the two edges of the ruler.
(4) Label the intersection of the edges C and D, and draw line segment CD. The point where segments AB and CD intersect is the midpoint M of AB.
(5) Have the students measure the lengths of segments AM and MB to assure themselves that M is indeed the midpoint. How close was their estimate of the actual midpoint?

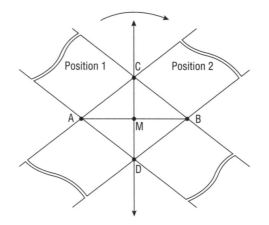

Discussion: Since the opposite edges of the ruler are parallel, the figure ADBC is a parallelogram, with AB and CD as the diagonals. Since the diagonals of a parallelogram bisect each other, M is the midpoint of segment AB (and, of course, the midpoint of CD also). Take time to review all the properties of the parallelogram with the class.

Summary: In this lesson, students discover an unusual method for bisecting a line segment. The lesson also provides an opportunity for them to practice their estimation skills and measurement skills. In addition, they were able to review the properties of a parallelogram.

Lesson 22: Value for Pi

Objective: To perform an experiment that will lead to an approximate value for pi (π)

Materials: A pi sheet (as shown in the figure) and a table on which to record the data. (The pi sheet shows an array of dots, each of which is exactly the diameter of a penny from its neighbor.) In addition, each group of students will need a penny to toss.

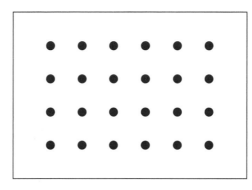

Introduction: Pi is a very important number in mathematics. It is the ratio between the circumference of a circle and its diameter. It has many other uses in mathematics and appears in many places. This experiment enables students to determine an approximate value for pi.

Development:
(1) Divide the class into groups of four to five students. The activity can also be done having students work in pairs.
(2) Place the pi sheet on the floor and have the students stand around it. Have each student toss a penny onto the pi sheet. Count only those pennies that land within the borders of the pi sheet.
(3) If the coin lands on a dot or touches a dot, it will be considered a "hit." If the coin does not touch a dot, it is called a "miss." Have each student in the group toss the penny 10 times and record the results in the table:

Penny tossing table	
Hits	*Misses*

(4) Have each student use the formula $\pi = (4h)/t$ to find an approximate value for pi. (In the formula, h = number of hits; t = number of tosses.)

(5) Next, combine the data for all the students and use the same formula to find another approximation for pi. This number should be closer to 3.14 than the individual numbers found by the students. Be certain to emphasize that 3.14 is only an *approximation* for π. Since π is an irrational number, it is a nonterminating, nonrepeating decimal. The more times the penny is tossed, the closer the approximation to 3.14.

Discussion: Pi is probably one of the first irrational numbers that middle school students come across in their study of mathematics. As soon as they are introduced to the circle, π appears in both the formula for the circumference as well as the formula for the area of the circle. Some textbooks equate π to $3\frac{1}{7}$ or $\frac{22}{7}$. This would make it a rational number and a repeating decimal. We prefer to use the true meaning of π—namely, π is an irrational number and thus cannot be represented exactly by a finite number of digits. Its value is only approximated for computational purposes.

Summary: This lesson provides students with an opportunity to conduct an experiment involving the gathering and recording of data. It also requires them to make use of their data in a mathematical formula to find the approximate value of π. This shows how mathematicians and scientists actually work in the real world.

Lesson 23: Square Numbers

Objective: To perform an experiment involving square numbers, examine the data, recognize number patterns, and generate the formula n^2 = the sum of the first n odd numbers

Materials: A supply of at least 36 square tiles cut from poster board or manila folders for each group of students

Introduction: The square numbers are an interesting and important set of numbers. Students should be able to recognize these numbers and note that the differences between successive terms are the odd numbers. Students will use square tiles to build squares with sides increasing from one to six units. They will record the number of additional tiles needed for each progressively larger square. By recording the results of this experiment and examining the data, students will be able to generalize their findings.

Discussion: (1) Divide the class into small groups of four to five students.
(2) Distribute 36 tiles to each group. Inform them that each tile represents one square unit of area.
(3) Before beginning the actual experiment, have the students "play" with the tiles and form different size squares. Ask them to state the area of each square they form. They can do this by counting the number of squares used or by using the formula A = L × W. (*Note:* Since a square is a rectangle, they can also use the formula $A = s^2$.)
(4) Now begin the formal experiment. Have the students begin with a square consisting of one tile. Have them prepare a table as shown below and enter the data in their table.
(5) Have students add as few tiles as necessary to form the next larger square. They should see that three tiles were needed to form a second square, and that this new square has a side of 2 and an area of 4 square units. Ask a student to estimate how many tiles must be added to form the next larger square. Have the students do this and enter the data in their table.

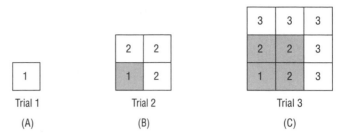

Trial 1   Trial 2   Trial 3

(A)   (B)   (C)

(6) Have the groups continue forming squares by adding the necessary number of tiles and recording the data in the table each time. (In the example table, the first three rows of data have been entered.)

(7) Carefully review with the students the table and its headings:

Trial	Number of tiles added	Total number of tiles recorded as a sum of tiles added during each trial	Total number of tiles (area)	Dimensions
1	1	1	1	1×1
2	3	$1 + 3$	4	2×2
3	5	$1 + 3 + 5$	9	3×3
4				
5				
6				
n	$2n - 1$	$1 + 3 + 5 + \ldots + (2n - 1)$	n^2	$n \times n$

Column 1—Trial: The entries in this column refer to the order in which the squares are made. 1 means the first square, 2 means the second square, and so on.

Column 2—Number of tiles added: The entries in this column represent the number of tiles that were added to the previous square to form the new square. That is, add 3 squares to the first square to form the second one.

Column 3—Total number of tiles added, recorded as the sum of tiles added during each trial: The entries in this column show how many tiles were used to make the square; the number is recorded as the sum of the tiles in each preceding trial.

Column 4—Total number of tiles (area): The entries in this column represent the total number of tiles that were used to form this square (or the area of the square).

Column 5—Dimensions: The entries in this column tell the length and width of the square.

(8) Now that the students understand the table, have them continue the experiment, recording the information for the next three squares in the table. When they have completed the experiment for six squares and have entered the data in their table, help them to analyze the table by asking such questions as:

(a) How would you describe the set of numbers in column 2?

(b) What number will go in column two for the tenth trial? for the fiftieth trial?

(c) Can you write a rule that will give us the number in column two for each trial?

(9) Continue with this line of questioning until all of the patterns have been recognized and all of the rules for ascertaining the terms in each column have been stated.

(10)   Conclude the lesson by putting a variable n in the first column, and have the students complete the entries in this row using the rules they have developed.

Discussion: This lesson involves students in an activity that permits them to generate data for a table, record the data, analyze it, and generalize to a set of formulas. When mathematicians look at a table of information, they also look for patterns and relationships so they can predict what will happen in future trials, without actually performing the experiment each time. After they recognize certain patterns, they try to write the formulas to show these relationships. In this lesson, students should recognize that perfect squares are formed as the sum of the set of the odd numbers.

Summary: This lesson is rich in mathematics. A table is created, and data created by the activity are entered. The table contains patterns of whole numbers, odd numbers, and perfect squares. Rules are stated (both in words and in symbols) that connect all three sets of numbers. The lesson provides students with experience in numbers, statistics, number theory, and elementary algebra in addition to good mathematical thinking.

Lesson 24: A Game of Chance #1

Objective: To explore probability in a game of chance

Materials: Two spinners, as shown in the figure.

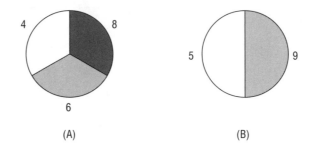

(A)   (B)

Introduction: The students are going to spin the two spinners. Whoever has the spinner with the higher number scores one point. The game ends when the players have spun their spinners a total of 20 times. The player with the higher point score is the winner.

Development: (1)   Divide the class into pairs of students. Have each pair of students make a set of spinners as shown. They can use a paper clip and a thumbtack (or a pencil) to actually make the spinners work.
(2)   Have the students play the game 20 times and record their results. Using these results, students should decide who is more likely to win the game and why.
(3)   Next, have students make a table of the possible outcomes when they spin (the sample space).

Spinner A	Spinner B	Who wins?
4	5	B
4	9	B
6	5	A
6	9	B
8	5	A
8	9	B

(4) Which player is more likely to win? Why?

(5) Could you change just one number on spinner B, leaving spinner A unchanged, and make this a fair game—that is, so the expected outcomes are equal?

Discussion: The player who spins spinner B is more likely to win. The sample space shown in the table reveals that B wins 4 times out of 6, while A wins only 2 times out of 6.

Summary: This lesson, taken from discrete mathematics, enables students to perform an experiment that leads to a discussion of the concept of a "fair game" (one in which each player has an equal chance to win). By performing this experiment, they are able to collect the data to show which spinner is more likely to win. In addition, the concept of a sample space is presented.

Lesson 25: A Game of Chance #2

Objective: To explore probability in a game of chance

Introduction: Tell the students that they will be rolling a pair of dice. However, instead of adding the two numbers that appear, they will be subtracting them. Which difference do they feel is most likely to occur?

Development: (1) Divide the class into groups of four to five students. Give each group a pair of dice.

(2) Inform the students that they are to roll the dice a total of 30 times. They are to subtract the smaller number that occurs from the larger. Keep track of the results. The differences that appear (the sample space) are 0, 1, 2, 3, 4, and 5. Which occurs most often? Which least often?

(3) Have the students make a table to determine the probability of each element in the sample space:

	1	2	3	4	5	6
1	0	1	2	3	4	5
2	1	0	1	2	3	4
3	2	1	0	1	2	3
4	3	2	1	0	1	2
5	4	3	2	1	0	1
6	5	4	3	2	1	0

(4) The probabilities of each number occurring are:

$P(0) = 6/36$ $P(3) = 6/36$
$P(1) = 10/36$ $P(4) = 4/36$
$P(2) = 8/36$ $P(5) = 2/36$

Discussion: Have students examine their tables and decide which difference is most likely to occur. Which is least likely? What would happen if they multiplied the two numbers on the dice? Now which product would most likely occur? Which would least likely occur?

Summary: This lesson in discrete mathematics provides students with an opportunity to make some conjectures about probability when rolling a pair of dice. Since they are not using the usual operation, namely adding the two numbers, the probabilities will differ from the traditional ones. Once again, the use of a sample space is most helpful.

Lesson 26: Inscribed and Circumscribed Circles

Objective: To determine the difference in areas of inscribed and circumscribed circles and squares

Introduction: We have often heard the expressions "It's like putting a square peg in a round hole." or "Try putting a round peg in a square hole!" Well, which do you think would be a better fit? Would a square peg in a round hole leave less waste than a round peg in a square hole?

Development: (1) This lesson can be done having the students work alone or in pairs.

(2) Have each pair of students draw the two figures involved. The left-hand figure (A) below shows a circle with a 2" diameter circumscribing a square. The right-hand figure (B) shows a circle with a 2" diameter inscribed within the square. In each case, the area between the two figures will be considered the waste.

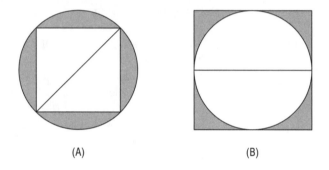

(A)   (B)

(3) Have students find the two areas in each figure and determine which is the better "fit."

(4) For Figure A (square inscribed inside the circle), the diameter = 2, radius = 1, the area of the circle = πr^2 (π = approximately 3.14 square inches). The side of the square = $\sqrt{2}$ and the area of the square = 2 square inches. The difference (the waste) = 3.14 – 2 or 1.14 square inches.

(5) For Figure B (circle inscribed inside the square), the diameter = 2, the radius = 1, and the area = π, or approximately 3.14 square inches. The side of the square = 2 and the area = 4 square inches. The difference (the waste) = 4 – 3.14 = .86 square inches. Thus, more waste occurs in the first case, and the round peg in the square hole is the better fit.

Discussion: The information given in the problem includes the diameter of the circle, but not the dimensions of the square. In the first case, the length of the diagonal of the square equals the length of the diameter, or 2. The length of the side is $\sqrt{2}$. The length of the side of the square in the second case is equal to the diameter, or 2.

Summary: This lesson presents an excellent opportunity for students to practice their knowledge of the two geometric figures, the square and the circle. The diagonal of the square is known, and the side can be found using the relationships of the 45°-45°-90° right triangle. In this case, the leg equals one-half the hypotenuse multiplied by $\sqrt{2}$.

Lesson 27: Number Curiosities
and Geometry

Objectives: To have students observe an interesting curiosity of our number system and relate it to geometry and also to see that mathematics is still an alive and growing field of study

Materials: A ruler or straightedge and a pair of compasses for each group of students, as well as a set of nine circles with a diameter of about 4", with the numbers from 0 through 9 spaced approximately equally along the circumference, as shown in the figures on the next page.

Introduction: Over the ages, mathematicians have discovered a great many curiosities as they studied our number system. Many of these numerical curiosities have been explained, but many others are still being examined. Mathematicians today are still seeking answers to many problems. This lesson examines one of these curiosities.

Development:

(1) Divide the class into groups of four to five students.
(2) Have each group begin by drawing a set of circles each with a diameter of approximately 4". Have them place the numbers from 0 through 9 along the circumference, as equally spaced as possible.
(3) Have the students write out the first 10 multiples of 1.

  1, 2, 3, 4, 5, 6, 7, 8, 9, 10

(4) Now rewrite the sequence, replacing any two-digit numbers by the units digit of that number. The sequence now reads:

  1, 2, 3, 4, 5, 6, 7, 8, 9, 0

(5) On the first circle, connect these numbers in order.
(6) Next, have each group write the first 10 multiples of 2.

  2, 4, 6, 8, 10, 12, 14, 16, 18

(7) Replace any two-digit number with the last digit of the sequence.

  2, 4, 6, 8, 0, 2, 4, 6, 8

(8) On the second circle, connect these numbers in order.
(9) Next, have the groups write the first 10 multiples of 3.

  3, 6, 9, 12, 15, 18, 21, 24, 27

(10) Replace any two-digit number with the units digit.

  3, 6, 9, 2, 5, 8, 1, 4, 7

(11) Connect these numbers in order along the circumference of the circle.
(12) Continue in this manner, finding the first 10 multiples of 4 through 9 and replacing the two-digit numbers by their units digit. Then connect the numbers in order on one of the circles.

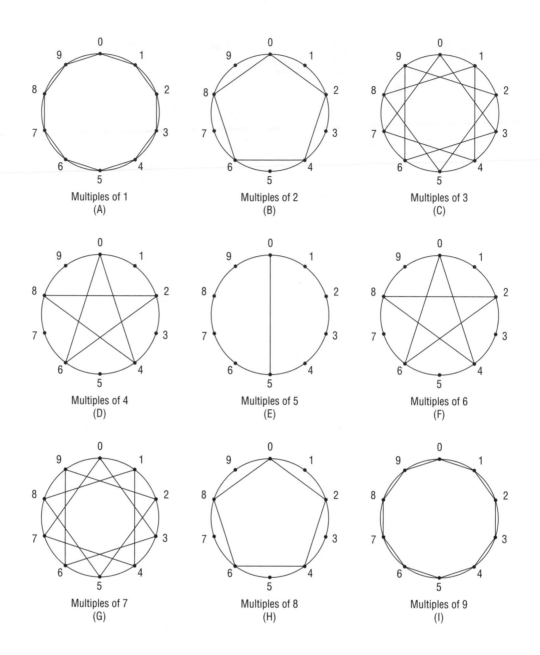

Multiples of 1
(A)

Multiples of 2
(B)

Multiples of 3
(C)

Multiples of 4
(D)

Multiples of 5
(E)

Multiples of 6
(F)

Multiples of 7
(G)

Multiples of 8
(H)

Multiples of 9
(I)

Discussion: Have students show their drawings. Discuss with the class which sets of multiples show the same drawing. Ask students to explain why this occurs. Have them examine the sequences they arrived at for each set of multiples. What would happen if this experiment were continued for numbers and their multiples beyond 9?

Summary: Your students are performing an experiment much like a pure mathematician would. That is, they are using numbers to observe a sequence of patterns and seeing what occurs as they draw the geometric figures that correspond to each sequence. Emphasize that much of mathematics begins in this way, often as a novelty with no practical use. It is only later on that the applied mathematician sometimes finds a practical application for these mathematics.

Lesson 28: Linear Relationships

Objective: To develop and explore a linear relationship that occurs within a physical model

Materials: Several dozen styrofoam cups of the same size

Introduction: Ask students how many cups they think could be stacked in a cupboard that is exactly 48" high. Would an entire package of 100 cups fit? A package of 50?

Development: (1) Divide the class into groups of four or five students. Distribute a different number of cups to each group.
(2) Have the students measure the "rim" and the "hold" part of one cup.

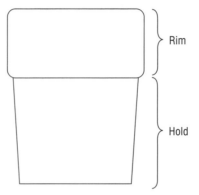

(3) Ask the students to stack their cups and measure the height of their stack.
(4) Now collect these data from the groups and prepare a table.

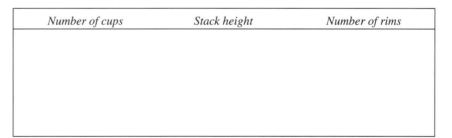

Number of cups	Stack height	Number of rims

(5) From these data, have the class arrive at a formula for the total height of any stack of n cups. (Height = n × measure of one rim + the measure of one hold.) Or, S = nr + h where S = the height of the stack, r = the measure of one rim, n = the number of rims, and h = the measure of one hold. Use this formula and check to see if this agrees with the height of their stack previously measured.

Discussion: Have students examine the formula they have developed. What is the slope of the function? (the measure of one rim.) What is the y intercept of the function? (the measure of one hold.) Now answer the original question: What number of cups would fit into a cupboard that was exactly 48" high?

Summary: The students have used a common object, a styrofoam cup, to develop a formula for the linear relationship between the number of cups and their height. Emphasize that they will find a great deal of mathematics in the everyday objects they find around their homes. The lesson also provides experience with algebraic thinking and discussion.

Lesson 29: Permutations and Combinations

Objective: To have students examine combinations in a familiar setting

Introduction: New cars are sometimes equipped with a keyless entry system. This is usually a keypad with a series of letters and/or numbers on it and a code to give the owner access. Suppose you have purchased such a car and are designing your own code. Let's assume your new car comes with a keypad with the four letters A, B, C, and D. The owner's manual clearly states that your entry code to lock or unlock the door must consist of four letters, with no letter appearing more than once in the sequence. Also, the sequence of A followed by B is different from B followed by A. Design all the possible codes you might create. How many possible codes would there be?

Development: (1)   Divide the class into small groups of four or five students.
(2)   After the class has worked for a while, begin the following discussion. Suppose there had been only one letter needed. How many different codes could there be? (Answer: 4)
(3)   Suppose there was to be a two-letter code. Now how many codes could there be? (Answer: $12 = 4! / 2!$ or 4×3)
(4)   What if the code contained three letters? (Answer: $24 = 4! / 1!$ or $4 \times 3 \times 2$)
(5)   How many four-letter codes would there be? (Answer: $24 = 4! / 0!$ or $4 \times 3 \times 2 \times 1$) There would be a total of $24 + 24 + 12 + 4 = 64$ possible codes with a four-letter keypad.

Discussion: Suppose the owner's manual did not exclude repeating a letter. Now how many one-letter, two-letter, three-letter, and four-letter codes would there be? How many different codes altogether?

(1-letter codes = 4)
(2-letter codes = 4^2 or $4 \times 4 = 16$)
(3-letter codes = 4^3 or $4 \times 4 \times 4 = 64$)
(4-letter codes = 4^4 or $4 \times 4 \times 4 \times 4 = 256$)

There would be a total of $4 + 16 + 64 + 256 = 340$ codes with a four-letter keypad.
    If there is time, have the students discuss the possibilities with a five-letter code consisting of A, B, C, D, and E.

(1-letter codes = 5)
(2-letter codes = 20)
(3-letter codes = 60)
(4-letter codes = 120)
(5-letter codes = 120)

There would be total of 325 possible codes with no repeating letters.

Summary: This lesson introduces the concepts of permutation and combination to students, when order is and is not important. These concepts, important in discrete mathematics, are ones that students usually grasp quickly. The model of the keyless entry pad system provides a setting with which most of your students will be familiar.

CHAPTER 10

The Role of Homework

One of the important decisions you will have to make is whether or not to assign homework on any given day and, if you decide to do so, what kind of an assignment you should give and how you will deal with it when it is handed in. Assigning homework on a daily basis is an accepted practice by most mathematics teachers. Homework is often considered to be the natural extension of the daily lesson. For many teachers, homework is where the real learning takes place.

Why do we assign homework? First, homework provides the student with the opportunity to more fully grasp the concepts and/or skills that were presented in class. Students can work at their own pace and carefully dissect the elements of the day's lesson, making for a fuller understanding. After seeing the topic presented in your class, and even participating in the lesson itself, it is only at home that many students fully come to comprehend the material.

Another reason for assigning homework is to prepare students for the next day's lesson. By "stumping" the students or presenting them with an introduction to what is coming, you may stimulate their interest in the next day's material. Thus, some teachers make the last problem of an assignment the lead-in for the next day in class.

Homework provides an opportunity for you to assign review materials to your students. Your class lesson, no matter how carefully planned and executed, often does not leave any time to review topics that were taught several months ago, several weeks ago, the previous week, or even the previous day. A carefully structured, or spiral, assignment will give the students a wide variety of topics to review.

A final purpose in assigning homework is to provide the students with some drill and practice of the new skills they learned in class. A careful selection of the problems assigned can help the students master the skills they were taught and make them an integral part of their arsenal of mathematics tools. This is particularly important when a new algorithmic skill has been taught—for example, factoring a polynomial in algebra, adding fractions with unlike denominators, and so on.

This is not to say that homework is only valuable when it involves mastery of an algorithmic or computational skill. This is definitely not so! And it certainly is not the impression we wish to convey to our students. In the middle school especially, homework can help students reflect on the ideas and concepts presented in class that day. Homework is a natural extension of the class lesson. Presenting students with interesting or unusual problems to investigate or an experiment to perform and collect data are some of the things that you can assign other than drill-and-practice exercises. This kind of homework helps build self-reliance, since students can't ask you to explain something they don't quite understand. Most of the time, they resolve their questions on their own. This tells students that you know they are capable of handling the problem. Early adolescents need this kind of encouragement.

Is homework important? According to the Third International Mathematics and Science Study, homework assignments affect the grades of 95 percent of our students.

Obviously, teachers place a great deal of value on their students' homework. Furthermore, homework is an excellent way to involve parents in students' everyday work. Parents of most middle school students want to help their children learn. Students become persistent mathematics learners when their parents exhibit the same traits. Encourage your students to ask their parents for help. You might even consider sending home an explanatory note to all parents outlining how they can best help their children do the assignments each night. You might suggest the appropriate format for the homework, and whether it should be written in pen or pencil. Ask the parents *not* to do the homework for the students or simply give them the answer. Rather, they should "admit" that the problem is a bit difficult for them also but suggest "let's work it through together." If the parent and child are both stuck on a particular problem, the parent should help the child find where the difficulty lies and encourage their child to ask about it in class the next day. In this way, parents become part of the student's learning team along with the teacher. Above all, instruct parents never to say "It's OK. I was never good at math either." This sends a wrong message to the child, encouraging them not to do their best to unravel any problems they might be having.

WHAT SHOULD A HOMEWORK ASSIGNMENT INVOLVE?

Unfortunately, many teachers regard homework as something to be easily brushed off or made up hastily to help keep students busy. If students are to regard their homework as important, then give homework the time it deserves when planning the daily assignment. First of all, determine which problems pose special difficulties and which you might not wish to assign for that lesson. The difficulties might tend to mask the concept or skill you are trying to emphasize. For example, when students first learn how to solve linear equations, you might not want to assign problems with several different operations in one equation the first day. Such problems can be reserved for another assignment, when students are more comfortable with linear equations.

One technique is the *spiral* approach—that is, the assignment spirals back over work that was learned throughout the semester. The spiral assignment permits students to master the newer material taught that day in class and, at the same time, to review material they may have forgotten. For example, if the new work is in geometry, you might assign some problems involving addition of mixed numbers or percent problems as review. In any case, you should keep a record of which problems have been assigned so as not to assign them again.

Another approach to making homework assignments is to include a wide variety of problems. That is, don't regularly give an assignment such as "page 156, problems 1 through 20." The students quickly realize that this is a busywork assignment. After all, if students can do problems 1 through 5, they will reason that they can do them all. If they can't do 1 through 5, they probably can't do the rest anyhow, so why bother? Variety in an assignment means including some thought problems, some practice/drill exercises, some construction or measurement problems, and some thought questions. For example, you might assign the following problem to a class studying division of fractions:

1.   How many half-dollars are in one dollar?

2.   How many quarters are in one dollar?

3.   What is $1 \div \frac{1}{2}$?

4. What is $1 \div \frac{1}{4}$?

5. What is $\frac{1}{2} \div \frac{1}{2}$?

6. What is $\frac{1}{2} \times 2$?

7. What is $\frac{2}{3} \div \frac{4}{5}$?

8. What is $\frac{2}{3} \times \frac{5}{4}$?

9. Write a general statement explaining to one of your friends a procedure they might follow when dividing a number by a fraction.

Another kind of assignment might be to perform an experiment at home and keep a record of the results. This could serve as a preview of the next day's lesson. For example, if you intend to introduce the concept of empirical versus theoretical probability in class on a given day, you could make the following assignment the evening before:

1. You are going to toss a fair coin a total of 20 times. Make a guess as to how many times the coin will land with heads showing and how many times with tails showing.

2. Take a quarter and toss it 20 times.

3. Use a table to keep a record of how many heads you get and how many tails.

4. Write a statement explaining why you think the number of heads and number of tails did or did not come out the same as your original guess.

Or, suppose you are going to introduce the concept that the circumference of a circle can be found using the formula $C = \pi d$. You might assign students to use a piece of string and a ruler to measure the distance around several circular objects, such as a circular wastebasket, a tin can, a dish, and so forth. Then have them measure the diameter of each and keep a record of their results. You might even give them a table like this to fill in:

Object measured	Circumference	Diameter	C/d
Wastebasket			
Dish			
Tin can			

When students bring their data to class the next day, you can have them combine all their data and make a conjecture of what the ratio C/d will be. From this data, you then move into the formula $C = \pi d$. In this way, you provide the interest factor for the day's lesson by using the previous evening's homework assignment.

You might even consider a writing assignment in which students research the history of mathematics and write a brief biographical sketch of a famous mathematician, such as Pythagoras, Euclid, Eratosthenes, or Kovaleski. This will help them to realize that mathematics is not dry numbers alone, but also has human interest.

How Much Time Should Each Assignment Require?

This is not a question that can be answered easily or in general terms. The length of each assignment will vary. If your assignments are too long, students will not complete them. On the other hand, if they are too brief, then the assignment will not achieve your goals. The exercises and problems you select for each assignment should have a clear-cut intent and should meet the objectives of the assignment. If you assign too many problems of the same type, students will quickly realize that they are merely repeating the same thing. They will become bored and will only do the assignment "to get it over with." They may even decide to just copy someone else's work the next day. As a result, little learning will take place. Many teachers also fail to keep in mind that theirs is only one of the several assignments students will have on a given day. After all, students do take other courses besides mathematics. Make your assignment cover the work you wish it to cover, but keep the work short but sufficient. Avoid repetitive problems, and be certain to include a variety of types of problems. Limit the homework to no more than half an hour to forty minutes a day.

Should All Your Students Do the Same Homework?

All the students in your class should do the same basic assignment. However, variations must be made to accommodate the different abilities in your class. The basic assignment should be within the capabilities of all students in your class. And the expectation is that all students should do it!

Challenge the bright students. Within the class assignment, put an asterisk (or some other symbol) to indicate a "Challenge Problem." These are optional for everyone; however, it is hoped that the better mathematics students will accept the challenge and attempt to solve them. Unusual solutions to these challenge problems could occupy space on your bulletin board.

Be certain that your assignment includes some experiences within the capabilities of the slower students. The old adage "Nothing succeeds like success" was never truer than when assigning homework to students.

REVIEWING THE HOMEWORK

There is no question that homework done regularly will help students achieve in mathematics. However, unless homework is gone over and graded either overtly or mentally, students probably will attach little importance to the homework assignments. They may either copy it from someone else, do it as quickly as possible with little or no thought, or not do it at all. If you collect the homework every day and spend many hours grading each paper, you will be wasting a great deal of your own time and encouraging students to copy from one another. Thus, you must devise a system to check the homework regularly to see that it is being done and that the questions raised by the homework get answered. Homework must be considered important if students are to be willing to spend the time necessary to think about the problems and work each of them out carefully. There are several procedures you might consider. Keep in mind, however, that different kinds of questions should be gone over in a different manner.

For example, questions that require single-word answers or oral responses can be done out loud at the start of the class period. The solution to other questions that require more careful thought must be written out for everyone to see and then discussed.

One system that many teachers find effective is to have any student who has had some difficulty or has a question about a particular problem write the page number and problem number on the chalkboard before class starts. As students arrive, they will see these problems listed. Anyone who understands the problem can go to the board and write the correct solution. This can be done during the first five or ten minutes of class while you are performing the usual clerical details, such as making announcements, taking attendance, and so on. You can have the rest of the class work on the opener problem. As time permits, you can walk around the room and glance at the other students' homework papers to see that they have attempted the work. In this way you can get an idea of which problems do not need explanation. You can also take a few minutes to talk with individual students if you notice any problems on their papers. When the problems are all on the board, you can have each student explain the problem and have the discussion needed. You must take care to see that it is not always the same few students who answer the questions.

Another procedure followed by some teachers is to assign problems in advance, when the assignment is made. If you have assigned five problems for homework as an example, the first five students in the first row are responsible for placing the solutions on the board the next day, with student number 6 "on deck" in case someone is absent. These five students will explain their solutions to the rest of the class. The next day, you begin with the next group of students, rotating assignments around the room over a period of a week or several days. This approach has several benefits. First, it assigns problems to students at random, which eliminates any complaints of "You always pick on me for the hard ones!" Second, it saves class time by having all the homework problems put on the board at the very beginning of class. Third, it gives you an opportunity to walk around the room and survey the papers of each student. It also allows all students to participate.

An alternative to this procedure is to ask for volunteers to put their solutions on the board. This is done at the beginning of the class period while students are working on the class opener. Be certain not to use the same volunteers every day; spread the work around. Students then can present and discuss their solutions to the class.

Another system many teachers have found successful is to give students a blank piece of overhead acetate and a pen at the start of the semester. Assign homework problems to specific students either the night before or as they walk into class. These students then place their solutions on their transparencies for the overhead projector. When the particular problem is called for, the student places the problem on the overhead projector and explains it to the class. Be certain that the solution remains in view for the rest of the class for a sufficient length of time for everyone to understand what is being explained.

Still another method is to collect the homework papers of the students seated in a given row or section of the room on different days. The row to be selected is chosen at random. Thus, all students must do their homework, since they will not know beforehand which row will have the papers collected. Again, this is not to be taken as a punishment but merely a means of selectively examining some homework papers each day.

Collecting homework after going over the problems is not always the best technique to use. Keep in mind that your students should be learning from the errors they might have made in their homework. The corrected homework papers provide a tool for students to use when they are preparing for a test.

When homework is basically conceptual in nature, time should be spent discussing students' approaches to the problems. What were they thinking? How did this affect their solutions? What kinds of answers would be acceptable? Trying to resolve an assigned thought problem in many different ways is a good use of class time. Students become more self-reliant as they learn to match their own work against the ideas of their classmates.

EVALUATING HOMEWORK

Evaluating every student's homework every day can't be done. However, every student's homework should be reviewed at least once a week. Collect the papers from one-fifth of the class each day and review them carefully for computational accuracy, correct strategy selection and solution, and completeness.

You *must* make some written comments on each paper. The comments should be both positive and negative, but should be constructive in nature. Even simply writing "Nice work!" or "Clever approach!" when an unusual solution is suggested will serve as a stimulus to keep up the good work. Your careful attention to the homework will show students that you consider homework to be a vital part of your class.

Keep a careful record of your comments and reactions to each student's homework. Place these reactions and comments in the student's folder. You will use these when making up your final evaluation at the end of the semester or school year as well as for any parent conferences held during the year.

Activities

1. You are going to introduce your class to the Pythagorean theorem tomorrow. Prepare an exploration activity to assign for homework the evening before.

2. Read about the life of a famous mathematician. Then write a brief (no more than two pages) biography of that person. Select your person from the following list:

Pythagoras	Karl F. Gauss
Aristotle	Benjamin Banneker
Euclid	Sonja Kovaleski
Johannes Kepler	Isaac Newton
René Descartes	Albert Einstein

3. There are many books based in mathematics and written at a level appropriate for students at the middle school level. Students can read one of these, and write a book report for their portfolios. Prepare a list of books that have to do with mathematics that you feel are appropriate for middle school students.

4. Here are some student excuses for not doing the homework. How would you react to each one?

" I didn't understand the homework so I couldn't do it!"

"I left my homework at home."

"I didn't have time last night. I had too much homework in my other subjects."

"I forgot I had an assignment."

"I forgot to copy the assignment in class."

5. You are going to teach a lesson on adding fractions with unlike denominators. Which topics would you include in a "spiral assignment" the night before?

6. A student complains, "You give too much homework!" How would you react?

7. A teacher tells her class, "You've been so well behaved, there is no homework for tomorrow." What is your reaction?

8. A teacher tells his class that the assignment for tomorrow is "Do a few problems from each of the four sections in this chapter." What is your reaction?

9. A teacher asks his class, "Are there any questions on the homework?" What is your reaction?

10. What would you consider a reasonable length of time for middle school students to spend doing their mathematics homework? How can you determine if your assignments are too long or too short?

11. Of the methods suggested in this chapter for checking homework, which would you select as your favorite? Why?

Bibliography

Beaton, A. E., Mullis, I. V., Martin, M. O., Gonzalez, E. J., Kelly, D. L., and Smith, T. A. *TIMSS: Mathematics Achievement in the Middle School Years.* Chestnut Hill, MA: Center for the Study of Testing, Evaluation and Educational Policy, 1996.

Eves, Howard. *An Introduction to the History of Mathematics.*

Mclean, E. "Tips for Beginners: Steps for Better Homework." *Mathematics Teacher* 86, no. 3 (November 1993): 212.

Testing and Assessing: How Did They— and You—Do?

CHAPTER 11

Testing and Evaluating Students

If we expect our students to learn something, we must find out how they did—that is, did they learn it? If so, how well? If they didn't learn it, why not? This is the area of teaching mathematics that often concerns new teachers—namely, testing. In the past, it was relatively easy to develop tests to assess your students' learning. Test questions could be taken directly from the textbook and the numbers changed. Teachers counted how many the student got correct, and based the score on the number right. However, the change in focus of the mathematics curriculum has made this process more complex. An effective mathematics teacher must make use of a variety of assessment strategies to determine how students have grown and how much they have learned.

There are two basic kinds of testing programs you will encounter as a middle school mathematics teacher. The first kind is *external* testing—tests that are mandated by an outside agency, usually the city or state. The second kind is *internal* testing— the classroom test, usually prepared by you.

EXTERNAL TESTS

The eighth grade of the middle school marks the end of the children's pre-high school career. The mathematics program during the middle school years is expected to have prepared students for high school mathematics, where more advanced work in algebra, geometry, probability and statistics, and calculus takes place. The middle school provides an ideal place and time to assess how well the children are doing. The external test is constructed by an outside agency or by the state education department. It usually has a multiple-choice format and is an electronically scored examination. The agency or group that constructs this kind of test usually has only a general knowledge of the student population being tested. As a result, for many years, these tests concentrated primarily on algorithms and skills rather than on thought processes. Once completed, the tests are forwarded to the agency that constructed the test, where they are usually scored by machine. The scores are then changed into local and state norms and the results presented in numerical fashion. The classroom teacher only sees a single or sometimes a series of numerical scores that may or may not have any real meaning to the teacher. After all, what does a score of 6 mean? How much more has this student learned than the student who scored a 4 or a 5?

A primary purpose of this type of testing program has been to see how well each school is doing when compared to the others in the state or school district. Rarely is the work of an individual child of consequence. The state or school district uses the results of these tests to decide how well the state curriculum guidelines are being met. The test results are also often used to compare individual schools within a particular school district. In some situations, the scores may also be used to determine how effective the teaching-learning process has been. The emphasis of external tests is usually on what students do not know rather than what they do know.

A weakness of these tests is the heavy focus on timed use of computation, a skill that NCTM's *Standards 2000* has suggested be de-emphasized. This emphasis is highly dependent on rote learning and memory, and little time is provided for thinking or reasoning. In addition, the use of multiple-choice questions with only one single correct item (or the choice "None of the above") does not provide for someone who may interpret the question differently and thus arrive at a different answer. For example, suppose a child is asked to solve the problem $500 \div 33$. The child who is used to thinking through problems in a context would begin by dividing 500 by 33, getting 15.1515. If the question is put in terms of how many busses are needed to carry 500 people, and if each bus carries 33 people, then the answer would be 16. If the student interprets the context to be dividing 500 balloons equally among 33 children, then each child would receive 15 balloons with 5 balloons left over. In either case, the student might select "None of the above," and this choice would be marked as incorrect.

Several widely used external tests that assess achievement in mathematics of middle school youngsters follow:

1. **TerraNova.** The TerraNova is a new, comprehensive, modular assessment series that offers multiple measures of academic achievement for both English-speaking and Spanish-speaking students. The series covers grades K through 12 and is available in two forms. It has sections on achievement in mathematics skills and in problem solving.

2. **Stanford Achievement Tests Series (ninth edition).** This test is referred to as the SAT9, and consists of a series of norm-referenced achievement tests covering grades K through 13. The SAT9 combines multiple-choice and open-ended questions in subtests. The various subjects are aligned with national standards, projects, and models.

3. **The Iowa Test of Basic Skills (ITBS).** The ITBS was designed and developed to measure skills and standards important to growth across the curriculum. National norms are available for the 13 grade levels of K through 12.

4. **National Assessment of Education Progress (NAEP).** This test, known as "the Nation's Report Card," is the only nationally representative and continuing assessment of what America's students know and can do in various subject areas. The test is given periodically and includes students drawn from both public and nonpublic schools. The results are reported for students from grades 4, 8, and 12.

INTERNAL TESTS

The internal, or classroom, test is usually prepared by you, the teacher. It is most often a set of problems and/or exercises taken directly from the content that has just been taught. It may also be a test prepared by the textbook publisher that is designed to be administered at the end of a given section of work. Credit is usually assigned on a partial basis, as determined by the teacher. A major advantage of the teacher-made test is that it is constructed entirely within the context of the classroom teaching situation by someone who knows the students and who knows what material has been taught.

Teacher-made tests have two distinctly different purposes. The first purpose is an *evaluative* one. There is no denying that each child in your mathematics class must receive a grade at the end of the marking period. The parents expect it, the school expects it, and even the children expect it. Thus, the tests you construct will provide a major part of the grade the child earns. These tests provide you with a reliable record of what the student has learned.

The second purpose (and, some feel, the major purpose) of any assessment should be *diagnostic*. Diagnostic assessment allows you to improve the learning of each individual child. This diagnosis helps inform you of how well your students are doing in class and how well they are learning what they are being taught. Because you have taught the concepts and skills in a particular unit, you are the natural person to make up the test to find out how well these skills and concepts have been mastered.

This kind of assessment also helps diagnose how well you are doing. If a large percentage of the children in your class miss question number 4 on your test, does the problem lie with the wording of the question? Or is it possible you forgot to teach that topic? Or perhaps your teaching was not done slowly or clearly enough for students to understand it. One thing is certain: the topic has not been learned adequately, and you should take the time to reteach that concept or skill. The internal test aids you in making these kinds of instructional decisions on an ongoing basis.

As a beginning teacher, you should seek some guidance in designing your tests. Consult with your chairperson, other teachers, and the teacher's edition of your textbooks. You may even find a file of examinations from previous semesters in the departmental office that you can examine for ideas.

Constructing the Test

Your first step in constructing the test is to decide what you wish to test. Every test should have clearly defined objectives. The test can be short. The short test usually is referred to as "quiz," either announced or unannounced, and takes approximately 10 to 15 minutes of class time. Short tests are designed to test a single skill or concept. On the other hand, a full period test is designed to determine student mastery of a particular topic or series of related topics. Before you give a long test, you should inform the students several days in advance so that they can prepare and study for the test. Be certain to let them know the material to be covered on the test and, if possible, provide them with sample questions similar to the actual test questions. You should select questions that are similar in type to those discussed in class or on the homework assignments. Questions should not be the most difficult or unusual, but rather should be middle-of-the-road in difficulty. Avoid "trick" items. After all, you are not trying to "trap" or surprise your students. Rather, you are providing them with an opportunity to demonstrate how much they know about the topics being tested. A sample test on decimals and fractions is shown on the next page. The test is designed to see if the students have mastered the basic concepts and operations with fractions and decimal fractions. Notice that the questions go beyond merely examining skills; there are some thought questions as well, which are intended to test mastery of the concepts.

Writing good test items is a difficult and creative task. The questions on the test should be clear, concise, and straightforward and should relate directly to the objectives of the unit just completed. Each question should test only one concept or skill.

Sample Test on Decimals and Fractions

1. In the fraction $\frac{2}{3}$, the number 3 is called the _____ of the fraction, while the number 2 is called the _____ of the fraction.

2. Change each improper fraction to a mixed number.

    a. $\frac{13}{9} = 1\frac{?}{9}$ b. $\frac{27}{5} = \underline{\ ?\ }$ and $\frac{2}{5}$ c. $\frac{18}{7} = ?$

3. Place the correct symbol (<, =, >) between the two fractions.

    a. $\frac{2}{3}$ $\frac{3}{4}$ b. $\frac{1}{2}$ $\frac{3}{5}$ c. $\frac{2}{4}$ $\frac{7}{14}$

4. Add:

    a. $2\frac{3}{8}$ b. $5\frac{7}{10} + 4\frac{3}{5} = ?$

        $+ 3\frac{5}{8}$

5. a. From $8\frac{3}{4}$ subtract $2\frac{1}{4}$ b. From $12\frac{1}{5}$ subtract $3\frac{3}{5}$

6. Arrange the following fractions from smallest to largest:
    $\frac{2}{3}, \frac{1}{2}, \frac{5}{8}, \frac{6}{7}$

7. A recipe calls for $2\frac{2}{3}$ cups of blueberries. Alise has $1\frac{1}{2}$ cups of blueberries. How many more cups of blueberries does Alise need?

8. Subtract 17.23 from 32.

9. Find the perimeter and the area of each rectangle shown.

    2.3 [   ]   .7 [   ]
              8.2   12.02

10. Poor Ramon. He missed the school bus. Now he has to walk 4 miles to school. He can walk at the rate of .15 mile a minute. It is now 8:15. He must be in school by 8:45. Will he make it?

Extra Credit: This question is worth only 3 extra points. Do not spend time on this question until you have completed the rest of the test.

   The diagram below shows a spinner. What is the probability that the arrow will land on a part of the spinner that is *not* red?

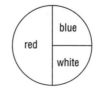

The questions should be presented in ascending order of difficulty (easiest questions first), in order to build the child's self-confidence. The language used on the test should be simple enough for students to readily understand. After all, you are not testing reading. Write your questions in the same language that you and the student have been using in class. This is especially important if you are selecting questions from different sources. Be certain that each question is couched in language that is clear, concise, and unambiguous. Once you have constructed the item, you should ask yourself if there is more than one way to interpret the question.

The test items should test the student's ability to recall information as well as to think. You should work out each question clearly and carefully in order to recognize—and remove—any stumbling blocks that might mask the intent of the question, including any typographical errors. For example, erroneously substituting an addition sign for a multiplication sign could easily make the problem too difficult for students to solve. Furthermore, in constructing the test item, you should try to eliminate the possibility of a student getting the correct answer by guesswork. For example, suppose you wish to see if the students understand the concept of perimeter. It would not make sense to ask them to find the perimeter of the polygon shown below.

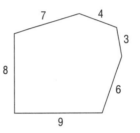

When a students see a polygon with all sides labeled with a given length, there is very little else the student can do except to add the numbers. Giving the correct answer (37) does not indicate whether or not students understand the concept of perimeter. Suppose, instead, that you ask students to draw a rectangle and label the lengths of the sides if the perimeter is 24. This is an open question, one with more than one correct answer. In order to answer this question, students must know what is meant by the perimeter of a rectangle. It would be difficult for students with no concept of perimeter to bluff their way through this question.

You may decide to include some review items on your test. Inform your students of this fact so they can study material learned earlier. This will provide an opportunity to see if your students have forgotten the earlier material or if they are keeping up with the work. You should not have more than one-quarter of the questions on any test be review items. The basic purpose of the test is to assess how well students are doing on the new work, work that has been covered since the last test.

How long should a test be? As a teacher, you don't want it to be too lengthy, since you are the one who must mark all the papers. If one asks the students, they usually will reply that they prefer a longer test, so that each error they make will not count as much. However, if the test is too lengthy, students will feel that they cannot finish it in the time allotted and may not even try. The basic rule is that the test should be just long enough to do its job—to find out if the material has been mastered by the students. You will also have to give some consideration to the length of the class period. One general rule of thumb is the 4:1 or 5:1 ratio. After you have designed the test, sit down with a blank sheet of paper. Now time yourself, taking the test in the same manner as your students will do it. That is, write the heading you want and complete each problem in the same way your students will probably do it (no shortcuts, please) and using the same tools, such as ruler, compasses, and protractors. Then take the time it took you to complete the test and multiply it by 4 or 5. The result should be the approximate time it will take your students to do the test in an acceptable manner. You can now either shorten or lengthen the test accordingly.

Most of the tests you create for your classes will include essay questions requiring longer answers. There should also be multiple-choice questions on your tests. Most of the external examinations your students will take will have multiple-choice formats. Constructing multiple-choice items is extremely difficult. Usually, the question consists of a *stem,* followed by four or five possible answers to complete the stem. Constructing the four responses to the stem is the difficult part. One of the four is the correct answer. At least two of the remaining three, however, must not be obviously incorrect; they should require some thought on the part of the student. For example, look at the following questions:

(1) What is the area of this sheet of paper? (usually, $8\frac{1}{2}"\times 11"$)
  (a) 39 inches
  (b) 39 square inches
  (c) 93.5 inches
  (d) 93.5 square inches

The question is designed to test whether or not the student understands the concept of area versus perimeter. Thus, the choices 39 or 93.5. Furthermore, the question will determine if the student understands that area is measured in square units. Thus, the correct answer is (d), 93.5 square inches.

(2) Tanya is buying hot dogs and buns for her barbecue this weekend. Hot dogs come in packages of 8, while the hot dog buns come in packages of 12. What is the smallest number of packages of hot dogs and buns Tanya can buy to be certain that she has the same number of hot dogs as buns?
  (a) 2 packs of hot dogs and 2 packs of buns
  (b) 3 packs of hot dogs and 2 packs of buns
  (c) 12 packs of hot dogs and 8 packs of buns
  (d) 8 packs of hot dogs and 12 packs of buns

This question is designed to test the concept of lowest common multiple. Notice that choice c, while yielding the same number of hot dogs and buns (96 of each), is not the smallest number. The correct answer is the LCM of 8 and 12, or 24. Thus, Tanya must buy 3 packs of hot dogs and 2 packs of hot dog buns, choice b.

Administering the Test

Unless it is a short quiz, begin distributing the test as soon as the bell rings to begin the class period. This will give students the entire period for the test. If they are to answer the questions on separate sheets of paper, pass these out as well. The test should be duplicated so that students have their own copies. This helps eliminate most of the errors in copying the questions from the board or in reading directions.

During the test, attempt in advance to eliminate the possibility of any cheating. If possible, arrange the desks to provide adequate room between students. Caution the students to keep their eyes on their own papers. If you see someone cheating, you can walk over and quietly make an appropriate comment to the student. If the violation is repeated, you might make a notation on the student's paper and add a penalty when correcting the test. You should walk around the room during the test or sit in the back of the room. Students usually turn around to locate the teacher's whereabouts and the movement of their heads will attract your attention so that you can look directly at them.

Provide for the student or students who finish early. Present them with an extra credit problem that requires careful thought and consideration. Inform the class that this extra credit problem is only worth a few points and should not be attempted unless the entire test has been completed. Tell them it will be better for them to spend their time on the questions of the test rather than on the extra credit problem worth only two points. A student with a perfect paper who completes the extra credit problem as well might receive a grade of 100 + 2, allowing the 2 points to be used on a future test. At the end of the class period, students should be instructed to put their pencils and pens down and turn in their papers.

Grading the Test

The test papers should be marked and returned *promptly*. A test can be an excellent learning device for students. However, if the test is to provide a valid learning experience, it should be returned within a day or two at most and gone over carefully in class. If you merely return the papers and do not go over the test with the class, little learning will take place. Furthermore, if several days have gone by before you return the test papers, the class will have moved on, and the test material will not be fresh in their minds.

Unfortunately, no matter how well you have constructed your test, it is only a one-day glimpse of how well a student is doing on a set of items you have written. For one thing, some students are not good at test taking; they can "freeze up" when confronted with a test. Or they may understand the concepts being tested but may be unable to present their knowledge.

How the test is graded will vary from teacher to teacher. Each person grading a test will see different things in different students' work. For example, here is one student's solution to this question on an eighth-grade algebra test: Solve this equation $x/3 + 7 = 21$.

$$x/3 + 7 = 21$$
$$x/3 = 14$$
$$x = 32$$

The answer is 32.

The answer is incorrect; it should be 42. However, the error made by the student was a relatively minor one. In the third step, the student multiplied 14×3 and got 32 instead of 42; otherwise, the problem was done correctly. On the basis of 10 points, how many points has the student earned? Some teachers will give 0, claiming that the answer is either right or wrong, with no in-between. Others may take off one or two points for the error and give the student eight points for the work. You must make a decision and apply it consistently.

Here is another student's solution to this question: Solve this equation for x: $7(x + 3) = 24$

$$7 (x + 3) = 24$$
$$7x + 3 = 24$$
$$7x = 21$$
$$x = 3$$

The answer is 3

Once again, the error is made early in the solution. The student failed to multiply 7×3 when removing the parentheses. (The correct answer is 3/7.) Decide in advance how much should be taken off for this type of error and apply this approach consistently. To ensure consistency when scoring a test, you may wish to use a scoring rubric. Rubrics are discussed in Chapter 12.

If the test is to be a midterm or final examination, you may wish to prepare the test in conjunction with other teachers in your department. Often, these tests are prepared by a committee of teachers for use with students in several classes, all of whom are taking the same course. The tests are designed to assess whether or not the concepts and skills of the entire course have been mastered.

Finally, consider this. A weekly test or unit test is really not sufficient to determine how well your students are doing. New nontraditional assessment strategies have been developed to address this lack. These will be discussed in more detail in Chapter 12.

Activities

1. Give an example of a test question you feel is inappropriate for a test. Explain why.

2. Give some possible values for x and y, so that the expression $-5xy$ will be

   (a) positive   (b) negative   (c) zero

3. Sometimes your students will ask a question you did not anticipate. You have two options: (a) you can ignore the question, putting it on "hold" for later, or (b) you can leave your planned lesson for later and move the discussion to the question that has been asked. Which would you do? Why?

4. In groups of four or five students, select a unit from a middle school textbook. Design a test that your group feels would adequately assess whether the children have achieved the goals of the unit. Have the rest of your class take the test. Discuss the results.

5. Here is a ten-point test item and one student's solution. How would you grade this solution? Share your results with the other students in your class. Do they agree with your grade? Why or why not?

   Marcela bought a skateboard that was originally priced at $49.00. It was on sale for 20 percent off. How much was the sale price of the skateboard?

   Solution: 20% = .2
   $49.00 \times .2 = \$9.80$
   $49.00 + 9.80 = \$58.80$

Bibliography

Cai, J., Lane, S., and Jakabscin, M. S. "The Role of Open-Ended Tasks and Holistic Scoring Rubrics: Assessing Students' Mathematical Reasoning and Communication." In *Communication in Mathematics*, (P. C. Elliott Ed.). Reston VA: National Council of Teachers of Mathematics, 1996.

Popham, W. James. *Classroom Assessment: What Teachers Need to Know.* Boston, MA: Allyn and Bacon, 1995. (especially Chapter 6: "Selected-Response Tests").

Related Research

Beaton, A. E., Mullis, I. V., Martin, M. O., Gonzalez, E. J., Kelly, D. L., & Smith, T. A. (1996). TIMSS: *Mathematics achievement in the middle school years.* Chestnut Hill, MA: Center for the Study of Testing, Evaluation, and Educational Policy.

Belcher, T, Coates, G. D., Franco, J., & Mayfield-Ingram, K. (1997). Assessment and equity. In J. Trentacosta (Ed.), *1997 yearbook of the NCTM: Multicultural and gender equity in the mathematics classroom: The gift of diversity* (pp. 195–200). Reston, VA: National Council of Teachers of Mathematics.

Cooney, T. J., Badger, E., & Wilson, M. R. (1993). Assessment, understanding mathematics, and distinguishing visions from mirages. In N. L. Webb (Ed.), *1993 yearbook of the NCTM: Assessment in the mathematics classroom* (pp. 239–247). Reston, VA: National Council of Teachers of Mathematics.

Driscoll, M. (1995). Implementing the professional standards for teaching mathematics: "The farther out you go . . . ": Assessment in the classroom. *Mathematics Teacher* 88 (5): 420–425.

EQUALS and California Mathematics Council Assessment Committee. (1989). *Assessment alternatives in mathematics: An overview of assessment techniques that promote learning.* Berkeley, CA: EQUALS, Lawrence Hall of Science, University of California.

Kulm, G. (1990). *Assessing higher order thinking in mathematics.* Washington, DC: American Association for the Advancement of Science.

Lambdin, D. V. (1995). Implementing the assessment standards for school mathematics: An open-and-shut case? Openness in the assessment process. *Mathematics Teacher* 88 (8): 680–684.

Mathematical Sciences Education Board National Research Council. (1993). Measuring counts: A conceptual guide for mathematics assessment. Washington, DC: National Academy Press.

Mayer, J., & Hillman, S. (1996). Implementing the assessment standards for school mathematics: Assessing students' thinking through writing. *Mathematics Teacher* 89 (5): 428–432.

National Council of Teachers of Mathematics. (1996). *Emphasis on assessment: Readings from NCTM's school-based journals.* Reston, VA: Author.

National Council of Teachers of Mathematics. (1995). *Assessment standards for school mathematics.* Reston, VA: Author.

National Research Council. (1993). *Measuring up: Prototypes for mathematics assessment.* Washington, DC: National Academy Press.

Office of Educational Research and Improvement (OERI). (1997). *Pursuing excellence: A study of U.S. fourth-grade mathematics and science achievement in international context.* Washington, DC: OERI, U.S. Department of Education.

Romberg, T. A. (1992). *Mathematics assessment and evaluation.* Albany, NY: SUNY UP.

Stenmark, J. K. (1991). *Mathematics assessment: Myths, models, good questions, and practical suggestions.* Reston, VA: National Council of Teachers of Mathematics.

Webb, N. L. (Ed.). (1993). *1993 yearbook of the NCTM: Assessment in the mathematics classroom.* Reston, VA: National Council of Teachers of Mathematics.

CHAPTER **12**

Comprehensive or Alternate Assessment

Because the curriculum in the middle grades has changed from a strictly skill-oriented curriculum to one that emphasizes problem solving and reasoning, testing must also shift from the skill-oriented test alone to other assessment devices that will enable you to examine the thought processes your children are using as they resolve problem situations. As we have stated before, the middle school mathematics curriculum is placing more and more emphasis on increasing students' ability to think and reason. Problem solving is now a major thrust of the middle school mathematics curriculum. Helping your students become better problem solvers and reasoners has become one of the primary goals in the teaching of mathematics in the middle school.

As a result of this change of focus in the curriculum, other forms of assessment must be used in addition to the traditional teacher-made test. Let us put your mind at rest. The teacher-made test will still be a major part of your assessment program. It will still be created by you as you complete teaching parts of your curriculum and will still serve a major role in determining how well your students are doing. These written tests will still be important in assessing skill acquisition. However, just as the focus and content of the mathematics program have changed since you were in school, so must the focus and content of your assessment program change as well. For one thing, the current view of assessment goes beyond testing and grades. As a rule, tests are given after the student has completed some portion of work. Assessment is current and ongoing, a process of collecting information on a continuous basis as teaching takes place. There is now an emphasis on what students do know, rather than what they don't know. There is an intensified interest in how students are thinking and reasoning as well as how well they have mastered skills and algorithms. Where the use of technology was once completely excluded from the assessment process, calculators and even computers are being used in assessing student achievement. These many additional methods of assessment help give a better and more complete picture of how well our students are mastering the process skills. These new methods are referred to as alternate or comprehensive assessment. Comprehensive is actually a better description, since it is in addition to traditional forms of assessment, not an alternative to them.

Comprehensive assessment can be divided into two major types: ongoing tasks and snapshot tasks. (See the listing below.) *Ongoing tasks* are continuous and recur in your classroom on an ongoing basis throughout the school year. These tasks let us examine the progress the child makes over an extended period of time. Most of these items are produced by the students and include portfolios, folders, journals, notebooks, and so on. *Snapshot tasks,* much like a photograph, occur singly or one at a time. They permit us to examine the child's knowledge and understanding of a topic at a given instant. Accumulating a series of these "snapshots" gives a good picture of the child's growth and progress.

Ongoing Tasks	*Snapshot Tasks*
Portfolios	Formal observations
Folders	Interviews
Journals	Projects
Notebooks	Forced-choice responses
Informal observations	Formulated responses

Portfolios

The one item that seems to have made the greatest impact on assessment at all levels, but especially in the middle school, is the portfolio. Portfolios are relatively new to the mathematics classroom. However, they are rather common in many other areas of endeavor. For example, artists, architects, photographers, journalists, and models present their work in portfolios. Their portfolios contain examples of their best work as selected by them. (It would hardly make sense to show their poorest work when trying to demonstrate their abilities in their respective fields.) Similarly, a mathematics portfolio should contain examples of the student's best work, as determined by the student. The portfolio provides an opportunity to demonstrate growth over an extended period of time. By its nature, the portfolio emphasizes what the child has been successful in achieving, rather than relying on a single test score. The portfolio remains in the hands of the child and is constantly being added to or modified as the year progresses. In some schools, the portfolio moves along with the child as the child progresses from grade 5 to 8.

Physically, the portfolio can be a large artist's-type envelope or a large manila folder. Students can decorate the outside of their portfolios with their original and creative work.

Although students should decide what work goes into the portfolio, the content is still somewhat controlled by the teacher. The goal is to include a wide variety of student achievement, presented in as many forms as possible. Another important goal is to represent how the student has grown over the year. The student will make the final decision as to what specific example to include in the portfolio, but the teacher should decide what areas should be represented. You want to be certain that the portfolio includes examples that demonstrate conceptual understanding, skill mastery, problem solving and reasoning, as well as good communication skills. Permitting students to select the specific work to be included in each category helps them develop their metacognitive abilities, as they think about what to include and why to include it.

What are some of the things students should place in their portfolios? You might ask students to include some of their homework assignments from different months over the year. For example, they might be asked to select one of their best assignments from October, one from January, one from March, and one from May. This selection is widespread enough to demonstrate growth throughout the year.

You can assign long-term or short-term projects to be done in groups of four or five students. Students can then place a copy of their group's final report on this project into their portfolios. This item reflects the students' social skills, showing how well they work within a group setting and how they organize their work and bring the pieces together to form a comprehensive report. Examples of topics for long-term projects follow:

1. *How many students in your grade are left-handed?* This is a survey project connected with social studies. Of the population of the United States, approximately 12 percent are left-handed. How does your grade (or school) correspond with this percentage?

2. *Bananas in a local supermarket sell for 49¢ a pound. How much of a banana is thrown away?* This project is connected to science. Students should actually use bananas and decide what part is thrown away. They should investigate the cost of the part of the banana that they actually eat.

3. *The traffic lights near your school are supposedly timed to turn red, yellow, and green based on the traffic pattern at the intersection. Are the traffic lights near your school timed correctly?* This is a social studies and civics project. Students should use stopwatches and calculators to actually count the number of cars and the timing for the traffic lights near the school.

4. *Each of the Federal Reserve Banks that issue paper money has a specific letter designation:*

A = Boston	E = Richmond	I = Minneapolis
B = New York	F = Atlanta	J = Kansas City
C = Philadelphia	G = Chicago	K = Dallas
D = Cleveland	H = St. Louis	L = San Francisco

   Which banks would you expect to have the most paper money in circulation in the area near your home? Why? How would you test your answer? This is a social studies survey involving the concept of sampling. The research would be done at home.

5. *Newspapers sell advertising to make money. Approximately how much space in your local newspaper is occupied by advertising?* This project connects economics and mathematics. Students should use pages selected from several newspapers to determine which one devotes the most space to advertising.

You can find more of these projects connecting mathematics to other topics in *Assessing Reasoning and Problem Solving* (Krulik and Rudnick, 1998).

Each student's portfolio should also include solutions to several problem-solving activities they have engaged in throughout the year. These might include their unusual solutions to difficult problems, how they approached a particular problem situation as well as their hypotheses, and how they tested them. Examples of original or creative thinking should also be included. For example, how students approach extensions of the given problem provide a picture of students' thought processes.

Portfolios should contain anything else that students wish to place in them that they feel demonstrates their best achievement during the year. After all items are in the portfolio, have students prepare a table of contents for their portfolios as well as brief descriptions of why they chose to include each item. Doing so will demonstrate their communication skills.

Portfolios provide an opportunity to involve parents in their children's mathematics education. Parents want to know how their children are doing in class and in comparison with what is expected. Be certain to tell parents the purpose of the portfolio so that they can help their children select appropriate works to include and review and discuss the contents of the portfolio with their children. At parent-teacher conferences, the portfolio can help show parents how their children are doing—which areas of mathematics they need help with and which they have mastered.

The portfolio should not be evaluated or given a grade. After all, the students selected what they considered to be examples of their best work. Think how devastated a student would be if this *best* work is graded a C or a D. The purpose of the portfolio is not to provide a grade but rather demonstrate students' growth over a period of time. You should examine the portfolios several times during the year and possibly review items with some students. You can also use the portfolio to assess such skills as working with others and use of technology in problem solving.

Folders

Unlike the portfolio, which stays in the hands of the student, the folder remains in the hands of the teacher. You should have a folder for each student in your class. This folder is your property and includes all the information you have gathered about the child during the year. You can keep a list of grades on tests or even the actual test papers in the folder. Observations made from time to time can be written on slips of paper and placed in the folder. Any information about the child should be placed in the folder. At the end of the grading period or the school year, the contents of this folder will provide a wealth of information to help you assess each student's progress during that year.

Journals and Notebooks

Both the journal and the notebook may be housed in a looseleaf binder, but what goes into each is different. The journal usually contains items concerning the affective domain—such as students' opinions, reactions, reflections, feelings, difficulties, successes, and so on. The notebook usually contains items more from the cognitive domain—such as classwork, notes taken in class, homework, explanations, definitions of terms, and so on.

The journal is a collection of the student's writings. It enables students to express their feelings about what has been learned, what is and is not understood, and their reactions to what has been taking place in class. The journal provides an opportunity for students to practice their writing and communication skills and to take the time for reflection on the assignments. The topics for the journal, often referred to as "journal prompts," are usually assigned by the teacher, either on a daily basis or as often as you wish. Examples of journal prompts follow:

- What was the most challenging thing you learned in today's class? Why?

- What did you learn in class today that you did not know before?

- How might you use what you learned in class today outside of school?

- How well do you think the other members of the class learned today's lesson?

- Did you find the homework assignment difficult? Why or why not?

- Can a fraction be reduced to more than one "simplest form"? Why or why not?

- What did you think was the most interesting part of today's lesson?

- What is the difference between estimation and mental arithmetic?

- Explain why any composite number of dots can be placed into a rectangular array having at least two rows.

You should read the student journals periodically, which will provide insight into how well your lessons have been received and how well the child is growing mathematically. However, once again, do not grade the journals. Since most of the entries will involve the students' feelings or opinions, a grade is not appropriate.

The notebook is an inventory of what is taking place in the classroom. Middle school students should be learning effective note-taking techniques in preparation for high school. Algorithms taught, formulas learned, and definitions and models should all be kept in the notebook. In the case of a problem-solving activity, each problem should be shown along with the solution process. If the assignment is for homework, students should write a brief paragraph explaining their thought processes as they attacked the problem. Middle school is a time when students begin to think about their thinking, or metacognition. Metacognition is important in helping children become better reasoners and problem solvers. Since metacognition is a process of monitoring one's own thinking, students should answer the following questions whenever they are assigned a problem to solve:

1. What was I thinking while I was attempting to solve the problem?

2. What led me to proceed in the manner I did?

3. If the approach was not successful, why wasn't it?

Students' notebooks should be evaluated regularly, examined holistically, and a grade assigned. You should write comments where appropriate. In fact, if students wish to include the notebook in their portfolio, they may wish to rewrite some items in order to improve them.

Informal Observations

Informal observation is one assessment technique that teachers have always used. As you teach, you will constantly be looking at your students, watching their faces as they try to grasp and absorb the material. You will ask questions and observe how the students respond. They will ask you questions and ask questions of each other. If the students are working in groups, you will be able to observe them as you walk around the room and listen to the group discussion. These informal observations enable you to diagnose problems as they arise rather than wait for the results of a written test. This form of observation is a natural part of the teaching process and has the advantage of providing immediate feedback.

You can use a seating chart to record your informal observations. Prepare a chart of your room with the students' names in the appropriate cells. A + symbol can indicate a positive response or comment, a – can indicate a negative response, and a ? can show that the student asked a particularly insightful question. A quick glance at the chart will reveal which students respond most often and which rarely, if ever, take part in the discussion.

Sometimes, you might want to make a more informative record of informal observations. In this case, you can make a quick comment or note on a small piece of paper and later place it in the student's folder. It is wise to wait until after class before placing the slip of paper into the student's folder so as not to call attention to this action at the time. But don't leave the recording of observations until later in the day, when you may have forgotten what happened. These notes often prove revealing when examined together with the other items in the student's folder.

Formal Observations

Formal observations are not done on an ongoing basis but rather several times during the school year. These observations are extremely valuable in assessing students' problem-solving abilities because you can examine how students employ the heuristic process.

If you are going to use formal observations for grading purposes, then some form of "evidence" must be kept. You should create a form to use, similar to the one shown in the figure on the opposite page. This form enables you to examine how students approach each part of the problem-solving process.

Whatever form you decide to use, complete the form as quickly as possible, while the observation is fresh in your mind, and place it into the student's folder. Don't observe more than one or two students in a class period. Rather, try to spread these formal observations out over a period of two to three weeks, observing every student in the class so that each is observed at least three times during the year.

Interviews

The interview is an opportunity to work closely with an individual child who may be having some problems or with a small group of two or three children. Interviews provide important information about students' thought processes, how they feel about mathematics, and what their work habits are. Interviews are especially valuable with students for whom English may not be the original language or for students who have trouble reading. Students can talk to you and often reveal things that are not apparent on paper-and-pencil tasks. Interviews are informal and permit students to talk freely as they work. They should be carefully structured around some mathematical task. Prepare a list of general questions in advance. You may decide not to use them, but they are valuable to have if the interview seems to lag. Be flexible. Present a problem to solve and ask students to think out loud so you can better understand their approach to solving the problem. The questions students ask of you while attempting to solve a problem often provide a significant amount of data about their problem-solving abilities. Try not to dominate the conversation or talk too much and avoid facial expressions indicating either praise or impatience. Tell students you may ask some questions but only to help them understand the problem.

During the interview, do not take extensive notes. This can be unnerving to the early adolescent and will foreclose their spontaneity. Rather, make some quick notes on a piece of paper and, after the interview is concluded, write a more formal report for the student's folder. Do this immediately after the interview, since you will probably forget a great deal if you wait.

The purpose of the interview should be discussed with students in advance and a convenient time and place decided upon. Since every child should be interviewed, you may find this process quite time consuming. However, the results are well worth the time and effort involved.

Student's name _____   Date _____

Observation Assessment Form

0 = inadequate   1 = satisfactory   2 = good   3 = exemplary

Category	0	1	2	3	Illustrations
Understands the Problem Facts, questions; illustrates by means of manipulatives, drawings, etc.					
Selects a Plan Appropriate strategy; alternative strategy.					
Carries Out the Plan Carries out strategy; arrives at an answer; effectively does work; carefully organized.					
Reflects Checks computation; reasonableness; answers the question; extends the problem.					
Communicates the Solution Expresses ideas clearly; orally and/or written; uses appropriate mathematical language; asks appropriate questions.					
Attitude Patience; perseverance; uses time productively; willing to take risk; enjoys problem solving.					

Source: S. Krulik and J. A. Rudnick, *Assessing Problem Solving and Reasoning* (Boston, MA: Allyn & Bacon, 1998) p. 107. Reprinted by permission.

Projects

Projects are one of the items to be placed in the student's portfolio. A project is a real-life situation or problem that requires students to devise a solution using their knowledge of mathematics. Usually, projects are assigned to small groups of four or five students. The projects should not be a short assignment that can be completed in a single night. Rather, it should involve the students in an ongoing task that takes about two weeks to complete. Project topics help make the connection between mathematics and other subjects that students study. As they work on their projects and prepare to write their final report, students develop their communication skills.

Once they have been assigned a project, students must first clearly define exactly what the problem is and what they are being asked to find. This is the way problems occur in the real world; rarely are they clearly stated in advance. Once they have defined the problem, students must decide how they are going to do it—what procedures they will follow. They must then divide up the tasks so that every member of the group takes an active part. When students have completed their projects, they should present their results and findings in class, either in written form or orally, or possibly both.

You should examine the final presentation to see if students have clearly defined the problem. Have they approached it logically? Have they clearly outlined the steps they intended to follow? Did they collect the correct data? Did they collect it in a logical manner? Was it interpreted correctly? Was it presented in an appropriate manner? Is the mathematics being used correct both in concept and in actual use? Were the outcomes stated clearly? Student projects and your evaluative comments provide you with an additional assessment tool for use with your students.

Forced-Choice Responses

The forced-choice response is usually referred to as either a multiple-choice question or a true-false question—that is, the student is forced to select an answer from among the given choices. These questions are usually quite difficult to construct, but they help determine if a student has mastered computation or algorithmic skills. If the question is not carefully constructed, in some cases the correct answer may be obtained by merely recognizing a choice. In fact, sometimes erroneous reasoning can lead to a correct answer. For example, consider the following multiple-choice question:

> 40% of 20 is:
> (a) more than 15
> (b) equal to 15
> (c) less than 15
> (d) cannot be found

The student might reason that 40 percent is equal to .4, and .4 is less than 15. Thus the student would select the correct answer (c), but for the wrong reason. The student does not understand the concept being tested yet has given the correct answer. This kind of question and its responses are of little value. To avoid this situation, you can obtain some of the study booklets designed to help students do well on a standardized test. These booklets usually contain many examples of forced-choice responses. You need only select questions that are based on the material you are teaching and adapt them for your own use. An additional advantage to using these types of questions is that they help prepare your students for the standardized tests they will be taking.

Formulated Responses

The formulated response question (sometimes referred to as the essay question or performance task) requires students to construct a response based on their knowledge. This is an opportunity for the students to demonstrate how much they know and how well they can use what they know. A problem is presented as a stimulus. Students must solve the problem, present their solutions, and *give explanations for the solutions*. This latter explanation is most important because it provides an opportunity for students to communicate their thinking to the reader. In the middle school, such communication skills must be emphasized.

Rubrics

In the past, when the emphasis was on algorithms and skill mastery, it was easy to score a test. The teacher simply deducted points for each arithmetic error made by the student. Unfortunately, the deduction was not always made fairly or accurately. Often, the amount deducted was affected to some extent by the neatness of the paper, on who the student was who made the error, and sometimes even on the time of day when the teacher was scoring the paper. Now, with the current emphasis on problem solving and reasoning, we need a more formal method of scoring to ensure that all students receive the same amount of credit for the same amount of work. This has led to the use of the scoring rubric.

A *rubric* is a grading scale that establishes, in advance, the appropriate criteria for evaluating students' work. A rubric enables the user to score a performance in a holistic manner (judging the work as an entirety by examining its parts and arriving at an overall score) or in an analytic manner (allowing the scorer to assign a score to each part of the student's performance). A rubric can be used to asses any task, from the traditional solving of an equation graphically to a problem-solving or performance task, such as dividing a square into four equal parts in many different ways. A typical analytic rubric is presented in the figure on the next page. This rubric follows the four-step problem-solving heuristic model discussed in Chapter 7.

To construct a rubric for a specific problem, first decide in advance what will constitute achievement in each of the categories. You must inform students of what these generic criteria are and discuss them in advance so that students know what they are being held responsible for doing. Next, you should write the specific criteria for each category in straightforward terms and assign point value to each. Finally, you should try out your rubric on a model solution to ensure that you have included all the critical ideas and computations.

Here are a problem, a typical solution, and some of the characteristics that must be accounted for in a rubric:

1. *Problem:* There are new baby puppies just born at the local pet shop. The owner weighed them two at a time, and the scale showed weights of 13, 14, and 15 pounds. How many puppies were there, and how much did each weigh to the nearest pound?

2. *Solution:* In order for there to be three weights, there must have been three puppies. They were weighed A-B, A-C and B-C. Using the guess-and-test strategy, the weights are determined to be 6 pounds, 7 pounds, and 8 pounds.

Student's name _____   Date _____

Analytic Rubric

Characteristics	Criteria	Score
Understands the Problem a. Illustrates the problem with drawing, table, equation, etc. b. Identifies the necessary data or information c. Identifies the question to be answered	3 = a, b, and c 2 = any 2 of a, b, or c 1 = any 1 of a, b, or c 0 = no meaningful responses	
Selects a Plan a. Selects appropriate strategy and initiates implementation b. Selects appropriate strategy with no implementation or initiates implementation of a questionable strategy c. Inappropriate strategy selected and not implemented d. No meaningful plan shown	3 = a only 2 = b only 3 = c only 0 = d	
Carries Out the Plan Implements plan and shows: a. Correct answer with appropriate work b. Appropriate work with minor computational or interpretation error c. Major interpretative or computational error d. No meaningful response	3 = a only 2 = b only 1 = c only 0 = d	
Communicates the Solution a. Gives the correct answer and a complete, logical explanation of how it was achieved, using appropriate mathematical vocabulary b. Work neatly and carefully presented with the answer labeled c. Tables and/or diagrams clearly labeled	3 = a, b, and c 2 = any 2 of a, b, or c 1 = any 1 of a, b, or c 0 = no work shown	
Shows Creativity a. Unusual or unique solution given b. More than one solution c. A generalization	1 = a or b or c	

Source: S. Krulik and J. A. Rudnick, *Assessing Problem Solving and Reasoning* (Boston, MA: Allyn & Bacon, 1998), p. 111. Reprinted by permission.

3. *Rubric:* These specific items should be included in the rubric:

   (a) Did students determine that there were exactly three puppies in order for there to be three weights?

   (b) Did students indicate that no two weights could have been the same or there would not have been three different sums?

   (c) Did students indicate how they arrived at an answer and what strategy was used?

   (d) Did students arrive at the correct weights?

   (e) Did students explain how they did the work?

Each of these items should be present in students' responses to ensure that they understood the problem and were able to answer it correctly.

Activities

1. Answer the following questions and explain your answers:

   Are all numbers that are divisible by 4 also divisible by 8?

   Are all numbers that are divisible by 8 also divisible by 4?

2. Devise a rubric for scoring problem 1. Then apply your rubric to the solution you gave. How well did you do?

3. Write a description of a project you would like to research.

4. A card is drawn from a standard 52-card deck, and a coin is tossed. What is the probability of drawing a queen and of getting a head? Explain your answer.

5. Prepare a rubric to score problem 4. Apply it to your solution. How well did you do?

6. A candybar was cut into equal pieces. Ramon ate $\frac{1}{4}$ of the pieces. Then Kaisha ate $\frac{1}{2}$ of what was left. Finally, Vicky ate the remaining 6 pieces. Into how many pieces had the candybar originally been divided?

7. Prepare a rubric to score problem 6. Apply it to your solution. How well did you do?

8. Select one of the comprehensive assessment techniques discussed in this chapter. Prepare a list of the advantages and disadvantages of the strategy you have selected.

9. A favorite question of students has always been "Is this going to be on the test?" If you answer no, students often stop listening. What answer would you give to an eighth-grade student who asks this question?

10. Describe the value of the various types of assessment techniques: observation and questioning, performance-based, teacher-made, group problem-solving, standardized tests, and textbook tests. When is one technique more important or less important?

Bibliography

Krulik, S., and Rudnick, J. A. *Assessing Problem Solving and Reasoning.* Boston: Allyn and Bacon, 1998.

Lesh, R. A. (Ed.). *Assessment of Authentic Performance in School Mathematics.* Washington, DC: American Association for the Advancement of Science, 1992.

National Council of Teachers of Mathematics. *Assessment Standards for School Mathematics.* Reston, VA: Author, 1995.

Raywid, Mary Anne. "Accountability: What's Worth Measuring?" *Phi Delta Kapan* 83, no. 6 (February 2002): 433–436.

Stenmark, J. K., Beck, P., and Asturias, H. "A Room with More Than One View." *Mathematics Teaching in the Middle School* 1, no. 1 (April 1994): 44–49.

Stylianou, D. A., Kenney, P. A., Silver, E. A., and Alacaci, C. "Gaining Insight into Students' Thinking through Assessment Tasks." *Mathematics Teaching in the Middle School* 6, no. 2 (October 2000): 136–144.

Thompson, Alba G., and Briars, Diane J. "Assessing Students' Learning to Inform Teaching: The Message in NCTM's Evaluation Standards." *Arithmetic Teacher* (December 1989): 22–26.

Webb, Norman (Ed.), *1993 Yearbook of the NCTM: Assessment in the Mathematics Classroom.* Reston, VA: National Council of Teachers of Mathematics, 1993.

Related Research

Barton, J., & Collins, A. (1997). *Portfolio assessment: A handbook for educators.* Menlo Park, CA: Addison-Wesley.

Becker, J. P., & Shimada, S. (1997). *The open-ended approach: A new proposal for teaching mathematics.* Reston, VA: National Council of Teachers of Mathematics.

Bryant, D., & Driscoll, M. (1998). *Exploring classroom assessment in mathematics.* Reston, VA: National Council of Teachers of Mathematics.

California Assessment Program. (1989). *A question of thinking: A first look at students' performance on open-ended questions in mathematics.* Sacramento: California State Department of Education.

Clarke, D. (1997). *Constructive assessment in mathematics.* Berkeley, CA: Key Curriculum.

Cross, M. (1995). *How to's in getting started with assessment and evaluation using portfolios.* Barrie, Ontario: Exclusive Educational Products.

Danielson, C. (1997). *A collection of performance tasks and rubrics: Middle school mathematics.* Larchmont, NY: Eye on Education.

Freedman, R. L. (1994). *Open-ended questioning: A handbook for educators.* Menlo Park, CA: Addison-Wesley.

Hart, D. (1994). *Authentic assessment: A handbook for educators.* Menlo Park, CA: Addison-Wesley.

McIntosh, M. E. (1997). Formative assessment in mathematics. *The Clearing House* 71: 92–96.

Stiggins, R. J. (1988). Revitalizing classroom assessment: The highest instructional priority. *Phi Delta Kappan* 69: 363–372.

Index